The
Spectacle
of the
False-Flag

THE SPECTACLE OF THE FALSE-FLAG:
PARAPOLITICS FROM JFK TO WATERGATE

Eric Wilson

Thought | Crimes

2015

THE SPECTACLE OF THE FALSE-FLAG: PARAPOLITICS from JFK to WATERGATE

First published in 2015 by
Thought | Crimes
an imprint of

punctum books * brooklyn, ny

punctumbooks.com

ISBN-13: 978-0988234055
ISBN-10: 098823405X

and the full book is available for download via our Open Monograph Press website (a Public Knowledge Project) at:

www.thoughtcrimespress.org

a project of the
Critical Criminology Working Group,
publishers of the Open Access Journal:
Radical Criminology:
journal.radicalcriminology.org
Contact: Jeff Shantz (Editor),
Dept. of Criminology, KPU
12666 72 Ave. Surrey, BC V3W 2M8

[+ design & open format publishing: pj lilley]

I dedicate this book to my Mother,
who watched over me as I slept
through the spectacle in Dallas
on November 22, 1963
and who was there to celebrate
my birthday with me during
the spectacle at the
Watergate Hotel on June 17, 1972

Contents

Editor's Preface
"On Parapolitics and a New Criminology"

C riminology is a strange discipline. For an area of
study focused overwhelmingly, obsessively even,
on state activity, criminology has perhaps as much as
any social science, outside of psychology, completely
and utterly undertheorized the state. The character of the
state is largely misunderstood or only slightly understood within criminology (even as the criminology of
figures like Pierre-Joseph Proudhon and Nicos
Poulantzas, who wrote much on law and the state, remain mostly unread by criminologists). Too often the
state is simply taken for granted without real critical
analysis. It is accepted straightforwardly, unproblemati-
cally, as the legitimate social authority, the social arbitra-
tor.

Where critical approaches to the state are pursued
there has been a tendency toward instrumentality or uniformity in discussing and explaining state activities.
That is, the state is typically portrayed as a rather direct
expression of the repressive needs of capital as a whole.
And this, again, is the case only in critical approaches in
which the state is interrogated or even problematized at

all, most criminology taking the state, its legitimacy if not its neutrality, for granted.

Philosophically inclined criminologists like Bruce Arrigo have remarked on the underdeveloped nature of criminological theory in general. So this under-theorization of the state is part of a larger problem in criminology. Arrigo suggests a philosophical turn in criminology that could engage with philosophical works, particularly the critical philosophies of the post-1968 period in social thought. For too much of criminology it is as if the waves of post-68 social theorizing (and associated contemporary developments) never happened.

Thankfully we have trailblazers like Eric Wilson who on the one hand seek to broaden the theoretical and political horizons of criminology while on the other giving a more nuanced and deeper reading of the state and the relations and practices that animate it. Wilson is too perceptive, his work too subtle to present a uniform view of the liberal democratic state. Wilson offers a presentation of state operations of power as conflictual, contradictory, competing, confused. His is a robust conception of power that is rarely encountered in criminology.

Wilson goes outside the theoretical bounds of what is typically in criminological thought. He makes use of insights from Guy Debord's works on social spectacle to re-read literature on deep state practice and its (spectacular) false flag representations. Wilson, following Debord, moves away from notions of static, uniform power.

Wilson's work, in addition to shifting thinking about the liberal democratic state, challenges us to rethink the subject(s) of criminology. This is a step, on one hand, toward rethinking criminology as analysis of states and state criminality. More than that, it challenges us to move beyond analyses of the simple or naïve view of states.

In a sense Wilson's book in *Spectacle(s) of the False Flag(s)* is solidly in the tradition of C. Wright Mills works like *The Power Elite* and *White Collar* (other offerings that are too little read by criminologists). In Mills' work the hidden or shadow networks are presented as the fabric of the modern state—always in action behind the screen (or wishful dream) of the formal democratic institutions of government. Mills work makes clear that ruling groups centered in the state often have driven interests—moving and shifting specific alliances as interests shift and specific players gain or lose influence.

Criminology needs works like this to develop its focus on state relations, networks of (counter)governance. Criminology has a long way to go to be adequately or effectively attuned to deep state relations. Whether from critical or uncritical, heterodox or orthodox perspectives, our understandings of the state have, for the most part been too superficial, too shallow. In place of simple instrumentality we may speak of instrumentalities, often competing and contradictory if converging at important points.

Clandestinity is the health of the state. Yet it is rarely understood or acknowledged as such. A critical criminology, let alone a radical one, must offer more insightful, nuanced, informed readings of the complexities of the state as the object of crime *par excellence*. One can envision future criminological undertakings that apply such parapolitical spectacular analyses to issues of state-corporate crime, transnational crime, or security studies as only a few examples. In this understanding, criminality, far from being a distortion of state practice is the character of state practice (with the state as fragmented and uneven).

The current work is an important step along these paths. It offers an example for all of criminology to approach. It hints at the possibility of a new criminology, a parapolitical criminology that looks beyond the surface of the spectacle that has so hypnotized and distracted mainstream and orthodox criminology.

It is work that carries certain risks. Thus, a final note on conspiracy. Even the threat of being labeled conspiracy theory can dissuade serious researchers from pursuing topics of great importance. This is, of course, partly how power operates to silence or defuse criticism. We know—intuitively—that conspiracies exist, yet we shrink from naming them as such. We need to conceptualize conspiracy not as strange, atypical event, but conspiracy as a manifestation of everyday pursuits of often mundane design. This is what Wilson does. This and much more.

Jeff Shantz
Kwantlen Polytechnic University
Surrey, unceded Coast Salish Territories
November 2014

Foreword
"The New Politology of Eric Wilson"

E ric Wilson put it clearly: if one wants to craft a realistic theory of political violence, one will find oneself *entre dos aguas*. On the Right, one will get no cooperation whatsoever from conservative hawks whose job is to salute the advent of the modern Liberal State as a teleological master-stroke: Liberalism, they affirm, is all humans have ever striven for ("democratic consensus"), and now it is here. In their vision, an organism as flawlessly balanced and efficient as the modern Liberal State is *ipso facto* immune to conspiratorial activity: the mere possibility of degenerative internecine feuds at the top is averted by the joint operation of transparency and democratic turnover. In this perspective, (political) crime is always the result of the psychopaths' and misfits failure to adapt to the rigors of a fast-paced, individualist, "free" society. On the Left, progressive hawks (plus the doves, red-white-and blue) will also rebuke one's inquiries because one should know that it would be illogical for elites, whose business it is to protect/further their (economic) interests behind the impersonal façade of governmental protocol, to frame, defame, or liquidate their own (one or many, highest or low) in order to achieve whatever hidden end they might have on their putatively "secret agenda." Again, political violence is construed as a pathological disorder that is essentially foreign, extraneous to the conventional management of the modern State.

Being all "theoretical" space is thus obstructed, what is the skeptical politologist to do? *Il peut tricher*; one can cheat French-Style, like, say, Baudrillard. Like Baudrillard, one could argue that momentous, unusual events are the nightmares of our collective mind; they are the theatrical production of our collective subconscious. And it is because our collective subconscious is so corrupt, neurotically torqued, and terrified of holding up the mirror to its savage self that the shows of our day-to-day chronicles appear delirious, or, as they say, "irrational." The delirium and "irrationality" of it all is to be interpreted as the oneiric labor of these demons we westerners have crammed, hidden in the basement of our psyche. It is astonishing to think that this post-Freudian chicken-halibut could have had any mass-traction at all—as it did, in fact, during the propagandistic campaign of Gulf One, (Iraq, 1990-1991); traction, say, over and beyond the usual Foucauldian fare of "there is no power at the center, but only at the margins." In any event, all of these are just extravagant "literalized metaphors," whose primary, obvious propagandistic goal is to efface political responsibility (authorship: whodunit and why? To such questions the postmodern reply is: it is irrelevant; it is one big, "liquid" nightmare, and the demons are ours anyway). They are subtle to the extent that they include the issue of guilt, if tangentially, but defuse that line of thinking forthwith by drowning it in an avowal of public culpability, and immediately thereafter negate the issue wholesale with the suggestion that the political making of history is nothing but a virtual (video-)game. The computer's gone crazy; and as for the machine's wiring, we all contributed to it, and eventually lost technical track of what we did, letting the Matrix run the programs and screw it all up, because we were the psychologically screwed-up engineers originally in charge of the project. This insane spectacle is, in the end, the unintended and sick phantasy of some "other," impersonal process, which, occasionally, the little deacons of Liberal academia describe, piously, as "the great forces of history."

The irony of the postmodern, post-Freudian twist is that in order to pre-empt in the spectator the temptation to indulge the anti-oligarchical drift (viz. they lie to you, they fabricate "events," and if it is politically expedient, they will kill you and your children too), the Captains of Discourse (i.e., the Maecenases of all successful "public intellectuals") have often run ahead of themselves by sponsoring (unknowingly?) the adoption of the metaphorizing of *theosophy*. (And was not Hegelism the most famous and shameless parody of spiritualist esotericism?). All these presumed phantasms and impersonal "processes," which are deemed capable, *by themselves and despite ourselves*, of conjuring the surreal scenarios of present-day wars and social and environmental cataclysms, are what theosophists customarily designate as "archangelic forces." Queer but simply true: one way or another, we never seem able to rise beyond our aboriginal attraction to mythologizing and archetypal mystery. And it could not be otherwise; Fernando Pessoa had said it: because it does not possess the knowledge of humanity's beginning, all "social science" is, in essence, mystique. In this sense, the unforgivable sin of these late politological "theories" is not so much that they are bogus, corrupted and corrupting—in arguing that, barring greed (which all conservatives mischievously worship anyway), the modern elite is guiltless by democratic default—but that they are aesthetically atrocious: they are the miserable rip-offs and "trans-vestitures" by artless hacks of esoteric and religious lore, always.[1] They fool no one.

In the face of such institutionalized disingenuousness and various standardized *tricheries*, the task Eric Wilson has set out to achieve is remarkable: he is creating a politology of subversion, which satisfies all the chrisms of scientific inquiry, while retaining on the one hand a commitment to truth, without sacrificing on the other the concern for giving proper expression to the mystical dimension of collective behavior. Of the one, truth, the modern-day academic has no motivated apprehension, and of the other, mysticality, the late postmodernists have made so fantastic a bamboozlement as to have managed to reclaim, on the Left, all the vast discursive/propagandistic acreage once tenanted by Marxism (& its derivatives). Eric is driving a wedge into the gentrifying concrete of the discursive space to open a "third pasture" in which we may regroup and begin to understand.

In spinning the narrative yarn linking JFK's assassination to Watergate—covering one of the crucial decades of the Cold War (1963-1974)—the first step he undertakes, and it is the most important, is to *identify the battling factions*. He re-adapts Carl Oglesby's scenario according to which much of the political instability of the time was due to the uncomfortable cohabitation of the imperial designs of two U.S. clans, an Eastern, Anglophile, finance-driven brethren versus a fraternity of Southwestern oil-men. To this, he then superimposes Peter Dale Scott's *"parapolitical"* schematics, whereby historical events may be viewed

---

1 In a different context, this is also true of Marxism and Libertarian (Liberal) teleologism.

as the reverberations of *"deeper"* machinations—hidden from public view, that is. In the making of such machinations, the "parapolitical" comes into play when the elite shifts gears, allowing an osmosis which permits the introduction of criminal elements into the secret of princes, and, reversely, shoves the princes into the lower layers of the gutter. The alliance resulting from this two-way trafficking—your standard tale of the functionalism of Mafia and crime in modern society—is, in point of academic etiquette, inadmissible. But, de facto, confess it or not, it is routine, and in this story of "false-flags," it is analyzed in detail in order to explain how it played in the overarching confrontation between "Brahmins" and "cowboys." The "osmosis" occurring in the bowels of the technocratic apparatus elicits, in turn, the further assumption that the State is, in fact, "dual"; in other words, the regime is organized in such a way that, under "exceptional" circumstances—Eric's extensive work on the politology of Carl Schmitt bears on this aspect—, some of its "bureaus"—generally, the political offices of the security apparatus—may spawn a variety of clandestine cells, whose task is to wage civil battle outside the legal perimeter of the State. This means that all "regular" administration—of justice, information, and security—is suspended as the rival factions proceed to cut all administrative nodes in half, as it were, re-appropriate and re-direct them in view of the forthcoming season of escalating hostilities. The fictionalizing beauty of the set-up is that while the fight among clans unfolds "deeply," i.e. entirely hidden from public scrutiny, there concomitantly "forms" on the media stage, as if inevitably bubbling over, a game of theatrics for mass consumption. The game is designed to sway "public opinion" with the final objective of topping off the "deep" victory with popular acclaim. All terrorist activity (whether it pits, say, Neo-

Fascists vs. Communists in a civil confrontation, or patriots vs. Islamists in a geostrategic deployment) is, in this case, the theatrical production with which the Intelligence bureaus impress, shock the crowds, and mold the "word on the Street." At this juncture, Eric applies Guy Debord's "situationist" critique to emphasize how these "games" have a weird habit of taking on a life of their own, replicating themselves in recognizable patterns and symmetries, which appear dictated over time by the choice of actors (agencies) and locales ("situations," "geography"). It is here that we find a hint of that sensation of being *cosmically* played—everybody, that is, not just the masses but the players too—by tricksters "bigger" than all of us.

Stenographically, Eric's thesis is the following: fundamental disagreement over the proper policy vs. Cuba—the conventional contraposition of maximalist hawks vs. pragmatic doves—leads to a half-baked plan of invasion, which fails miserably at the Bay of Pigs in 1961. According to the Pentagon hawks, Kennedy's lack of firmness on this front is such that the situation further degenerates until it reaches a full-blown state of red-alert nuclear crisis in 1962. Determined to get out of the way what they perceive as a double-crossing incompetent, the secret squads of the "Dual State," with a little functional help of the Mafia, resolve to eliminate Kennedy in a grand spectacle featuring the manipulation of a (suicidal) "political idiot" (Oswald), "manifestly" linked to America's pro-Castro Communist underground—the final objective being that of prompting a mass popular outrage with which to launch a full-scale and, this time around, fail-safe invasion of Cuba. The design fails but, with the cowboys solidly in charge, Dallas's regicidal build-up finds ("situationist") release a year later, in the (fabricated) incident of the Gulf of Tonkin—a completely different sort of theater, yet one featuring identical actors still driven by 1963's subversive momentum. A decade of incineration and slaughter in Vietnam seals a generational catastrophe and a season of bungled political maneuvers, which have eventually brought to center stage a pivotal protagonist of this saga, Richard Nixon, a Californian "cowboy." Something of a political visionary, Nixon plays his hand creatively by isolating, on the one hand, Russia's economic deadweight with a new round of détente, and by wagering, on the other, America's imperial future on an overture to China. To him, this last policy means sacrificing, in part, Europe, which he acrimoniously resolves to confront, financially and commercially. So acrimoniously, in fact, that the Europe-patronizing Brahmins (Rockefeller's "Trilateralist" front), by way of a "situationist" reversal, orchestrate the grand Watergate scandal to oust Nixon ignominiously from the White House.

I keep restating how lamentable it is that we plow through current affairs, daily, doing our best to understand the dynamics at play, and inevitably fail, because we have yet to understand fully what went down during that essential phase in the history of power that was the Cold War. Eric Wilson is perfectly aware of this, and his piece is an admirable *tour de force* that should set the tone for a new history, and politology, of that absolutely critical period. I say absolutely critical because all post-Soviet, but even more so, all post-9/11 historical developments are entirely rooted in the politics, deceptions, and maneuvers of the Cold War. It is as if the post-9/11 strategists had exhumed, or rather, recycled virtually all the sets, props, costumes, screenplays of the past to play anew the late dismal game to which we are all (dejected) witnesses: Arab terrorists, nuclear proliferation, pandemics, chaotic migratory flows, evil Russians, wars by proxy in Africa...Of course, there are differences as well, the chief one being that America's bellicose odium toward Russia, these days, seems real enough, rather than entirely feigned, as it once was. Which is to say that our era appears more unstable and frightening than the old one —and I assume that such is the conviction behind Vladimir Putin's declared nostalgia for the Cold War order.

Although I am by no means equal to contribute, *à la hauteur d'*Eric, anything insightful to the debate surrounding his captivating fresco of the Kennedy-Nixon epoch (my knowledge of the chronicles is yet too superficial), I shall nevertheless offer a series of disjointed observations on the Cold War, merely to round off the little I have just sketched.

I have never believed in the Cold War's ostensible antagonism of capitalist West vs. Communist East. Like Eric, I think that *domestic factional wars* are what explain virtually everything, but they are extremely hard to dig out, or guess, because Power's code of honor has bound, binds, and will forever bind all players to eternal silence. On the one hand, such literal "obscenity" (out-of-the-scene) of power, should fill us every day with revulsion— revulsion for the unspeakable corruptness of the powerful human being, and for the gloating pride and sense of perfect impenitence with which he usually takes his secrets to the grave; on the other, it is exciting in that it forces social investigators and politologists to become detectives and treat their research material like murder cases (if it were always so, how thrilling academic life would be!).

My guess is that the East-West contraposition was just one giant deceptive back-drop, set-up after the crushing of Germany, against which feuds of various geopolitical kind and import could be consummated in the face of diffuse popular cluelessness. And this applied just as well to the

Russians on one side of the fence as it did to the Europeans and the Americans on the other: the two enemies, in fact, were not to bother each other for matters of strictly political, and domestic, administration. Whenever they "clashed," it was because they were having (theatrical) recourse to the "inimical clause" of the Cold War to solve, settle some particular issue of domestic control, which, indeed, required a "popular shock." So, when they clashed, *they were actually (theatrically) helping one another*—"crises," in this sense, were born out of "favors" one faction, depending on the occasion, would do the other. In this regard, I am still not sure what the Bay of Pigs really was: many say it was unthinkable that the very country that had organized the Normandy landing of WWII could have forgotten seventeen years later to provide air cover for a full-fledged invasion of an infinitely smaller and virtually undefended area. Could it be that JFK set the whole operation in motion exclusively to make it fail, *publicize* it, and then leverage the whole shameful flop to decapitate, say, the CIA's leadership—merely for clannish advantage? And could it be, then, that the faction thus suckered, swearing revenge, planned Dallas, also as some kind of psycho-social experiment? An experiment, that is, designed to jolt the masses with a spectacle of raw, unmitigated violence[2]—as it turned out: JFK's splattered brain squirting out of his skull and being chased by Jackie to the far back of the limos' trunk— in order to effect desensitization in the viewers for purposes of tightened social domestication? As Eric and I have discussed, if it was a revenge murder, there was no need to take such incredible risks in staging the assassination so sensationally; a discrete death by lethal inoculation, which could have been easi-

---

2 And the ceaseless repetition of its televised footage.

ly passed off as "cardiac arrest," would have sufficed.

Planned spectacles of gruesome death aside—the discussion of such a fantastic thesis rather pertains to a dedicated exegesis of David Cronenberg's superb 1982 horror movie, *Videodrome*,—my reading of the 1962 Cuban Missile Crisis is that it was a side-show of pure pretense, fully pre-arranged by both sides, to strike geo-strategic, as well as dramatic balance, which the greater Cold War Game periodically required, after the 1961 crisis of the Berlin Wall. The symmetry is explicit: each block had (agreed to have) an annoyingly defiant speck, a thorn of the enemy in its side: the Soviets had to tolerate the "free-city" of West Berlin smack-in-the middle of their German protectorate, whereas the U.S. had to "suffer" Fidel Castro's antics 90 miles off the tip of Florida. All staged, all phony, with Castro being the phoniest of all—as if the mammoth apparatus in charge of clandestine operations in D.C. could not erase Cuba and crush its dictator of papier-mâché at will.

As for Richard Nixon, in hindsight, he comes out, in my view, as the most interesting, most intriguing elder statesman of this whole story. It turns out he had been right all along; he had seen much farther ahead than his (imperial) peers. Our "globalized" word is, indeed, a Nixonian world. Today, the American hegemon is, notwithstanding French jinxing, stronger than ever: it has managed to contain fairly well a quasi-reborn Russia, and harnessed almost perfectly China's enormous productive power (slave-labor) to its commercial sector (propriety of all remunerative patents). By foisting successfully its currency and multifarious financial securities on the rest of the world, the USA manages to dominate all markets for vital commodities, as well as to control its vassals' finances and savings, which it conveys to Wall Street for financing its budget and military expenses. Europe, for her part, finds herself spiritually sclerosed and economically paralyzed by a common, expensive currency that has undermined its world competitiveness and allowed her to be ravaged by Chinese imports, to the greatest delight of Anglo-America. These are all developments born of plans originally hatched by Nixon and his administration. He had been a great Neo-con Founding Father. It was only fair, then, that the (Brahmin) establishment would, somewhat apologetically, rehabilitate him. Not by accident did a fellow cowboy, President Bill Clinton of Arkansas, seek him out, late in life, as an officious adviser on foreign policy, and eventually attend Nixon's funeral in 1994 to pay his last respects to this unjustly disgraced prophet-warrior of the great Anglo-American Commonwealth.

The background to this key page of our recent history is richly detailed in the book you are about to read. In conclusion, it is my hope that such a contribution is Eric's first installment of a vast and sorely needed opus of historiographical reappraisal of the Cold War, which, in the final analysis, will provide the theoretical and methodological bedrock for an educated understanding of contemporary political dynamics. Within this new framework, we shall be expecting Eric to provide us with the "deeper," "parapolitical" significance of all the great mysteries of that time (in random order): the Rosenberg Case, the attempted assassination of John Paul II, the Dirty War in Argentina, the first terrorist wave (from the OLP to the RAF), De Gaulle and the OAS, etc. We very much look forward.

Buona lettura.

Guido Giacomo Preparata,
Rome, Italy
September 2014.

Acknowledgements

I owe much of this work to the assistance of four individuals. The first is my good friend Peter Dale Scott, author of what I consider the single greatest work on the assassination of John F. Kennedy; as befitting the dean of conspiracy researchers, Peter has mastered the *sine qua non* that has ultimately proven to have eluded my grasp: the minutiae of the interminable. The second and third are my colleagues and sometimes collaborators Guido Preparata and Jeff Kinkle; the present book emerged out of an extensive series of three-way e-mails concerning Castro, Kennedy and Dallas in late 2012 as we were completing our joint work on another text. The fourth is premiere JFK researcher Larry Hancock, who, at literally the last minute, provided me with invaluable assistance on the bottomless swamp of Lee Harvey Oswald in Mexico City; even if Oswald really was the lone gunman of Establishment orthodoxy, the necessary groundwork for the spectacle of Dealey Plaza was laid down in that most beautiful and remarkable of cities.

These four 'Goodfellows' (or 'wise guys' as they may prefer) each did their bit.

The resultant thing of darkness I acknowledge as mine.

Eric Wilson
(Faculty of Law, Monash University)

'Dealey Plaza is symmetrical.'
—Don DeLillo

Introduction

I n the following pages I do not attempt to supply any new evidence in support of or formulate any new theory or explanation of the three conspiratorial situations that I discuss—although I do provide what I feel to be the least implausible accounts of these events self-consciously understood as 'conspiracies'. I also do not undertake a thorough discussion of the nature and function of what is often dismissively referred to as 'conspiracy theory' within contemporary political and popular culture; the subject matter is vast (seemingly even greater than the substantive content of the manifold conspiracy theories themselves) and would require a separate book (probably redundant by now) to treat the topic adequately. Nor, finally, am I offering an argument for the objective rightness of any particular form of critical theory or research methodology; if my tone is at times polemical or didactic, this is simply the by-product of the close reading that I am undertaking of certain historical fragments that have managed to reach the public domain using the lenses of one particular school of radical thought —Situationism.

My purpose here is much narrower and wholly consistent with my purposes elsewhere: to demonstrate the practical usefulness of a number of critical theorists to the discipline of radical criminology whose work has, for whatever reasons, been largely underappreciated by those in the field. The subject of this monograph is the late writings of Guy Debord (1931-94), the ostensible founder and moving spirit (or, more precisely, the permanent general secretary) of the more than normally anomalous form of French critical theory known as Situationism, which lasted as a formal movement from 1957 to 1972.[1] Perhaps most accurately described as a neo-avant-gardist crypto-Dadist anti-Surrealist direct political action group,[2] Situationism, not surprisingly, fetishized the notion of the 'situation', a philosophically elaborate and poetically reified hybrid of street theatre and political combat.

> Our central purpose is the construction of situations, that is, the concrete construction of temporary settings of life and their transformation into a higher, passionate nature. We must develop intervention directed by the complicated factors of two great components in perpetual interaction: the material setting of life and the behaviors that it incites and that overturn it.[3]

Situationism is best understood not as an intellectual product of duration but as a glossary of terms, virtually all of which were derived from Surrealism: *dérive*, a sort of 'free flowing stream' of political consciousness; *dé-*

---

1 Although Situationism is frequently reduced to the work of Debord, the general consensus is that the first recognizably Situationist text is 'Formulary for a New Urbanism', written by Ivan Chtcheglov in 1953. See Chtcheglov generally.

2 One of the reasons why Situationism is so difficult to define is that during its life span Debord managed to expel virtually every other member from the group. Apart from Debord, the most important Situationists were Asger Jorn (1914-73) and Raoul Veneigem (b. 1934). See generally Wark.

3 Debord, 'Report on the Construction of Situations', 44.

tournement ('literary communism'), the freewheeling appropriation of any and all cultural materials at hand as a form of 'collective property'[4]; psycho-geography, the "study of the specific effects of the geographical environment, consciously organized or not, on the emotions and behavior of individuals"[5]; and unitary urbanism, the subordination of all architectural forms to a radically aestheticized Humanism.[6] But above all else, Situationism was a radical protest movement, in both abstract word and physical action, against the original sin of Modernity: *boredom.*

> Our action on deportment, in connection with other desirable aspects of a revolution in custom, can be defined summarily as the invention of a new species of games. The most general aim must be to broaden the non-mediocre portion of life, to reduce its empty movements as much as possible.[7]

The situation is ludic in essence, and, via the performative magic of both *dérive* and *détournement*, is to be directly realized through those forms of cultural materials most appropriate to it—film, photography, posters, graffiti (*'Ne travaillez jamais'*), comic books, and 'scandalous' speech. The paradox at work here is obvious: in order to negate the twin forms of modern (-ist) alienation—boredom and commodification—the situation must unconsciously replicate the cultural logic of entertainment, the very disease that the poetry-in-the-streets is attempting to cathartically purge. But it is also the case—and not only in Sicily—that the very best of all tactics is 'to keep your friends close and your enemies

---

4 Wark, 62.
5 Ford, 34.
6 Wark, 68.
7 Debord, 'Report on the Construction of Situations', 45.

closer'. And the arch-enemy, or Other, of the situation, as Debord brilliantly explicated near the end of the Situationist moment, is the *spectacle*, 'a sort of diplomatic representative of hierarchical society at its own court, and the source of the only discourse which society allows itself to hear.'[8] The spectacle is a congealing of the collective imagination of the masses, a totalitarian unification of the senses, the regimentation of 'the shutters of the eyes' (as Kafka described the cinema) sanctioned directly by the State. The situation and the spectacle are antinomies, and the future of cultural (= political) resistance in our so-called post-modern society depends solely on the way and means by which we negotiate the (post-) dialectical dance of the two mirror images.

My goal, therefore, is an extremely modest one—to argue for the richness of Situationist, and specifically Debordean, discourse for the field labor of a criminology that has become well and truly radicalized. For if it is true that 'Generalized secrecy stands behind the spectacle, as the decisive complement of all that it displays and, in the last analysis, as its most vital component,'[9] then who knows what criminological garden of delight lies just beyond our sight?

---

8 Debord, *Society*, 18-19.
9 Debord, *Comments*, 12.

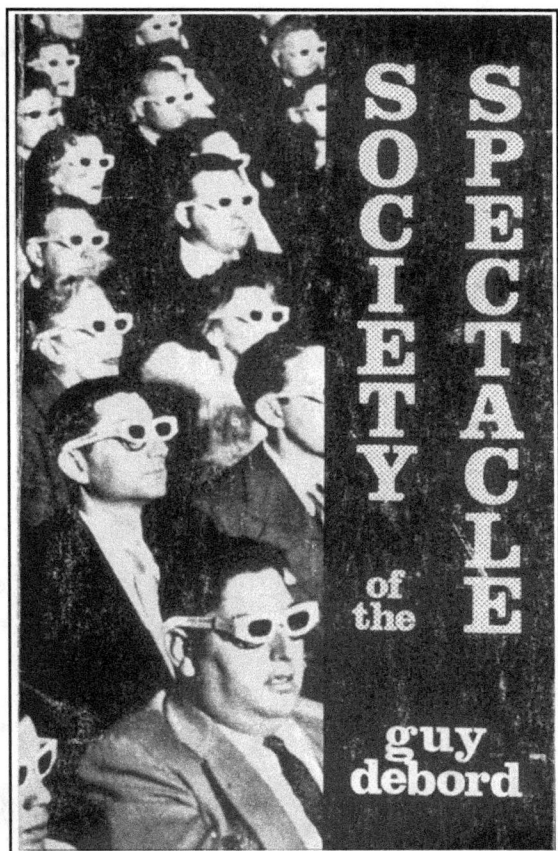

[Cover image of Guy Debord's "Society of the Spectacle",
1983 english edition by Black & Red press–translation and
cover design by Fredy Perlman (& friends); based on an
excerpt from a photograph by Life Magazine photographer
J. R. Eyerman taken November 26, 1952 of an audience at
the Paramount Theatre (Oakland, California).]

1 | Parapolitics and Spectacular Power

*'The more important something is, the
more it is hidden.'*—Guy Debord

A widely under-utilized source for the development of radical criminological theory is the work of the French post-Surrealist and Situationist philosopher Guy Debord. Of vital relevance to radical criminology is Debord's nuanced linking of the criminogenic with the mass politics of popular representation and perception, epitomized by his seminal notion of the Society of the Spectacle: "the autocratic reign of the market economy which had acceded to an irresponsible sovereignty and the totality of new techniques of government which accompanied this reign."[1] The hegemony of the Society of the Spectacle, in turn, is signified by the *integrated spectacle*, the cultural reification of mass media as the sole medium and arbiter of 'truth';

> the whole life of those societies in which modern
> conditions of production prevail presents itself as

1 Debord, *Comments*, 2.

> an immense accumulation of spectacles. All that
> once was directly lived has become mere repres-
> entation.'[2]

As a result, the overall relationship between the social
and the visual is governed by a radical functionality.

> If the spectacle—understood in the limited sense
> of those 'mass media' that are its most stultifying
> superficial manifestation—seems at times to be
> invading society in the shape of a mere apparatus,
> it should be remembered that this apparatus has
> nothing neutral about it, and that it answers pre-
> cisely to the needs of the spectacle's internal dy-
> namics. If the social requirements of the age
> which develops such techniques can be met only
> through their mediation, if the administration of
> society and all content between people now de-
> pends on the intervention of such 'instant' com-
> munication, it is because this 'communication' is
> essentially *one-way*; the concentration of the me-
> dia thus amounts to the monopolization by the ad-
> ministrators of the existing system of the means to
> pursue their particular form of administration.[3]

Once defined as integrated, the spectacle is understood
to be socially (and politically) unifying precisely because "the spectacle is not a collection of images; rather,
it is a social relationship among people that is mediated
by images."[4] But the spectacle, while unifying in effect,
is totalitarian in nature.

> For what is communicated are *orders*; and with
> perfect harmony, those who give them are also

---

2 Debord, *Society*, 12.

3 *Ibid*, 19-20.

4 *Ibid*, 12. I expand on this aspect of the spectacle in greater detail in my
discussion of the Don DeLillo novel *LIBRA* in Chapter Five.

those who tell us what they think of them...A virtually infinite number of supposed differences within the media thus serve to screen what is in fact the result of a spectacular convergence, pursued with remarkable tenacity. Just as the logic of the commodity reigns over capitalist's competing ambitions, and the logic of war always dominates the frequent modifications in weaponry, so the harsh logic of the spectacle controls the abundant diversity of media extravagances.[5]

The cultural logic of the spectacle is identical with the transition of the political economy, now increasingly 'virtual' in nature, towards a globalized form of what I have called 'cyber-capitalism';[6] 'The spectacle is *capital* accumulated to the point where it becomes image.'[7] Anticipating the excavations of both Jean Baudrillard[8] and Paul Virilio[9] on the para-covert effects of simulation upon public discourse, Debord openly postulates the infinite transformational potential of the mass 'mediated' multiplication of the commodity-form.

The spectacle corresponds to the historical moment at which the commodity completes its colonization of social life. It is not just that the relationship to commodities is now plain to see— commodities are now *all* that there is to see; the world we see is the world of the commodity... With the advent of the second so-called industrial revolution, alienated consumption is added to alienated production as an inescapable duty of the

---

5 Debord, *Comments*, 6-7.
6 Wilson, 'Criminogenic Cyber-Capitalism', generally.
7 Debord, *Society*, 24.
8 Baudrillard, generally.
9 Virilio and Lotringer, generally. I discuss Virilio in greater detail in Chapter Five.

masses.[10]

This intensive, or internal, colonization of social space by late industrial capitalism having been completed by the end of the 1920s.[11]

> The spectacle subjects living human beings to its will to the extent that the economy has brought them under its sway. For the spectacle is simply the economic realm developing *for itself*—at once a faithful mirror held up to the production of things [including 'events'] and a distorting objectification of the producers [and 'actors'].[12]

However, with the universalization of a digitalized, or 'virtual', neo-liberalism as the integrated (and integrating) component of post-Cold War globalization, we witness a parallel technocratization of all forms of governance, both public (political) and private (economic).

The ubiquitous growth of secret societies and net-

---

10 Debord, *Society*, 29.

11 Although he is notoriously imprecise concerning the historical evolution of the spectacle, in his *Comments* Debord writes that the society of the spectacle had been in existence for 'barely forty years' when he first wrote about in in 1967: this would place its genesis sometime during the 1920s. Debord, *Comments*, 3. Jonathan Crary has offered a fascinating explanation for this startling assertion: 1927 was the year of both the perfection of the television by Vladimir Zworkin and the release of Al Jolson's *The Jazz Singer*, the first film that completely synchronized the cinematic image with recorded sound, an event that signalled not only a new cinematic technique but an unprecedented industrial and financial conglomeration as well, the record industry largely subsidizing Hollywood's transition to 'talking' films; ' as with television, the nascent institutional and economic infrastructure of the spectacle was set in place.' Crary, 457-8. The late 1920s was also the period when both Stalinism and Fascism grasped the revolutionary potential of the new media technologies for political propaganda.

12 *Ibid*, 16.

works of influence answers the imperative demand of the new conditions for profitable management of economic affairs, at a time when the
state holds a hegemonic role in the direction of
production and when demand for all commodities
depends strictly on the centralization achieved by
spectacular information/promotion, to which
forms of distribution must also adapt. It is therefore only a natural product of the concentration of
capital, production and distribution. Whatever
does not grow must disappear, and no business
can grow without adopting the values, techniques
and methods of today's industry, spectacle and
state.[13]

The effective collapse of media into spectacular power
"means quite simply that the spectacle's domination has
succeeded in raising a whole generation molded to its
laws."[14] Spectacular government,

which now possesses all the means necessary to
falsify the whole of production and perception, is
the absolute master of memories just as it is the
unfettered master of plans which will shape the
most distant future. It reigns unchecked; it *ex-
ecutes its summary judgments*.[15]

The spectacle, therefore, is mediated through its primal
political form, *spectacular power*, which, not at all coincidentally, is "the historical moment by which we happen to be governed."[16] And, within this unbroken social
procession of mediating images dwells the hegemony of
the *clandestine*; "At the root of the spectacle lies that
oldest of all social divisions of labor, the specialization

---

13 Debord, *Comments*, 6.
14 Ibid, 7.
15 Ibid, 10.
16 Debord, *Society*, 15.

of *power*."[17] And with this comes the operational hegemony of covert agency; "Secrecy dominates this world, and first and foremost as the secret of domination."[18]

> We should expect, as a logical possibility, that the state's security services intend to use all the advantages they find in the realm of the spectacle, which has indeed been organized with that in mind for some considerable time; on the contrary, it is a difficulty in perceiving this which is astonishing and rings false.[19]

Accordingly

> Networks of promotion/control slide imperceptibly into networks of surveillance/disinformation. Formerly one only conspired against an established order. Today, *conspiring in its favor* is a new and flourishing profession. Under spectacular domination people conspire to maintain it, and to guarantee what it alone would call its well-being. This conspiracy *is a part* of its very functioning.[20]

It follows, therefore, that the ubiquity of the clandestine is itself the primary sign of the lurking presence of an extra-legal form of sovereignty; 'In a world that *really* has been stood on its head, truth is the moment of false-

---

17 Ibid, 18.

18 Debord, *Comments*, 60.

19 Ibid, 25. This neatly dovetails with the statement provided by CIA Director Richard Helms to the Church Committee (1975-6), the Senate body investigating the assassination operations (or 'wet work') undertaken by the CIA during the 1950s and 60s: '"When you establish a clandestine service [like] the Central Intelligence Service, you established [sic] something totally different from anything else in the United States government. Whether it's right that you should have it, or wrong that you should have it, it works under different rules...than any other part of the government."' Cited in Talbot, 112.

20 Debord, *Comments*, 74.

hood.'[21] Paul Hirst has stated this plainly:

> The nuclear-security apparatus reserves to itself considerable powers of control over economic resources, special police measures, etc., and has a capacity for secret policy-making whose limits are difficult to determine. If we take [Carl] Schmitt's claim seriously that 'sovereign is he who decides on the exception' seriously, then most of our formal constitutional doctrines are junk.[22]

'Junk' indeed, although 'spectacle' might be a more accurate term; 'Understood on its own terms, the spectacle proclaims the predominance of appearances and asserts that all human life, which is to say all social life, is mere appearance.'[23] Viewed through radical criminological lenses, contemporary onto-politics reveals a perpetual migration between antinomies: the public (political) and the private (covert) forms of decision-making. And it is precisely within this eternally unstable double movement that the covert power of the spectacle resides.

SPECTACULAR POWER, CRIMINAL SOVEREIGNTY, AND PARAPOLITICS

'Real power begins where secrecy begins.'
—Hannah Arendt

The (radical) criminological term for this hitherto nameless condition outlined by Debord is *criminal sovereign-*

---

21 Debord, *Society*, 14.
22 Paul Hirst, cited in Wilson, 'The Concept of the Parapolitical', 26.
23Debord, *Society*, 14.

ty and has been most thoroughly defined by Robert Cribb as

> [N]ot just a topic but an analytical conclusion. On the one hand, it goes significantly beyond the proposition that relations between security and intelligence organisations, international criminal networks and quasi-states are occasional and incidental, the work of 'rogue elements' and the like. On the other hand, it falls significantly short of grand conspiracy theory: it does not suggest that the world of visible, 'normal' politics is an illusion or that it is entirely subordinated to 'deep' politics. Rather, it proposes that the tripartite relationship between security and intelligence organisations, international criminal networks and quasi-states is systematic, extensive and influential.[24]

The multiple extra-judicial affinities between criminal sovereignty and spectacular power thoroughly subvert mainstream criminology's current preoccupation with models of good governance, transparency, and rule-compliance as benchmarks of social and political normality.

The great world-historical irony revealed by Debord is that the apparent 'regression' of the State into more archaic forms of governance is actually the supreme sign of the advancement of 'those societies in which modern conditions of production prevail'.

> It is precisely here that we can see the profound truth of the Sicilian Mafia's maxim, so well appreciated throughout Italy: 'When you've got money and friends, you can laugh at the law.' In the integrated spectacle, *the laws are asleep*; because they were not made for the new production

---

24 Cribb, 8.

techniques, and because they are evaded in distribution by new types of agreement. What the public thinks, or prefers to think, is of no importance. This is what is hidden by all these opinion polls, elections, modernizing restructurings. No matter who the winners are, the faithful customers *will get the worst of it*, because that is exactly what has been produced for them.[25]

As I have argued elsewhere,[26] any State that has been (extra-) constitutionally reconstituted under criminal sovereignty—or, in the alternative, has been socially and economically reduced to the pure functionality of the integrated spectacle—may be expected to exhibit the following four signs: governance as a substitute for government (the collapse of the distinction between 'public state' and 'civil society', resulting in an open-ended but clandestine 'privatisation' of the State); duality (the iterable relationship between 'law' and 'crime'); nomadicism (a chaotic proliferation of supra-statist, statist, and sub-statist entities, all of an indeterminate legal nature, that regularly transverse established juro-political boundaries[27]); and the irrational (the invisible co-option of the 'public interest' by the 'private actor'). The radical criminological term for this temporal dominium of criminal sovereignty—'the historical moment by which we happen to be governed'—is parapolitics, the study of 'criminals behaving as sovereigns and sovereigns behaving as criminals in a systematic way…The task of parapolitics as a discipline is to identify the dynamics of that

25 Debord, *Comments*, 69-70.

26 Wilson, *Government of the Shadows*, generally.

27 Here, I am employing 'nomadicism' in the sense of 'the nomadic' as developed by Deleuze and Guattari at 351-423. The nomadic denotes not only a free moving material agent or agency, but also the ontological indeterminacy of the nomadic force, the equivalent of the 'un-decidable' in Deconstruction.

relationship and to delimit precisely the influence that it has, or does not have, on public politics.'[28]

Most closely identified with the progressive scholarship of Peter Dale Scott, who strives throughout his work to formulate a new terminology, or even a poetics, with which to convey new understandings of hitherto un-describable political phenomena, the as yet still marginalized notion of the parapolitical lends itself supremely well to a Debordean application.[29] Scott defines parapolitics in the following manner:

> 1. A system or practice of politics in which accountability is consciously diminished. 2. Generally, covert politics, the conduct of public affairs not by rational debate and responsible decision-making but by indirection, collusion, and deceit. Cf. *conspiracy*. 3. The political exploitation of irresponsible agencies or para-structures, such as intelligence agencies.[30]

For Debord the reduction of media to the functionality of spectacle induces the collective loss of historical and political reason; 'under the rule of the integrated spectacle, we live and die at the confluence of innumerable mysteries.'[31] For Scott, the essence of the parapolitical is an 'intervening layer of irrationality under our political culture's rational surface.'[32] The submerged, or repressed, nature of covert agency is not only an ontological problem but an epistemological one as well; it is precisely because of its irrational nature that the parapol-

---

28 Cribb, 8.
29 See Kinkle in general.
30 Scott, *War Conspiracy*, 238.
31 Debord, *Comments*, 55; also, 25, 40, 69 and 74.
32 Scott, *Deep Politics*, 6-7.

itical evades cognitive recognition, with all of the attendant ideological implications.

> Just as politics as a field ('political science') studies the overt politics of the public state, so parapolitics, as a field, studies the relationships between the public state and the political processes and arrangements outside and beyond conventional politics. However, conventional, or liberal, political science assumes the normalcy of the state, both in its constitutional and normative dimensions, as a given and studies political phenomenon from the perspective of the state. Parapolitics, in contrast, constitutes a radically nominalist critique of conventional political studies. Parapolitics uses the varying levels of interaction between conventional states and quasi-statist entities as the basis for formulating an analytical perspective that privileges neither the state nor its alternatives as legitimate international actors. Although of no determinative political bias, parapolitics does foster a basic scepticism regarding the coherence of orthodox liberal understandings of the state.[33]

As a result of the clandestine application of spectacular power, mainstream scholarship is rendered thoroughly oblivious to the operational presence of the parapolitical mechanisms of governance, collectively denoted as the *Deep State*.

> Liberal political science has been turned into an ideology of the 'deep state' because undisputable evidence for the [national security] 'deep state' is brushed away as pure fantasy or conspiracy[34]... Thus, the problem with liberalism in political sci-

---

33 Wilson, 'Deconstructing the Shadows', 30.
34 Ola Tunander cited in Wilson, 'Deconstructing the Shadows', 29

ence and legal theory is not its ambition to defend
the public sphere, political freedoms and human
rights, but rather its claim that these freedoms and
rights define the Western political system.[35]

For Scott, parapolitical scholarship has enabled us to directly perceive two aspects of the Deep State.

The potentially larger condition of a shadow government, or a state within a state, is what we may
call the *deep state phenomenon*. But there [is]
also the more operational sense of the *deep state
connection*: a hard-edged coalition of witting
forces including intelligence networks, official
enforcement, illegal sanctioned violence, and an
internationally connected drug mafia.[36]

My own predilection, however, is to resist the totalizing
implications of the language of Scott's more recent
work; in place of the seemingly monolithic Deep State, I
prefer the radically pluralistic—if not latently schizophrenic—notion of Scott's earlier term, the *Dual State*.

The Dual State. A *State* in which one can distinguish between a *public state* and a top-down deep
state. The *deep state* emerges in a false-flag violence, is organized by the military and intelligence
apparatus and involves their link to organized
crime. Most states exhibit this duality, but to varying degrees. In America the duality of the state
has become more and more acute since World

---

35 Tunander, 68.

36 Scott, *American War Machine*, 21. 'Today everything that has ever been
labelled "invisible government", or "shadow government" can be
considered parts of that machine—not just the CIA and organized crime
but also such other non-accountable powers as the military-industrial
complex (now the financial-military-industrial complex), privatized
military and intelligence contractors, public relations experts, and even
Washington's most highly organized lobbyists.' *Ibid*.

War II.[37]

The dual nature, or duality, of the State signifies the suspension of political monism and the division of the residual 'State' into a public domain and a (quasi-) private 'para-state'. Even more subversive is the (potentially) unlimited sub-division of the para-state into multifarious and competing clandestine groupings. The duality of the State correlates precisely with spectacular power; any State under the aegis of the integrated spectacle suffers an absolute loss of onto-political meaning by that fact alone.

> So it is that thousands of plots in favor of the established order tangle and clash almost everywhere, as the overlap of secret networks and secret issues or activities grows ever more dense along with their rapid integration into every sector of economics, politics and culture. In all areas of social life the degree of intermingling in surveillance, disinformation and security activities gets greater and greater. The plot having thickened to the point where it is almost out in the open, each part of it now starts to interfere with, or worry, the others, for all these professional conspirators are spying on each other without really knowing why, are colliding by chance yet not identifying each other with any certainty…In the same network and apparently pursuing similar goals, those who are only a part of the network are necessarily ignorant of the hypothesizes and conclusions of the other parts, and above all of their controlling nucleus.[38]

---

37 Scott, *War Conspiracy*, 238. In turn, the 'Dual State' equates with a 'deep political system', which Scott defines as 'one which habitually resorts to decision-making and enforcement procedures outside as well as inside those publicly sanctioned by law and society. In popular terms, collusive secrecy and law-breaking are part of how the deep political system works.' Scott, *Deep Politics and the Death of JFK*, xi-xii.

38 Debord, *Comments*, 82-3.

But the truly vital connective thread between Debord and Scott lies within their respective meditations upon the primacy of the clandestine manipulation of public perception and social discourse for the domination of the politically irrational. For Scott, no less than for Debord, a stage-managed form of universal cognitive dissonance constitutes the highest form of parapolitical governance; in Scott's terminology, the mass production and consumption of *deep events*, 'events that are systematically ignored, suppressed, or falsified in public (and even internal) government, military, and intelligence documents as well as in the mainstream media and public consciousness.' Like Debord, Scott has conceived of modern civilization as '"a great conspiracy of organized denial"', the creation of a 'partly illusory mental space in which unpleasant facts, such as that all Western empires have been established through major atrocities, are conveniently suppressed.'[39] Deploying the deep event as an instrument of parapolitical hermeneutics, Scott has advanced the proposition that the integrated spectacle is the interpretative key of the national history of the U.S.

> In American history there are two types of events. There are ordinary events which the information systems of the country can understand and transmit. There are also deep events, or mega-events, which the mainstream information systems of the country cannot digest. I mean by a 'deep event' one in which it is clear from the outset that there are aspects which will not be dealt with in the mainstream media, and will be studied only by those so-called conspiracy theorists' who specialize in deep history.[40]

---

39 Scott, *American War Machine*, 3.
40 Scott, '9/11, JFK, and War', 1.

Understood not as an accumulation of episodic events but as manifestations of foundational systemic properties, these deep events 'suggest the on-going presence in America of what I have called a "dark force" or "deep state," analogous to what [Vincenzo] Vinciguerra described in Italy as a "secret force...occult and hidden, with the capacity of giving a strategic direction to the [successive] outrages."'[41] For Scott, then, 'national security state conspiracies' as deep events serve as 'components of our political structure, not deviations from them.'[42]

Especially germane for my purpose is Scott's arresting equation between the deep event and the (integrated) spectacle of the false-flag, best understood as a self-inflicted catastrophe within the public sphere as a means of: (a) controlling political perceptions; and (b) temporarily obviating conventional political operations in favor of enhancing the decisionism of the Executive branch—in other words Carl Schmitt's infamous 'state of exception'.[43] If deep events can be shown to periodically recalibrate the psychic economy of the collective post-political consciousness through the instantaneous and unending circulatory operations of mass media, then the hyper-intensive visuality and theatricality of false-flag spectacle may legitimately be considered an indispensable tool of clandestine suppression through the control of perception by means of media circulated imagery. In this sense, the false-flag resembles nothing so much as a media saturated variant of the much wider covert phenomenon of the strategy-of-tension, a parapolitical mode of governance mediated through catastro-

---

41 Scott, 'Systemic Destabilization', 4 of 18.

42 Michael Parenti, cited in Scott, *American War Machine*, 210.

43 Wilson, 'The Concept of the Parapolitical', generally.

phe. As Scott alludes, Italy is the contemporary birth-place of classic strategy-of-tension para-statism: Italy: the Piazza Fontana bombing in 1960, the Piazza della Loggia bombing in 1974, and the Bologna railway bombing of 1980, were all terrorist acts conducted by a clandestine far-right network embedded within the Italian military, national security, and police networks—and which, since this is Italy, included the Mafia—that were all re-presented by an hysteria obsessed media as manifestations of the homicidal will of the Far Left.[44] In the words of Vincenzo Vinciguerra, one of the convicted conspirators, the explosions were 'supposed to be the detonator which would have convinced the political and military authorities to declare a state of emergency.'[45] If the U.S., in turn, can properly be considered to constitute a Dual State—like Italy—then I should be able to point to instances of decisive political importance wherein the strategy-of-tension served as a mechanism of governance; equally, I should be able to provide evidence of false-flag spectacles having become embedded within the para-political landscape the Dual State.

YANKEES AND COWBOYS

> *"Clandestinism is not the usage of a handful of rogues, it is a formalized practice of an entire class in which a thousand hands spontaneously join. Conspiracy is the normal continuation of normal politics by normal means."*
> —Carl Oglesby

An acknowledged classic in the literature of so-called

---

44 Ganser, generally.
45 Scott, 'Systemic Destabilization', 1 of 18.

'conspiracy theory', Carl Oglesby's *The Yankee-Cowboy War* (1976) imposes a Debordean geo-political grid upon the parapolitical systems and networks of the U.S. Dual State, that most violently manifested itself in The War Between the States (1861-65).[46] Almost alone of works on American 'deep History', Oglesby's text radically prioritizes the legacy of the struggle over Secession, revealing it as the genetic determinant of the U.S. as a quintessential dual (-ist) State.

> [T]he cost of nationhood in the United States was not merely a sectional compromise but also a compact between two distinct elites—a modern [sic] capitalist class that increasingly recognized the advantages of a free labor system and a southern planter class already implicitly committed to the preservation and extension of slavery… Hence, the United States seemingly emerged from its revolutionary period without a national ruling class; it was in fact a federation of two regional ruling classes.'[47]

---

46 'That a power struggle of some kind is in fact necessary from the beginning [of American History] and that there has always been "a split at the top" is best evidenced by the struggle over secession.' Oglesby, *Yankee-Cowboy War*, 323 fn. 3.

47 George M. Frederickson, cited in ibid, 323 fn. 3. As Oglesby freely admits, the core of his thesis is taken directly from Caroll Quigley's magisterial work on the 'anglo-sphere', *Tragedy and Hope: A History of the World in Our Time*: 'The period since 1950 has seen the beginnings of a revolutionary change in American politics. This change is not so closely related to the changes in American economic life as it is to the transformation in social life. But without the changes in economic life, the social influences could not have operated. What has been happening has been a disintegration of the middle class and a corresponding increase in significance by the petty bourgeoisie at the same time that the economic influence of the older Wall Street financial groups has been weakening and been challenged by new wealth springing up outside the eastern cities, notably in the Southwest and Far West. These new sources of wealth have been based very largely on government action and government spending but have, none the less, adopted a petty-bourgeois

Almost alone in following Oglesby, Scott, in his seminal work on the John Kennedy (hereafter JFK) assassination, *Deep Politics and the Death of JFK* (1993), was the first to deliberately situate the locus for the potential for conspiracy within regionally based networks and factions that follow the broad excavations of Oglesby's post-Secessionist schema. This theme of regionalism-as-dualism continues straight into Scott's most recent work.

> [I]t is quite possible to acknowledge that there are both ongoing continuities in American policy and also important, hidden, and recurring internal divisions that have given rise to America's structural deep events. These events have repeatedly involved friction between Wall Street and the [Council on Foreign Relations] on the one hand, and the increasingly powerful oil- and military-dominated economic centers of the Midwest and the Texas Sunbelt on the other. At the time that General MacArthur, drawing on his Midwest and Texas support, threatened to challenge Truman and the State Department, the opposition was seen as one between the traditional Europe-Firsters of the Northeast and the new-wealth Asia-

outlook rather than the semi-aristocratic outlook that pervades the Eastern Establishment. This new wealth based on petroleum, natural gas, ruthless exploitation of national resources, the aviation industry, military bases in the South and West, and finally on space with all its attendant activities has centred in Texas and southern California. In existence, for the first time, made it possible for the petty-bourgeois outlook to make itself felt in the political nomination process instead of in the unrewarding effort to influence politics by voting for a Republican candidate nominated under Eastern Establishment influence.' Quigley, 1245-6. Naturally Quigley's state-centric account needs to be updated for our post-modern contemporary reality, primarily in the way in which the two regional/economic blocs have fused into a supra-statist entity labelled by Scott as 'the American War Machine', a hybridization underpinned by the transformation of high-velocity financial networks into cybernetic weapons systems; see Wilson, 'Criminogenic Cyber-Capitalism', generally.

> Firsters. In the 1952 [federal] election, the foreign
> policy debate was between Democratic 'contain-
> ment' and Republican 'roll-back'... [a split] even
> within the CIA, between 'Wall Street internation-
> alism' on the one hand and 'cowboy-style' expan-
> sionism on the other.[48]

Because of its obvious political symbolism, both Scott
and Oglesby naturally focus on the JFK assassination—
the spectacular murder of a New England liberal President in a reactionary southern state—as a pivotal micro-
event encapsulating macro-level parapolitical trends. But
The Yankee-Cowboy War is even more audacious in its
scope than *Deep Politics and the Death of JFK*: Oglesby
claims to have uncovered a hitherto unrecognized 'parapolitical symmetry' between the two great political scan-
dals of 1960s and 1970s America respectively: the
murder of JFK and the constitutional overthrow of
Richard Nixon.

> The assassination of John Kennedy and the down-
> fall of Richard Nixon have both been viewed as
> isolated and moral disasters for American demo-
> cracy... [In truth, the] two events are actually
> concrete links in a chain of related and ominous
> events passing through the entire decade in which
> they occurred and beyond. And this chain of
> events itself represents only the violent eruptions
> of a deeper power struggle of rival power elites
> identified here as Yankees and Cowboys. This
> book proposes to show that Dallas and Watergate
> are intrinsically linked conspiracies in a hidden
> drama of coup and countercoup which represents
> the life of an inner oligarchic power sphere, an
> 'invisible government,' capable of any act in the
> pursuit of its objectives, that sets itself above the

---

48 Scott, *American War Machine*, 208-9.

law and beyond the moral rule: a clandestine
American state, perhaps an embryonic police
state.[49]

In essence, Oglesby is suggesting that both dramas were
governed by a covert mechanism of parapolitical exchange; unable to successfully manage its international
transition to Hegemon because of the embedded, or
'deep' structure of factional regionalism within the domestic political economy, the U.S. from 1945 to 1973
underwent a kind of clandestine factional power struggle
'safely' mediated through the periodic staging of integrated spectacles.

> The Dallas-to-Watergate outburst is fundament-
> ally attributable to the breakdown [that took
> place] within the incumbent national coalition, the
> coalition of the Greater Northeastern powers
> [anglophilia; international finance capitalism;
> Wall Street; The Council on Foreign Relations;
> NATO] with the Greater Southwestern powers
> [anglophobia; the aero-space industry; The China
> Lobby; the petroleum industry; the manufacturing
> sectors of the 'military-industrial complex'], the
> post-Civil War, post-Reconstruction coalition, the
> coalition of the New Deal, of Yankees and Cow-
> boys.[50]

This is 'Civil War II', [51] a simulacrum of the earlier War
Between the States, but this time waged through clandestine agencies waving a false-flag of some sort, signifying the re-direction of covert agency from foreign into
domestic political space—the political nightmare of the
internationalization of Harry Truman's national security

---

49 Oglesby, *Yankee-Cowboy*, 3-4.

50 Ibid, 4-5.

51 Ibid, 14.

State.

> This is the theme, at bottom, of the entire narra-
> tion to follow. The agony of the Yankees and the
> Cowboys, the 'cause' of their divergence in the
> later Cold War period, is that there was finally too
> much tension between the detentist strategy of the
> Yankees in the Atlantic and the militarist strategy
> of the Cowboys in the Pacific. To maintain the
> two lines was, in effect, to maintain two separate
> and opposed realities at once, two separate and
> contradictory domains of world-historical truth. In
> Europe and the industrial world, the evident truth
> was that we could live with communism. In Asia
> and the [Developing World], the evident truth was
> that we could not, that we had to fight and win
> wars or else face the terrible consequences at
> home [in the form of civil unrest and radical left-
> ism]. As long as the spheres of détente and viol-
> ence could be kept apart in American policy and
> consciousness, as long as the Atlantic and the Pa-
> cific could remain two separate planes of reality
> wheeling within each other on opposite assump-
> tions and never colliding, then American foreign
> policy could wear a look of reasonable integra-
> tion. But when it became clear that the United
> States could not win its way militarily in [East
> Asia] without risking a nuclear challenge in the
> North Atlantic, the makings of a dissolving con-
> sensus were at hand.[52]

Essential to Oglesby's schema is the cathartic function
of the role played by spectacular power; the trauma of
the spectacular event was consciously intended to yield a
post-traumatic rehabilitation of political and cultural
consensus through a prescribed script of appropriation.
This becomes clear when we realize the depths of

---

52 Ibid, 5.

Oglesby's crypto-Debordean approach: 'The intensification of clandestine, illicit methods against racial and antiwar dissent [i.e., "The Spirit of 1968'] as a "threat" to the (secret) state precisely coincided with the intensified use of such methods in conflicts for power and hegemony taking place *within* the secret state, against a background of declining consensus.'[53] The language here is wholly Debordean; although *Comments on the Society of the Spectacle* appears nowhere within Oglesby's text, *The Yankee-Cowboy War* uncannily replicates Debord's post-cynical reconstitution of the primacy of covert power within the age of spectacular power: 'Clandestinism is not the usage of a handful of rogues, it is a formalized practice of an entire class in which a thousand hands spontaneously join. Conspiracy is the normal continuation of normal politics by normal means.'[54]

For Oglesby, both Dallas and Watergate 'book-end' the tumultuous decade of the 1960s, which ultimately culminated in the irreversible transition of domestic hegemony away from the North-East Yankee elites to the South-West Cowboy factions, solidified by the election of Ronald Reagan and the establishment of the U.S. as a 'pure war' State.[55] In the following chapters, I will offer a full-length Debordean reading of Oglesby's thesis, adding an important observation of my own—that Dallas and Watergate, the shift from Yankee towards Cowboy political economies—were linked by an under-studied integrated spectacle: the Gulf of Tonkin incident.

53Ibid, 5.

54 Ibid, 27-8.

55 Wilson, 'Criminogenic Cyber-Capitalism', generally; see also Wilson, 'Speed/Pure War/Power Crime', generally.

[PHOTO: November 24, 1963. Jack Ruby about to shoot Lee Harvey Oswald who is being escorted by Dallas police detectives Jim Leavelle and L. C. Graves. Taken by Ira Jefferson "Jack" Beers Jr. for The Dallas Morning News]

2 | False Flag I: JFK / Dallas

*'What cost Kennedy his life was his attempt
to impose the limits of Camelot
Atlanticism on a Frontier-minded defense
and security elite.'*—Carl Oglesby

The single most striking, but generally under-appreciated, aspect of Dealey Plaza, is also the most Debordean feature of the JFK assassination: the spectacularly *public* nature of the execution. In both the endlessly re-cycled iconic 'Zapruder film', as well as in Oliver Stone's monumental film *JFK*, a spectacular cinematic appropriation of a spectacle,[1] the collective impressions mediated through the imagery are those of the clandestine false-flag event: shock, trauma, disorientation, cognitive dissonance—all of the epistemo-cognitive affinities of a parapolitical deep event that, like Poe's purloined letter, is 'hiding in plain sight'. On closer reflection, it is the killing of Kennedy in such audaciously open space that itself raises the most intriguing questions. If the purpose of the assassination as an 'inside job' (i.e. U.S. intelligence services) was simply to

---

1 See Chapter Five.

kill JFK, then the murder both could and should have been conducted in private space.[2] However, the public spectacle of Dealey Plaza, a veritable outdoor amphitheater, itself provides compelling but indirect evidence of the false-flag nature of the event and it is in terms of the spectacular nature of the act that the assassination must be understood: a highly stage-managed act of clandestine theatre, consciously intended to manipulate public perceptions of reality so as to engineer a pre-given set of parapolitical outcomes.[3] In this section, I will outline a 'minimalist' theory of a conspiracy to assassinate the President; that is, in order for a deep event to be made out on the basis of the historical record before us, what conditions must have been fulfilled and what is the absolute minimum that must be true? My central thesis is that a 'minimalist' theory (following CIA nomenclature, hereafter referred to as JFK/DALLAS) would involve two necessary suppositions: (i) that the murder of Kennedy was a false-flag operation (the artificial cre-

---

2 I owe this keen observation to Guido Preparata. The Joint Chiefs of Staff were aware that JFK suffered from Addison disease and was addicted to cortisone and other pain-killers while J. Edgar Hoover had extensive files on Kennedy's sexual addiction, which easily could have been used as political blackmail, forcing the President to either resign or, possibly, to undergo impeachment. Talbot, 42. According to William Sullivan, the 'number three man' at the FBI under Hoover: "'I was sure [Hoover] was saving everything he had on Kennedy, and on Martin Luther King Jr., too, until he could unload it all and destroy them both. He kept this kind of material in his personal files, which filled four rooms on the fifth floor of headquarters.'" Cited in Talbot, 142.

3 Admittedly, following this logic, I would also be able to conclude that the 'in plain sight' spectacle of Dealey Plaza provides indirect support of Oswald as the lone gunman; public space was the shooter's only means of access to the President. Here, the sniper's physical space from the moving target correlates to the lone gunman's para-political distance from the Executive. However, as I shall show, the possible fact of Oswald as a lone gunman does not by itself disprove the existence of a 'conspiracy' or subtract anything from Dealey Plaza as a parapolitical spectacle.

ation of a 'state of exception' by the covert agencies of the State to further an otherwise politically unacceptable foreign policy objective, in this case the invasion of Cuba); and (ii) that the epicenter of the operation was within the disparate and myriad 'parapolitical' networks of Cold War Miami, New Orleans, Mexico City and Dallas (primarily the CIA and the anti-Castro Cuban networks with a possible subsidiary role performed by the Mafia).

THE DEEP EVENT AND PHILOSOPHICAL DENIAL

'I have always believed, and argued, that a true understanding of the Kennedy assassination will lead not to "a few bad people," but to the institutional and parapolitical arrangements which constitute the way we are systematically governed.'—Peter Dale Scott

Within 'mainstream' or orthodox political discourse, the possibility of a deep event—or, in somewhat pejorative terms, a 'conspiracy'—involving JFK or national politics altogether are ordinarily dismissed on grounds *a priori*. For the Right (of-center), such refusal is grounded on the axiomatic nature of the liberal-democratic consensus and the daily re-enactments of the (media regulated) transparent model of the modern Western State. For the Left (of-center), the *a priori* of the negative is the self-evident ideological uniformity of the political elites: the clandestine agencies of the State would never feel the need to assassinate its own Chief Executive precisely because the monolithic nature of the liberal State would preclude that that Chief Executive would ever act contrary to the self-interest and wishes of the Establishment

—the elite manufacturers of consent in Chomsky's famous phrase.[4]

What unites both positions, apart from their mutual rhetorical posturing through the media, is that both reject the pluralistic model of the Dual State, relying instead upon the orthodoxy of political monism, the preferred paradigm of the Western intelligentsia since Plato and, in the 20th century, reaffirmed most emphatically by Martin Heidegger.[5] For Heidegger, the inherently political nature of the relationship between the political being of the State and political reason (*ratio*):

> [S]prings from the essence of truth as correctness in the sense of the self-adjusting guarantee of the security of domination. The 'taking as true' of *ratio*, of *reor*, becomes a far-reaching and anticipatory security. *Ratio* becomes counting, calculating, calculus. *Ratio* is self-adjustment to what is correct.[6]

In Heidegger's view, political 'truth' that equates with

---

4 Chomsky's attitude towards Dealey Plaza is exemplary: the assassination is of historical importance only if it provides proof of 'a high-level conspiracy followed by a cover-up of remarkable dimensions'. As there is in fact no evidence, then conspiracy theorists must engage in empirically unverifiable counterfactuals to construct an *a priori* argument, such as an early U.S. withdrawal from Vietnam if JFK had *not* been murdered—all of which betrays a fundamental incomprehension of the nature of American political power and foreign policy. For Chomsky, all such hypothetical counterfactuals 'are baseless, and hold little interest. In the present case [Kennedy's approach towards Vietnam], there is a rich record to assist us in understanding the roots of policy and its implementation. People who want to understand and change the world will do well, in my opinion, to pay attention to it, and not engage in groundless speculation as to what one or another leader might have done.' Chomsky, 38. All of the institutions of the 'new mandarins' are both total and totalizing.

5 See Wilson, 'The Concept of the Parapolitical', 5-8.

6 Heidegger, *Parmenides*, 50.

correctness is both delimited by a homologous discursive space and subjugated to the political will to domination; 'The essence of truth as *veritas* [i.e. correctness] is *without space* and without ground,'[7] signifying the unreality of the heterogeneous, or the 'different'; 'The result is the *presence* of truth as self-evidence, or the presence of thought to itself in the manner of self-identity' within an exclusively homogenous discursive space.[8] *Veritas* is the ground of western jurisprudence's conflation of Law with Reason, establishing an undifferentiated chain of signifiers delimiting the parameters of 'orthodox' or 'common' legal speech. Homogeneity guarantees that whatever is not identical with *ratio* cannot constitute a portion of reality and, by political implication, cannot constitute an actual attribute of the 'true' State. Consequently, 'the idea of sovereignty, which clearly implies but one absolute power laying in the social order, with all relationships, all individuals...ultimately subject to it, has been the characteristic approach to the political community.'[9]

Nationalism is secular mythology.[10] The onto-political division that originated with Plato serves as the historical originary of the modern nationalistic myth of the homologous Nation-State. According to Heidegger, it is with Hegel that 'the transformation of veritas into certitudo is completed. This completion of the Roman essence of truth is the proper and hidden historical meaning of the nineteenth century.'[11] It is also, however,

---

7 Ibid.

8 'There is no space, no distance, between our true thoughts concerning a state of affairs in the world and that state of affairs: the two coincide.' Bell, 28.

9 Nisbet, 386.

10 See generally Anderson.

11 Heidegger, *Parmenides*, 58

very much the historical meaning of the 'long sixteenth century' (1492-1648), the critical incubating period for early modern international law; the Dutch Republic of the early 17th century had emerged as a self-grounding juro-political space, delimited by three undifferentiated signs: sovereignty (*potestas*), freedom (*libertas*), and right (*ius*).[12] Although Heidegger situates the historical victory of political monism in the post-Napoleonic period, it is clear that onto-political homogeneity—or what I have referred to as the indivisibility of sovereignty[13]— had achieved an irreversible ascendancy by the time of Jean Bodin (1529/30-1596), as Jens Bartelson has established.

> Since Bodin, indivisibility has been integral to the concept of sovereignty itself. In international political theory, this means that whenever sovereignty is used in a theoretical context to confer unity upon the state as an acting subject, all that it conveys is that this entity is an individual by virtue of its indivisibility [i.e. its homologous space], which is tautological indeed. What follows from this search for the locus of sovereignty in international political theory, however necessary to its empirical testability is thus nothing more than a logical sideshow; the essential step towards unity is already taken whenever sovereignty figures in the definition of political order. Whether thought to be upheld by an individual or a collective, or embedded in the State as a whole, sovereignty entails self-presence and self-sufficiency; that which is sovereign is immediately given to itself, con-

---

12 See Wilson, *The Savage Republic,* Chapters Five and Six. As the case of the Brothers Koerbagh (Johannes and Adriaen) reveals, contesting the delimiting effects of official terminology within the Dutch state could ruin one's life. See Israel, 185-96.

13 See generally Wilson, 'Deconstructing the Shadows'.

scious of itself, and thus acting for itself. That is, as it figures in international political theory, sovereignty is not an attribute of something whose existence is prior to or independent of sovereignty; rather, it is the concept of sovereignty itself which supplies this indivisibility and unity.[14]

Hegel notwithstanding, it was the early modern nation-state that acted as the discursive space of the identity of unity with political power (*potestas*). The presence of unity/monism equates with the absence of pluralism, which is the multiplication, or proliferation, of political identities and entities. According to Robert Nisbet

It has been the fate of pluralism in Western thought to take a rather poor second place to philosophies which make their point of departure the premise of, not the diversity and plurality of things, but, rather, some underlying unity and symmetry, needing only to be uncovered by pure reason to be then deemed the 'real', the 'true', and the 'lasting'.[15]

Yet the Platonic denial of difference contains within itself the very grounds of its actual reversal. The apparent falsity of the originary myth, the inversion of Bartelson's 'empirical testability', is affirmed by the historical continuation of difference(s). As contemporary anti-Hegelian thought insists, the Nation-State 'is not best and fully understood as a teleological unity, directed exclusively at attending some single end or as having a single function'[16]—a profoundly parapolitical insight. In other words, the persistence of difference is itself the

---

14 Bartelson, 28. See also Wilson, *The Savage Republic*, 189-93.

15 Nisbet , 386. Nisbet's language repeats the tenor of Platonic myth.

16 Geuss, 61.

space of contestation of the Platonic myth; this is the central assumption of Heidegger's anti-Hegelian project. For Heidegger, 'serious'—that is, metaphysical—thought within the post-Hegelian State demands a return to the early Hellenic concept of *aletheia* (the 'un-concealed'[17]) that pre-dated *veritas*,[18] which is both the awareness and the actively making aware of the governing presence of ontology (Being) in all forms of thought and speech, 'the uncommon within the common'; 'For us, the matter of thinking is the Same, and this is Being —but Being with respect to its difference from beings.'[19] Until this moment, what has been lacking in western *logos* is the primacy of heterogeneity, the 'essential space of *aletheia*, the unconcealedness of things...a space completely covered over by debris and forgotten.'[20] Ironically, the fatal flaw of the Heideggerian project lies within this very move towards the un-concealing of the heterogeneous: whenever Heidegger attempts to convey a positive definition of Being, as opposed to the mere invocation of it, he reduces it to a self-identical and (re-) unifying 'ideal of simplicity, purity and self-containment'.[21] To think about Being as such is to repeat, on another level, the original sin of Platonism: the fetishizing of the (self-) identical. The true substitution of homo-

---

17 That is, a non-correspondence notion of 'truth'.

18 Bell's commentary on this is excellent. 'Truth as *aletheia*, as the unstable Being and clearing which allows for the presencing of thinking and being, is stabilised and replaced by the Roman view of truth as *veritas*, as correctness.' Bell, 26.

19 Heidegger, *Identity and Difference*, 47; see also 50.

20 Heidegger, *Parmenides*, 50.

21 Bell, 150. Being 'is the unifying One, in the sense of what is everywhere primal and thus most 'universal; and at the same time it is the unifying One in the sense of the All-Highest (Zeus).' Heidegger, *Parmenides*, 69. 'Truth"—that which is un-concealed—is difference, the being(s) within Being. However, within the Heideggerian schema, beings are ultimately revealed as embedded within the primordial and universal One.

geneity with heterogeneity demands a radical and un-
conditional *rapprochement* with difference(s)/being(s):
the proof of the absence of political homogeneity is the
signification of the presence of a potentially radical and
discursively de-stabilizing heterogeneity. And it is precisely the uncovering of the concealed, the traumatic
revelation of the radical and irreducible heterogeneity of
the State that serves as the philosophical basis—whether
consciously expressed or not—of what is conventionally
referred to as 'conspiracy theory'.

Given, however, the philosophical pedigree of princi-
pled doubt concerning all things 'conspiratorial', I am
loathe to undertake a direct critique of this media-manu-
factured consensus. Rather, my own form of empirical
'testability' will be along lines more oblique: employing
Occam's Razor, I hold that the preferred explanation in
any theory of a possible deep event as political conspiracy is the one that most economically reduces the element
of implausibility—or, in the alternative, most lowers the
'threshold of resistance'—to the possibility of clandestine autonomy within the allegedly indivisible unity of
the State. My own interest in JFK/DALLAS stems in
part from my personal experience of the reverse application of Occam to Oswald, namely the improbably high
number of (seemingly) meaningful coincidences that,
accumulatively, constitute a body of persuasive circumstantial evidence, albeit on the lower evidentiary threshold of balance-of-probabilities rather than beyond-
reasonable doubt. Charles Pigden has articulated the implications of this beautifully: depending on the nature of
the event in question 'non-conspiracy theories may be
more complex. They may require an elaborate and unlikely sequence of coincidences or complicated social
mechanisms which *duplicate* the appearance of conspir-

acy.'[22] The notion of JFK/DALLAS as a false-flag spectacle provides the least implausible of the JFK conspiracy theories not only because of its innate simplicity but precisely because the strategy-of-tension that signifies constitutes empirical verification of the parapolitical governance within the Dual State. If JFK/DALLAS can be intelligibly read as a singular event within a broader pattern of strategy-of-tension enactments as an instrument of spectacular power, then not only can the requisite elements of the conspiracy be made out, but the assassination would be automatically invested with 'deep' political significance.

Oglesby situates the crux of the parapolitical dilemma of the Kennedy administration within the catastrophic implementation of the (spectacular) ZAPATA Plan—better known as the invasion of the Bay of Pigs (April 15-19, 1961)[23] –which served as the fulcrum of a dangerously precarious Northeast/Southwest divide within the elite coalition of the Kennedy administration (Massachusetts/Texas).[24]

> [The] Kennedy administration was in sharp internal conflict over what to do about Cuba, and... the formulation and implementation of Frontier Camelot Cuban policy were affected by this conflict or, as might be said, disfigured by it. That is the key point which the Cold War conception of the Bay of Pigs Fiasco cannot bring into focus: that the Cuban question and the question of hemispheric revolution so divided the Kennedy administration that the United States could neither accept Castro nor act with a will to destroy what

22 Pigden, 37.
23 Freedman, 123-48.
24 Oglesby, *Yankee-Cowboy*, 77.

Castro stood for.[25]

Strikingly, the deep politics both within the Kennedy administration itself as well as among diverse anti-Castro groups mirrors the contending paradigms of Cold War neo-colonialist warfare, between that of covert forms of para-military warfare favored by the Yankee CIA and more conventional but exceptionally large-scale exercises of direct military intervention endorsed by the more Cowboy Joint Chiefs of Staff (JCS) and the Pentagon. Even more unnerving, this debate over the correct strategy towards Cuba prefigured almost exactly the equally unresolvable debate over the nature, aims, and scope of military intervention in Vietnam during the 'Kennedy phase' of the war.[26] Enamored as the President was by the entire notion of clandestine power, General Maxwell Taylor's very covert friendly doctrine of the 'flexible response' proved to be the cornerstone of the strategic thought of Kennedy's administration.

> The strategic doctrine which I propose to replace Massive Retaliation is called herein the Strategy of Flexible Response. This name suggests the need for a capability to react across the entire spectrum of possible challenge, for coping with anything from general atomic war to infiltrations and aggressions such as threaten Laos and Berlin in 1959.[27]

Crucial to understanding the fiasco is that although presented as a covert operation, governed at all times by strict 'plausible denial'—a signature of the Kennedy administration[28]—there is little doubt that the ZAPATA

25 Ibid, 50.

26 Freedman, generally.

27 Taylor cited in ibid, 19.

28 Ibid, 133-5. Defined as intelligence operations 'that might cause

Plan was actually a carefully engineered trap, intended to commit the President to a full-scale military invasion of Cuba.

> Past experience suggested to the CIA and the military that these [executive] commitments were never fixed and that the pressure of events would oblige the president to bring American power to bear... [According to Allen Dulles] 'We felt that when the chips were down—when the crisis arose in reality, any request required for success would be authorized rather than permit the enterprise to fail.'[29]

In other words, a nominally 'Yankee' (CIA) operation was semi-consciously intended to yield 'Cowboy' outcomes (U.S. military intervention)—a micro-level restaging of the wider Yankee-Cowboy rift, which explains practically in toto the extreme indecisiveness exhibited by Kennedy during the crisis. On January 4, 1961 a preliminary paper on ZAPATA was drafted by two of the chief military planners, CIA officer Jack Esterline and Marine Colonel Jack Hawkins, making clear the operational assumption of the allegedly Cuban nationalist invasion as an immediate pre-text for full-scale U.S. attack.

> The primary objective of the [amphibious] force

---

embarrassment (because violate international law or for some other reason) should be planned and executed in a way that allow the head of government [or the Agency itself] to deny that he had anything to do with the activities or even know they were occurring.' Abram Shulsky cited in Albarelli, 438.

29 Freedman, 145 and 138. See also Blight and Kornbluh, 65-66, 69, 93, 94, 100 and 101. 'Few believed it—the CIA did not believe it—when Kennedy said that whatever happens, there will be no American military involvement. He meant it. They did not understand that he meant it.' Arthur Schlesinger in ibid, 65.

will be to survive and maintain its integrity on
Cuban soil. There will be no early attempt to
break out of the lodgment for further offensive
operations unless and until there is a general uprising against the Castro regime or overt military
intervention by United States forces has taken
place. It is expected that these operations will precipitate a general uprising throughout Cuba and
cause the revolt of large segments of the Cuban
Army and Militia...If matters do not eventuate as
predicted above, the lodgment established by our
force can be used as the site for establishment of a
provisional government which can be recognized
by the United States, and hopefully by other
American states, and given overt military assistance. The way will then be paved for United
States military intervention aimed at the pacifica-
tion of Cuba, and this will result in the prompt of
the Castro government.[30]

Oglesby's parapolitical interpretation of the Bay of Pigs
as a micro-deep event closely tracks the confused military nature of the Plan, which was, in turn, the external
manifestation of the underlying and unresolved tensions
of the Dual State.

---

30 Gleijeses, 17. For the system-wide cognitive 'dis-connect' between the
phase one planning of the invasion and the phase two mechanics of the
overthrow of the Castro regime, see ibid, 27-39. Hawkins later reiterated
the need for direct military action against Cuba in his post-mortem
assessment of ZAPATA, 'Record of Paramilitary Action Against the
Castro Government of Cuba', May 5, 1961, which replicated JFK's own
preoccupation with plausible denial: 'Further efforts to develop armed
internal resistance, or to organize Cuban exile forces, should not be made
in connection with a planned overt intervention by United States forces...
The Government and the people of the United States are not yet
psychologically conditioned to participate in the cold war with resort to
the harsh, rigorous, and often dangerous and painful measures which
must be taken in order to win.' Hawkin's report remained classified until
June 4, 1998. Kornbluh, 16.

> We see Kennedy's Cuban policy better if we
> simply recognize that it was formed under condi-
> tions of internal conflict, conflict within the exec-
> utive policy apparatus itself. Frontier Camelot
> was the Kennedy's attempt to transform an exag-
> geratedly wide *electoral* coalition—the
> Kennedy/Johnson, Yankee/Cowboy coalition—
> into an effective *governing* coalition, an attempt
> which failed at the Bay of Pigs, its first test, as it
> ultimately failed in Vietnam, its most tragic test.[31]

Compare this with Colonel Hawkins comments on the
Bay of Pigs, in discussion with historian Peter Kornbluh
in 1998.

> We should have done it so we could succeed. That
> was the whole thing. No one seemed to have suc-
> cess in mind. What they had in mind was is
> someone going to know about this. Success was
> what they should have been thinking about. It was
> a fundamental error that was really the underpin-
> ning of all the other errors made because every-
> body at the political level was trying for plausible
> deniability and that caused so many restrictions
> that the operation could not really be successful.[32]

Directly portending the future, and greater, catastrophe
of Vietnam, the Cowboy mind-set of the JCS on display
during ZAPATA clearly rendered it incapable of adequately planning and implementing a successful, large-
scale covert operation. According to Esterline,

> We [the ZAPATA Plan Task Force] would have
> debates and meetings among ourselves about the
> merits of this or that plan when, all of a sudden—
> and this had nothing to do with the White House

---

31 Oglesby, *Yankee-Cowboy*, 55.
32 Kornbluh, 265.

—but all of a sudden we would get a new order,
usually coming from a member of the Special
Group [on Cuba], telling us that we 'needed'
more of this or more of that—always more of
something. Very often, it would be generated by
some general who was a member of the Special
Group. It was often [Chairman of the Joint Chiefs
General Lyman] Lemnitzer for example, but others did this too. Those guys just didn't understand
anything about guerilla warfare. They wanted to
fight this thing as if it was World War II in
Europe, or something. You know, the whole thing
—land a huge invasion force and march forward
until you liberate the territory.[33]

The accentuating problem here, which is what made
Cuba the albatross of the Kennedy administration, was
that direct military intervention was the only truly reliable means of eliminating the Cuban government given
the overwhelming popularity and broad based support of
the Castro regime; predictably, Kennedy was 'looking
for the minimalist option when the only real possibilities
were maximalist in nature.'[34] Not surprisingly, then, the
Taylor Commission/Cuba Study Group drawn up by
JFK after the Bay of Pigs to provide post-mortem assessment of the fiasco concluded in no uncertain terms
that

A paramilitary operation of the magnitude of ZA-
PATA should not be prepared or conducted in
such a way that all U.S. support and connection
with it could be plausibly denied. Once the need

33 Blight and Kornbluh, 50-1.

34 Freedman, 145. A Special National Intelligence Estimate, released in
December 1960 'had foreseen no development "likely to bring about a
critical shift of popular opinion away from Castro." Any disaffection
would be "offset by the growing effectiveness of the state's
instrumentalities of control."' Ibid, 138.

> for the operation was established, its success
> should have had the primary consideration of all
> agencies of government...Operational restrictions
> designed to protect its covert character should
> have been accepted only if they did not impair the
> chance of success. As it was, the leaders of the
> operation were obliged to fit their plan inside
> changing ground rules laid down for military con-
> siderations, which often had serious operational
> disadvantages.[35]

The 'secret' reason for the fiasco was that clandestine techniques were employed in order to justify a U.S. military intervention in Cuba. Quite clearly, then, the seemingly autonomous debate over strategy was, in reality, little more than epiphenomenal; the governing truth is that covert versus invasion was the visible manifestation of Yankee versus Cowboy.

> This is why it is so important to see the Kennedy
> administration's record *not* in terms of its outward
> rationality, for it has none, and *not* as the expres-
> sion of Kennedy's will alone, for his will did not
> prevail, but in terms of the impassioned political
> in-fighting that in reality constituted its actual life.
> It is the relations of power *in America* that speak
> in Kennedy's apparent formula: If the Cuban ex-
> iles can make the invasion alone, let it be done,
> *but only if.* Or again: If the Vietnamese threat can
> be contained with a Special Forces-level commit-
> ment, and without disrupting North Atlantic rela-
> tions, let it be done, *but only if.* [36]

---

35 Bohning, 65.

36 Oglesby, *Yankee-Cowboy War,* 67. This touches directly upon a point of vital importance that, in my opinion, has been under-emphasized by scholars concerning the 'true intentions' of JFK with regards to Vietnam. As with so much else concerning the Kennedy presidency, the Vietnam debate took the form of a two track approach: not merely between intervention versus withdrawal, but also, and equally, between para-

It is at precisely this juncture that the parapolitical scholar is forced to confront what is perhaps the single most
disturbing series of documents of the Kennedy administration in regard to Cuba—the JCS proposal for OPERA-
TION NORTHWOODS.[37] Prepared by the Chief of the
JCS, Army General Lymon Lemnitzer, the operation
constitutes an unsettling hybrid of both covert and military measures—a clandestine form of parapolitical theatre to induce an integrated spectacle presaging a
military invasion of Cuba.

> U.S. military intervention will result from a peri-
> od of heightened U.S.-Cuban tensions which
> place the United Nations in the position of suffer-
> ing justifiable grievances. World opinion, and the
> United Nations forum should be favorably af-
> fected by developing the international image of
> the Cuban government as rash and irresponsible,
> and as an *alarming and unpredictable threat to
> the peace of the Western Hemisphere*.[38]

military counter-insurgency versus conventional warfare. See Johnson,
generally. According to Gareth Porter, JFK's much analyzed 'withdrawal
policy' of October 1963 was 'apparently prompted by new pressures
from the military to deploy combat forces to South Vietnam if necessary
to avoid defeat... [On 13 January 1963] the JCS sent McNamara a
memorandum that forcefully re-opened the issue of a commitment to
save the South Vietnamese regime by sending combat troops, if
necessary. It asserted that, if the Viet Cong could not be brought under
control, the JCS saw "no alternative to the introduction of U.S. military
combat forces" into South Vietnam.' Porter, 166. It would appear that the
bane of the Cuba Project—para-militaries versus armed forces—re-
surfaced in Vietnam. For discussion of JFK and Vietnam, see below, this
chapter.

37 It is important to note that some skepticism over the authenticity of the
OPERATION NORTHWOODS documents has been expressed by Carol
A. Valentine, who finds problematic the occasional use of British, rather
than American, English throughout the document. Cf. Valentine,
generally. However, most parapolitical scholars accept their authenticity.
Personal correspondence with Peter Dale Scott.

38 Lemnitzer, cited in Davis, 137. Italics added. It is important to compare

NORTHWOODS is an exceptionally grandiose example of the false-flag, the entirety of the operation embedded within the over-arching theatrical strategy of staging and managing public spectacle. It is, therefore, necessary to keep the nebulous relationship between the theatrical and the clandestine in mind at all times.

> The basis of the theatrical event is the encounter between different participants, where the boundaries between performer and spectator are in a state of flux. This fluid situation changes not only the context, but the quality of production and communication… [T]he sharing of the same space, which reveals a collective intent, can vary from a simple juxtaposition of presence that establishes a minimal level of connection, to a harmonizing common physical action… [T]he participant can shift role from actor to spectator and vice-versa, thereby determining each time a different level and quality of engagement and a varying degree of involvement.[39]

Somewhat in contrast to the convoluted counter-intelligence (i.e., psychological) operations of the actually implemented OPERATION MONGOOSE,[40] NORTHWOODS involved more overt elements of the brazenly theatrical.

> [N]ot just embodiment but enactment; not just a scheme of action but a plot of deceitful action; not just coordinated behavior but purposeful behavior for the creation of faith in illusion…the substitution, in some cases, of simulacrum for an event;

this passage with the language of the Gulf of Tonkin Resolution, 10 August, 1964; see Chapter Three.

39 Cremona, 'Introduction to Part One', *Theatrical Events*, 30, cited in Davis, 136.

40 See below, this chapter.

and manipulation of plot elements in order to
stimulate belief among persons necessary to (mis-
takenly) testify to the authenticity of the fabrication.[41]

Take, for example, the following.

> 4. We could develop a Communist Cuban
> terror campaign in the Miami area, in other
> Florida cities, or even Washington.

> The terror campaign could be pointed at
> Cuban refugees seeking haven in the
> United States. WE could sink a boatload of
> Cubans en route to Florida (real or simu-
> lated). We could foster attempts on lives of
> Cuban refugees in the United States even
> to the extent of wounding in instances to be
> widely publicized. Exploding a few plastic
> bombs in carefully chosen spots, the arrest
> of Cuban agents and the release of pre-
> pared documents substantiating Cuban in-
> volvement also would be helpful in pro-
> jecting the idea of an irresponsible govern-
> ment.[42]

As theatrical scholar Tracy C. Davis has rightly pointed
out

> The recognition of elements ubiquitous in dramat-
> ic writing and stage performance in [diverse] cul-
> tural manifestations—whether a written document
> or a news story, a community event or an interna-
> tional dispute, an ideological conflict or wit-

---

41 Davis, 144.
42 Ibid, 140.

> nesses' contrasting points of view—is not merely
> resemblance; it depends upon the borrowing or
> appropriation of elements from theatre and drama,
> as well as the ontology of 'script' or 'perform-
> ance'.

Wholly consistent with the parapolitical logic of the strategy-of-tension, Lemnitzer and the JCS, displaying a total misunderstanding of the nature of metaphor,

> [P]ropose ways to *stage* the provocation that
> could lead to war. In such a case, 'stage' is not
> only a verb indicating the calculated orchestration
> of events, but also stands for a process that delib-
> erately blurs the demarcations between simula-
> tions and their legitimization. Performance, by
> these terms, is not so much the context of North-
> woods as its precondition.[43]

In other words, NORTHWOODS is thoroughly Debor-dean in its assumptions; not only can spectacle be artful-ly deployed as a covert form of power, but that such a spectacle will perform an integrating function: the col-lective re-adjustment of perceptions towards a new, and effective, political consensus—the very thing that was absent from ZAPATA. And, following the ultra-cynical instrumentality of spectacular power, I might even be tempted to conclude that NORTHWOODS does, indeed, make a kind of parapolitical 'sense': the operation is it-self the necessary therapeutic device to resolve the inter-minable crisis of the Kennedy administration through a traumatic application of a form of 'shock therapy'—shock and disorientation, of course, being hallmarks of counter-intelligence operations. It is worth noting, then, that 'Psy-Ops', or counter-intelligence 'shock action', were the operational core of ZAPATA. In a CIA paper

---

43 Ibid, 145.

entitled 'Proposed Operation Against Cuba' (March 11, 1961), the authors held that, 'This course of action [i.e., the amphibious landing] has a better chance than any other of leading to the prompt overthrow of the Castro regime because it holds the possibility of administering a demoralizing shock.'[44] And it is also significant that Davis himself dismisses the parapolitical significance of the documents in an annoyingly naïve, or liberal, manner.

> From a conventional historical perspective, Northwoods is one among many curiosities pertaining to the Kennedy administration's handling of Cuba. From a conventional historical perspective, it is documentation of discussions, of a proposal, and perhaps of a point of view held by the Joint Chiefs. Beyond that, because it was not implemented...it is not 'history'. But from the perspective of a performance historian, it is a set of ideologically linked scenarios that demonstrate a line of thought ratified by the Joint Chiefs: thought made concrete as a set of actions that are templates for events that were—on some level—imaginable and advocated. Northwoods was not implemented, and in that sense it is not history, but neither is it fiction. Like a dramatic script, it exists as actions *in potential*, yet, like a dramatic script that is real, it results in imaginative acts that makes its reading historicizable. It exists as potential that was (once) acted upon insofar as Lemnitzer envisioned the scenarios and sought approval for them from higher authorities, and this in itself was a form of performance.[45]

The obvious question here is how can Davis be so certain that NORTHWOODS was never actually imple-

---

44 Kornbluh, 122.
45 Davis, 145.

mented, albeit in a different form? If certain historical events (JFK/DALLAS, LBJ/TONKIN, NIXON/WA-TERGATE) were really 'theatrical events'—and, by virtue of their false-flag status, deep events—then we are facing the prospect of a doubled form of Debordean spectacle: the manufacturing of a false reality that remains unidentifiable as illusion as prescribed by counter-intelligence orthodoxy. There is clear evidence that the germ of NORTHWOODS originated within the Eisenhower White House; according to James Bamford, Lemnitzer was directed to formulate a plan, using 'phony evidence, all of it [which] would be blamed on Castro, thus giving Lemnitzer and his cabal the excuse, as well as the public and international backing, they needed to launch their war.'[46] And the strong impression that Lemnitzer was merely following a formally prescribed form of thought actively encouraged by the Executive is further evidenced by the history of the production and distribution of the documents. The plan for NORTHWOODS was officially completed and submitted to the Secretary of Defense Robert McNamara on March 13, 1962.

---

46 Bamford, 82. 'The idea may actually have originated with President Eisenhower in the last days of his administration. With the Cold War hotter than ever and the recent U-2 scandal fresh in the public's memory, the old general wanted to go out with a win. He wanted desperately to invade Cuba in the weeks leading up to Kennedy's inauguration; indeed, on January 3 he told Lemnitzer and other aides in his Cabinet Room that he would move against Castro before the inauguration if only the Cubans gave him a really good excuse. Then, with time growing short, Eisenhower floated an idea. If Castro failed to provide that excuse, perhaps, he said, the United States "could think of manufacturing something that would be generally acceptable." What he was suggesting was a pretext—a bombing, an attack, an act of sabotage—carried out secretly against the United States *by* the United States. Its purpose would be to justify the launching of a war. It was a dangerous suggestion by a desperate president.' Ibid, 82-3. White House, Top Secret memorandum of meeting with the president, on January 3, 1961 (January 9, 1961).

MEMORANDUM FOR THE SECRETARY OF DEFENSE

1. The Joint Chiefs of Staff have considered the attached Memorandum for the Chief of Operations, Cuba Project,[47] which responds to a request of that office for brief but precise description of pretexts which would provide justification for U.S. military intervention in Cuba.

JUSTIFICATION FOR U.S MILITARY INTERVENTION IN CUBA

2. It is recognized that any action which becomes pretext for U.S. military intervention in Cuba will lead to a political decision which then would lead to military action.

APPENDIX TO ENCLOSURE A: DRAFT: MEMORANDUM FOR CHIEF OF OPERATIONS, CUBA PROJECT

3. This plan, incorporating projects selected from the attached suggestions, or from other sources, should be developed to focus all efforts on a specific objective which would provide adequate justification for U.S. military intervention. Such a plan would enable a logical build-up of incidents to be combined with other seemingly unrelated events to camouflage the ultimate objective and create the necessary impression of Cuban rashness and irresponsibility on a large scale, directed at other countries as well as the United States. The plan would also properly integrate the time phase the courses of action to be pursued. The de-

---

47 General Edward G. Lansdale of OPERATION MONGOOSE; see below, this chapter.

> sired resultant from the execution of this plan
> would be to place the United States in the appar-
> ent position of suffering defensible grievances
> from a rash and irresponsible government of Cuba
> and to develop an international image of Cuban
> threat to peace in the Western Hemisphere.

By this time, however, the White House had decided against a physical invasion, relying instead upon anti-Castro insurgents aided and abetted by the U.S. to either overthrow or assassinate Castro themselves; accordingly, at the March 16, 1962 meeting between Lemnitzer and JFK to discuss NORTHWOODS, 'President Kennedy told Lemnitzer that there was virtually no possibility that the U.S. would ever use overt military force in Cuba.'[48] However, in a memo sent to McNamara on April 10, 1962, Lemnitzer opined that

> The Joint Chiefs of Staff believe that the Cuban
> problem must be solved in the near future...Fur-
> ther, they see no prospect of early success in over-
> throwing the present communist regime either as
> a result of internal uprising or external political,
> economic or psychological pressures. Accord-
> ingly, they believe that military intervention by
> the United States will be required to overthrow
> the present communist regime.[49]

Lemnitzer's memo to McNamara not only replicated the past—a CIA document, 'Program of Covert Action Aimed at Weakening the Castro Regime' written on May 19,1961 openly stated 'There would be no intervention of U.S. armed forces except in response to aggressive

---

48 Bamford, 87; Department of State, Secret memorandum, written by U. Alexis Johnson and dated March 16; attached to 'Guidelines for Operation MONGOOSE' (March 14, 1962).

49 Ibid; JSC, Top Secret/Special Handling/Noforn memorandum, Lemnitzer to McNamara, April 10, 1962, pp. 1-2 (ARRB).

military action by Cuba directed at the United States'[50]—but it clearly anticipated the future as well.

> In May 1963, Assistant Secretary of Defense Paul H. Nitze sent a plan to the White House proposing 'a possible scenario whereby an attack on the United States' reconnaissance aircraft could be exploited toward the end of effecting the removal of the Castro regime.' In the event Cuba attacked a U-2, the plan proposed sending in additional American pilots, this time on dangerous, unnecessary low-level reconnaissance missions with the expectation that they would be shot down, thus provoking a war. '[T]he U.S. could undertake various measures designed to stimulate the Cubans to provoke a new incident,' said the plan. Nitze, however, did not volunteer to be one of the pilots.[51]

And it is quite telling that at the beginning of the Cuban Missile Crisis, it was the de facto Assistant President himself, Robert Kennedy (RFK), who vetted the option of running an improvised false-flag operation against Havana.

> [A]t a high-level White House meeting on the crisis [October 16, 1962], Bobby hinted at the possibility of a provoked or staged attack to justify removing the missiles from Cuba: 'One other thing is whether…whether there is some other way we can get involved in this through, uh, Guantanamo Bay, or something, er, or whether

---

50 Bohning, 72.

51 Bamford, 89-90; Department of Defense, Top Secret/Sensitive memorandum, Assistant Secretary of Defense for International Security Affairs to [McGeorge] Bundy, May 10, 1963 (JFKL, National Security Files, Meetings and Memoranda Series, Standing Group Meeting) (FRUS, Vol. XI, #337).

> there's some ship that, you know, sink the *Maine*
> again or something.'[52]

OPERATION NORTHWOODS, therefore, is highly revealing of the *systemic* nature of false-flag operations, an entrenched part of the spectacular power of Psy-Ops. Although somewhat dismissive of Lemnitzer, Bamford makes this clear in his authoritative discussion of the documents.

> Lemnitzer was a dangerous—perhaps even unbalanced—right-wing extremist in an extraordinarily sensitive position during a critical period. But OPERATION NORTHWOODS also had the support of every single member of the Joint Chiefs of Staff, and even senior Pentagon official Paul Nitze argued in favor of provoking a phony war with Cuba. The fact that the most senior members of all the services and the Pentagon could be so out of touch with reality and the meaning of democracy would be hidden for four decades.[53]

A fully sophisticated understanding and appreciation of strategy-of-tension and false-flag provides the 'missing link' of JFK assassination conspiracy theory. If it can be shown that the strategy-of-tension had in fact evolved as a systemic property of the U.S. Dual State by c. 1960, then I can argue much more easily for the inherent 'non-implausibility' of JFK/DALLAS as false-flag/spectacle. This approach has the added advantage of fully accounting for one of the central facets of conspiracy scholarship: if there was a conspiracy, then, on a purely

---

52 Bohning, 124. The phrase 'sink the *Maine* again' is interesting. According to then Under Secretary of State Chester Bowles, during the May-June 1961 crisis in the Dominican Republic Robert Kennedy espoused the explosive demolition of the U.S. Consulate as a pretext for a military intervention. Talbot, 81-2.

53 Bamford, 90.

planning and operational level, it would seem to have taken place on a medium-to-low level within the clandestine hierarchy, and that this covert agency was exercised on only the local level in several venues (Miami, New Orleans, Mexico City, Dallas) that formed important 'nodes' within the over-lapping parapolitical networks. Within the era of spectacular power one does not need to be very senior, or even very sophisticated, to appreciate the potency of its integrative function. So, deploying the strategy-of-tension re. JFK/DALLAS in the manner of Occam's Razor, I get the following.

'THE WILDERNESS OF MIRRORS': THE USUAL SUSPECTS

'We had been operating a damned Murder Inc. in the Caribbean.'—Lyndon Johnson

'Well, we took care of that son of a bitch, didn't we?'—David Sanchez Morales

As parapolitics necessarily supposes a radically pluralistic model of the State, the legal identities and organizational loyalties of the 'usual suspects' that loom large in conspiracy literature are never unitary or exclusive; here, I am confronted with the sheer 'giveness' of the radical nomadicism of the clandestine actor as a quasi-criminal sovereign. However, I am able to impose a degree of cognitive certainty upon these suspects through the rigorous application of Debordean principles: if the false-flag repeats the logic of the integrated spectacle, then the 'Cuba Project' self-evidently presents itself as the unifying thread of interpretation. The parapolitical network of linkages centered upon Havana provides the only epistemic apparatus that, in equal measure, both explains and is explained by the spectacle of public execution in Dealey Plaza.

THE JOINT CHIEFS OF STAFF

A/ GENERAL LYMON L. LEMNITZER

Commenting upon JFK's relationship with the Joint Chiefs of Staff at the time of his inauguration, Bamford writes that 'John F. Kennedy's election buttressed their worst fears.'[54] Apparently, Washington D.C. was on the brink of the state of exception in January 1961.

> Just below the surface, it was a dangerous time in America. For many in the military, the distrust of civilian leadership ran deep, to the point where a number of senior officers believed that their civilian leaders had ben subverted by international communism. It was a belief exacerbated by the election of Kennedy, a socially liberal democrat. 'The presence of a benign and popular General of

---

54 Bamford, 65-66. Although I follow the bulk of the secondary literature in focussing upon the Central Intelligence Agency as the main covert body implicated in Dealey Plaza, the reader should be aware at all times of the possible role of the Defence Intelligence Agency (DIA) in the events at Dallas. In many ways military intelligence services were the 'shadows' of the CIA which has often been used as a 'cover', or a 'front', for the machinations of much less well known organizations, such as the Office of Naval Intelligence (ONI). I strongly suspect, although I cannot prove, that many of the ubiquitous personalities of JFK/DALLAS, such as the notorious 'Maurice Bishop', may very well have been military intelligence officers. The possible but under-explored role of the CIA as a red herring might go far in explaining the maddening lack of clarity and exactitude concerning the Kennedy assassination, including the identities of the participants (provided, of course, that there actually were any). For Maurice Bishop see below, this chapter.

the Army in the White House [Dwight Eisen-
hower] had a calming influence on people and
kept the Rightist's audiences small,' said one account at the time.[55]

If we accept Lemnitzer, and the group of ultra-reac-
tionary military officials that he represents as possible
conspirators, then I can detect a possible motive for conspiracy in JFK's attempt to establish direct back-channel
communications[56] with the USSR following the near
catastrophe of the Cuban Missile Crisis (October 15-28,
1962).

Vladimir Semichastny, the Moscow head of the
KGB, reported to Nikita Khrushchev on October
2, 1963, that Kennedy wanted to re-open the
secret channel between them, using [Press Secretary Pierre] Salinger and a Washington-based
KGB agent as the conduit...Khrushchev then 'approved the use of the KBG as an intermediary to
exchange proposal [with Kennedy] that could not
go through regular diplomatic channels...The
President was well aware of how few people in
his administration he could trust with his peace-
making messages to their Communist enemies. As
he was forced to do repeatedly with his Cold War
bureaucracy, he simply bypassed the State Department's resistance to his dialogue with
Khrushchev in the fall of 1963 by creating an alternative means of communication.[57]

---

55 Donald Janson and Bernard Eismann, *The Far Right* (New York:
McGraw-Hill, 1963), 6, cited in ibid, 65-66.

56 A reliance upon back-channel diplomacy seems to have been one of the
hallmarks of the JFK administration just as it was, perhaps not
coincidentally, for Richard Nixon. Talbot presents evidence for Kennedy
back-channel efforts with Che Guevera (58-61), Fidel Castro (115-18),
the Soviet Union during the Berlin Wall Crisis of 1961 (70), the FBI
(141) and with the 'moderate' anti-Castro Cuban exiles (194).

57 Douglas, 291.

There is a growing body of scholarship indicating that JFK directly anticipated the detentist strategy of Richard Nixon and Henry Kissinger—in effect, 'Détente I'—by a full decade. And, as with Nixon,[58] Kennedy was threatened with subversion from within for having done so.

> Nevertheless, although the tactic was a familiar one for Kennedy, the means he sought out for his final effort to explore peace with Khrushchev is startling. For JFK to have to rely in the end not on his own State Department but on the Soviet secret police to convey secure messages of peace between himself and Khrushchev speaks volumes. Because of his own turn toward peace, the President had become almost totally isolated in his own government before he made his trip to Dallas.[59]

The notion of Kennedy as the first Presidential defector from the Cold War seems to have established itself as the 'grand narrative' of conspiracy theory—JFK as the martyred hero of noble failure. I tend to refer to this theory as the 'Garrison Thesis', as it formed the basis of Jim Garrison's own formal explanation for the political murder—an act which, like every other form of homicide, legally requires a motive (*mens rea*) in addition to the act (*actus reus*).

> This decision [to withdraw U.S. troops from Vietnam by the end of 1965], on top of the new [anti-intervention] Cuba policy, added up to nothing

---

58 See Chapter Four, below.

59 Ibid. JFK's alienation from his own government by November 1963 does, in fact, seem to be one of the defining features of his administration, which had in effect become a "'family affair'"; according to Peter Dale Scott, "'Kennedy couldn't work through the CIA, the Pentagon or even the State Department. There was so little institutional support in Washington for the Kennedys' policies. The bureaucrats were very committed to the Cold War...'" Cited in Talbot, 53.

less than a fundamental break with Cold War foreign policy, which had been the lifeblood of the
CIA. Here, it seemed to me, was a plausible
motive for the assassination. Though my thinking
at this stage was not very well developed, at least
I could see that the C.I.A.'s vested interest as well
as its ideological commitment were to the continuation of the Cold War…Along the way [Pres-
ident Kennedy] had made implacable enemies—
from top-level C.I.A. cold warriors like Allen
Dulles…and Richard Helms (then deputy director
in charge of covert operations[60]) down to anti-Castro Cuban exiles who felt betrayed at the
Bay of Pigs.[61]

As is well known, the Garrison Thesis provided the
para-political narrative spine of Oliver Stone's film
spectacle *JFK*;[62] it also, for all intrinsic purposes, forms
the argumentative core of James W. Douglass'
magisterial *JFK and the Unspeakable: Why He Died
and Why He Mattered.*[63] The main problem with
JFK/DALLAS as a pre-emption of Détente I as
engineered by the JCS and its subordinates within the
military intelligence complex is that, once again, it fails
to adequately account for the spectacular power
invoked: if terminating the back-channel itself was the
motive, then the murder would have been better handled
far more covertly as an 'inside job' performed in secret.
But, if I apply *a priori* reasoning and work axiomatically
from Dealey Plaza as Debordean spectacle, then it
becomes obvious that the parapolitical objectives of
JFK/DALLAS could not have been merely negative in

---

60 This is incorrect; Helms was Deputy Director for Plans (DDP) from
1965-66.

61 Garrison, 178.

62 For discussion, see Chapter Five, below.

63 Douglass, generally.

its nature—that is, the derailment of Détente I—but must necessarily have been positive, which required the presence of the theatre of the false-flag. And this could only have been the psycho-political inducement for the military invasion of Cuba. Even if I hypothesize that the implication of Castro in the death of JFK was the means selected by Lemnitzer et al to create the strategy-of-tension necessary to undermine U.S.-Soviet rapprochement, I am still left with the task of having to explain the not inconsiderable residue of the centrality of Cuba to the successful staging of the clandestine spectacle.

B/ GENERAL EDWARD G. LANSDALE

Air Force General (and former advertising executive) Lansdale was director of OPERATION MONGOOSE (November 1961-January 1963) the formal Operations Branch of the Cuba Project (1959-62),[64] initiated by the Eisenhower administration and officially discontinued by JFK following the Cuban Missile Crisis of October, 1962. Although Lansdale's real-world record of self-promotion and border-line incompetence largely fails to substantiate his far more spectacular one as an omniscient dealer of covert death,[65] Lansdale constitutes a 'usual suspect' through his connection to MONGOOSE, a vast umbrella organization that provided clandestine

---

64 See Russo, 3-84, generally.

65 See discussion of Oliver Stone's *JFK* in Chapter Five. In the estimation of CIA officer Sam Halpern, Lansdale was a "'con man, absolutely perfect. He's the man in the grey flannel suit from Madison Avenue in New York. I think he could sell refrigerators to Eskimos or...the Brooklyn Bridge to people who don't have cars. I betcha he could sell that, too. He was very good. You got to give him credit for that.'" Bohning, 85.

cover to virtually all of the other suspects.

On November 4, 1961, following the Bay of Pigs, a special meeting between RFK and CIA Deputy Director of Plans Richard M. Bissell took place; consistent with JFK's (now strengthened) aversion to military intervention, both 'agreed that large-scale sabotage actions would be carried out by both CIA-controlled assets and independent Cuban groups as quickly as possible.'[66] This meeting signals the Kennedy administration's choice of covert para-military and insurgency operations as the prescribed norm of the Cuba Project; in the words of RFK, 'My idea is to stir things up on [the] island with espionage, sabotage, general disorder, run & operated by Cubans themselves with every group but Batistaites & Communists.'[67] The 'beauty of such an operation over the next few months' wrote White House aide Richard Godwin in a memo to JFK, 'is that we cannot lose. If the best happens, we will unseat Castro. If not, then at least we will emerge with a stronger underground, better propaganda and a far clearer idea of the dimensions of the problems which affect us.'[68] In December, 1961 Allen Dulles was removed as Director of the CIA for his role in the Bay of Pigs and was replaced by John McCone, who appointed Richard Helms as the new head of Cuban affairs. Helms then replaced the disgraced Richard Bissell as Deputy Director for Plans several weeks later; 'Helms split Cuban affairs off from the rest of the Western Hemisphere branch, and in February [1962] William Harvey...took over Task Force W, the new CIA office charged with Cuba.'[69] It was during this pivotal transi-

---

66 Kaiser, *The Road to Dallas*, 100.

67 Freedman, 153.

68 Blight and Kornbluh, 244.

69 Kaiser, *The Road to Dallas*, 100. Apparently, Task Force W was named

tion towards new personnel committed to covert as opposed to military action that RFK formally established
OPERATION MONGOOSE. A generic term for a loose
network of anti-Castro proxies and para-military forces,
MONGOOSE was nominally under the direction of
General Lansdale, but the real decision-making power
lay with the Special Augmented Group (SGA) whom
Lansdale reported to, which was supervised by RFK and
included the Heads of all of the branches of the Armed
Forces, most importantly the new Chief of the JCS, General Maxwell Taylor, the author of 'flexible response'.[70]

As would be expected, 'Operation MONGOOSE focused on utilizing a Cuban and Cuban-exile political
base opposed to Castro, infiltrating the island, and insti-
gating sabotage in order to spark the overthrow of the
regime by internal revolt.'[71] On August 7, 1962, CIA liaison Harvey drafted the official 'Covert Activities' Mission for the operation: '"Exert all possible diplomatic,
economic, psychological, and other pressures to overthrow the Castro-Communist regime without overt U.S.
military commitment."'[72] Although MONGOOSE clearly anticipated eventual U.S. military intervention, the
prevailing assumption throughout was that such an invasion would only take place in response to a wholly 'indigenous' uprising against Castro—this under the
blanket of plausible deniability.[73] MONGOOSE provides
the needed context to JFK's rebuff to Lemnitzer over
NORTHWOODS on March 16, 1962; however, it also

---

in honour of William Walker, the 19th century American filibuster who set
up a mercenary state in Nicaragua from 1856-7. Talbot, 103.

70 Ibid, Chapter Five, 97-122.

71 Davis, 135.

72 Blight and Kornbluh, 251.

73 Bohning, 84 and 88.

renders painfully obvious the operation's 'fatal flaw':
under RFK's tenure, the Cuba Project, while officially
favoring the clandestine, was in fact always implicitly
slanted towards military force, replicating perfectly the
underlying parapolitical dynamics that undermined the
earlier ZAPATA Plan. At all times, primary operational
control lay with the Defense Department; MONGOOSE
was 'masterminded by the Pentagon. The Joint Chiefs
were motivated by the desire to prevent Castro from
spreading Communism elsewhere in Latin America. For
them, time was of the essence.'[74] The alarming element
at work here was the Pentagon's concern with the build-
up of Russian nuclear forces; military planners for the
JCS had openly stated that the optimal time for any hypothetical pre-emptive nuclear attack against the Soviet
Union would be by the end of 1963.[75] Accordingly, the
March 14, 1962 guidelines for MONGOOSE drafted by
General Maxwell Taylor and approved by the SGA,
clearly stated that although the U.S. will make '"maximum use of indigenous resources...final success will require decisive U.S. military intervention..."'; therefore,
domestic anti-Castro forces were to '"prepare and justify
this intervention, and thereafter to facilitate and support
it,"'[76] prompting Sam Hurwitch, the State Department liaison to MONGOOSE, to argue that '"the concentration
of attention upon the employment of U.S. military force
against Cuba runs counter to the basic concept of Mongoose, which is to bring down the Castro regime from
within."' [77] The parapolitical dilemma of ZAPATA had
not been resolved by MONGOOSE precisely because of
the fractured nature of the Dual State—and, as before,

---

74 Davis, 134.
75 Douglass, 234-42.
76 Blight and Kornbluh, 170.
77 Bohning, 115.

the centerpiece of Civil War II was Cuba.

THE CENTRAL INTELLIGENCE AGENCY

Long the favorite of conspiracy scholars who prefer a domestic origin of JFK/DALLAS—what I call the 'enemy-from-within' school—this group of suspects is the most difficult to discuss with certainty because of the intensely compartmentalized nature of the Agency coupled with the standardized operational procedure of refusing to leave paper trails for covert operations.[78] Although I will discuss many of these suspects later in this essay, I have tentatively grouped them together along the following lines.

A. SENIOR LEVEL OFFICERS

Allen Dulles (Director of Central Intelligence, 1953-61); Lt. General Charles Cabell (Deputy Director of CIA during the Bay of Pigs and brother of Earle Cabell, Mayor of Dallas from May 1961 to February 1964[79]); Richard M. Bissell (Deputy Director for Plans/DDP 1958-62; head of the Cuba Project, 1961-62 and initiator of CIA/Mafia assassination operations); Richard Helms (DDP chief of operations 1952-65, creator of ZR/RIFLE); and James Jesus Angleton (Associate Deputy Director of Operations for Counterintelligence, 1954-75).

Dulles, Cabell and Bissell—Dulles' most likely suc-

---

78 Three of the most salient points concerning plausible denial, the bane of assassination researchers and theorists, were laid out by William Harvey himself: 'no projects on paper', 'strictly person-to-person, singleton ops', and 'never mention word assassination'. Pease, 'James Angleton', 162.

79 Albarelli, 151.

cessor—where all scapegoated and then sacrificed by JFK following the failure of ZAPATA.

B. *MIDDLE LEVEL OFFICERS*

William Harvey (head of special operations CIA international assassination team ZR/RIFLE and supervisor of Task Force W, the CIA operations component of MON-GOOSE, which included joint assassination efforts with Chicago Mafiosi Johnny Roselli[80]); Theodore Shackley (operational head of JM/WAVE, the Miami based CIA station for MONGOOSE); David Atlee Phillips, a.k.a. 'Maurice Bishop'[81](CIA chief of Covert Action in Mexico City from 1961 through the Fall of 1963); and Tracy Barnes (Assistant Director of Plans to Richard Bissell for ZAPATA; Head of Domestic Operations Branch under Angleton from 1962-63).

---

80 See below, this chapter. Simpich has made the most powerful argument that I have ever read for Harvey as a leading suspect as a conspiracy planner. Although Harvey was taken off MONGOOSE and appointed head of the CIA station in Rome by Robert Kennedy in June 1963, there is clear evidence that Harvey continued to participate in anti-Castro counter-intelligence operations. Furthermore, as Simpich has shown, Harvey also served as head of the CIA's Staff D which ran a series of major wire-tapping operations in Mexico City and, apparently, liaisoned with the National Security Agency (NSA). The two most important of these wire-tapping operations were LIENVOY, which targeted the Cuban and Russian Consulates and Embassies in Mexico City, and LIFEAT, which focused on the residences and private telephones of Cuban and Russian Foreign Service staff. Simpich, Chapters Two and Four. For the possible significance of these wire-tapping operations for JFK/DALLAS, see below, this chapter. Even after his 'exile' to Rome, every four to six weeks Harvey travelled to Miami to visit his friend and accomplice Johnny Roselli; Roselli would reciprocate by visiting Harvey every time the latter was in Washington. Morley, 163-4.

81 On Phillips' possible identity as Bishop see below, this chapter.

C. LOW LEVEL OFFICERS

E. Howard Hunt ('Chief of Covert Operations' for the Domestic Operations Branch under Barnes); James Mc-Cord: operational liaisons with anti-Castro field agents. (Note: both Hunt and McCord share the code-name 'Eduardo'); David Sanchez Morales (field chief of JM/WAVE 'secret war' operations including all Cuba penetration teams; provided operational support to Task Force W assassination operations through both Harvey and Roselli).[82]

COSA NOSTRA (A.K.A. 'THE WISE GUYS')

These include, but are not limited to, the following:

Johnny Roselli (Los Angeles, Las Vegas; liaison with William Harvey, Task Force W[83]), Santo Trafficante (Tampa; Miami; Havana), Robert Maheu (Las Vegas; connection with Howard Hughes), Carlos Marcello (New Orleans; Dallas); John D. Martino (personal courier between Trafficante and Marcello[84]); Sam Giancana (Chicago); Jimmy Hoffa (the Teamsters); and last, but certainly not least, the assassin-of-the-assassin Jack Ruby (Trafficante courier to Cuba and Mafia liaison with Operation MONGOOSE operations in Louisiana/Lake Pontchartrain[85]).

Although I consider the 'Made Men' of the American

---

82 Fonzi, 366-90; Hancock, 513-14.

83 For an exhaustive account of Roselli's quite extraordinary history of collaboration with national security agencies, see Rappleye and Becker generally.

84 Kurtz, 209-11.

85 Hancock, Chapter 11, 185-98.

Mafia as lacking the requisite degree of gravitas to successfully plot and to perform the assassination of the Chief Executive, the Goodfellas merit inclusion in my line up not only because of the ferociously 'Cuba-centric' nature of their motives, but also for the sheer constancy of their nomadic migrations through the covert spaces of central and military intelligence. The deep meaning of these peregrinations were certainly not lost on Fabio Escalante, the director of the official Cuban investigation of JFK/DALLAS.

> The more details revealed...concerning the conspiracy of Giancana and many others, the clearer it became that there were no lines of demarcation between the Mafiosi organization and the CIA. There were no white hats or black hats; everything was a farce 'for the use of fools,' as Giancana would say. On many occasions the organization and the Mafia were one and the same thing. That was the case with Frank Fiorni, Giancana's lieutenant, who was simultaneously working for the government's espionage agency and was later implicated in the Watergate scandal under the alias of Frank Sturgis.[86]

Mafia involvement with the Cuba Project officially commenced in August 1960 when DDP Bissell began to

> [E]xplore the possibility of mounting a sensitive operation [i.e., assassination] against Fidel Castro. It was thought that certain gambling interests which had formerly been active in Cuba might be willing to assist and might have intelligence assets in Cuba and communications between Miami, Florida and Cuba. Mr. [Robert] Maheu

---

86 Escalante, *JFK*, 188. Sturgis was an informant for the CIA. Hancock, 77. For more on Fiorni/Sturgis, see this chapter and Chapter Three.

was approached and asked to establish contact
with a member or members of the gambling syndicate...Mr. Roselli showed interest...indicated
he had some contacts in Miami that he might
use...*met with a courier going back and forth to
Cuba...never became part of the project current
at the time for the invasion of Cuba...no memoranda...no written documents...orally approved by
said Senior Officials of the Agency.*[87]

Cosa Nostra is of interest for two additional reasons.
Firstly, in the event that there actually were additional
shooters, either single or in teams, along with Oswald in
Dealey Plaza, then it seems almost certain that the
snipers were Cuban.[88] Escalante himself strongly insinu-

87 *Foreign Relations of the United States, 1961-1963, Volume X,
Department of State 337 Memo, May 14, 1962* cited in Hancock, 142-3.
Italics in the original.

88 Dallas may, in fact, have been the third site on the list for the staging of
the homicidal/patricidal spectacle. On November 22nd in Chicago Secret
Service agents intercepted a four man sniper team (including two
Cubans) who were, apparently, planning to assassinate JFK while he was
watching the annual Army-Air Force football game held in Soldier Field.
Most striking of all was the shadowy presence of a Chicago-based
version of the 'patsy' Oswald: Thomas Arthur Vallee, a former Marine,
'disaffiliated' member of the John Birch Society and alleged paranoid
schizophrenic, who worked in a warehouse that the presidential
motorcade was to pass by on the way to the sports stadium—which, as in
Dallas, would have required Kennedy's limousine to make a slow,
hairpin turn. Vallee was arrested on the basis of a tip that he 'had
threatened to kill Kennedy in Chicago.' The President's trip to Chicago
was cancelled at the last minute. Two of the snipers, whose names have
never been de-classified, were arrested but refused to talk during
interrogation and were subsequently released; the other two have never
been identified. Douglass, 200-7 and 213-17. In their book *Ultimate
Sacrifice*, Lamar Waldron and Thom Hartmann discuss another possible
attempt on JFK, this one planned for November 19 in Tampa and, once
again, involving a right-wing FFPC anti-social patsy, this time 'Gilberto
Lopez'. Waldron and Hartman, 652-65 and 684-96; they also provide a
series of comparisons (and a few contrasts) between Lopez and Oswald
at 478-82. However, as Hancock has pointed out, all of the CIA reports
on Lopez are second and third hand, apparently originating with David
Morales' death squad unit within JM/WAVE. I find his conclusion

ates that the two actual JFK shooters were the violently anti-Castro Eladio del Valle Gutierrez and Sandalio Herminio Diaz Garcia,[89] both of whom doubled as members of Santo Trafficante's 'Havana crew', the Wise Guy most intimately connected to the Cuban underworld: del Valle Gutierrez was involved with Trafficante's heroin smuggling network[90] and Diaz Garcia served as Trafficante's bodyguard in Havana.[91] Also, both seem to have been connected with Operation 40, the homicidal Cuban counter-intelligence unit established in Miami.[92] Secondly, there is strong circumstantial evidence to suggest that Trafficante was actually protecting Castro by providing

---

persuasive: 'All in all, the saga of Gilberto Lopez more probably reveals the creation of another Cuban associated suspect than a lead in a Cuban conspiracy.' Hancock, 14-15.

89 Escalante, *JFK*, 162-5 and 165-6. Del Valle was murdered in February 1967, shot through the heart and partially dismembered by a machete; at the time, New Orleans District Attorney Jim Garrison was seeking to question him as part of his investigation into the Kennedy assassination. Hinckle and Turner, 321.

90 Dietche, 162.

91 Ibid, 168. If del Valle Gutierrez and Diaz Garcia really were the extra shooters at Dealey Plaza, then this may provide the simplest possible explanation of all of one of the most frequently discussed aspects of JFK/DALLAS: that both Trafficante and/or Marcello seemed to have possessed some degree of prior knowledge of the assassination; Trafficante allegedly declared in the fall of 1962—the same time as the missile crisis—that JFK was going to be 'hit'. Talbot, 122 and Hancock, 59.

92 Ibid. Albarelli repeats the theory of two Cuban snipers at Dallas, but identifies one of them as Nestor Izquierdo, a former Brigade 2056 member and a veteran of the Bay of Pigs. Albarelli, 230. Operation 40 originated as an ultra-covert branch of the ZAPATA Plan, intended to operate as a death squad within the 'liberated' Cuba, eliminating all political rivals to Manel Artime, the administration's preferred leader of post-Castro Cuba. Hancock, 6 and 522 fn. 14. Although officially disbanded after the Bay of Pigs, it continued to operate domestically in clandestine form throughout the Kennedy presidency, continuing its activities as an extremist counter-intelligence unit—with extensive ties to organized crime—up to the 1970s. Ibid, 21.

him with information on the assassination plots, all of which ended in farcical failure; if this is correct, then Trafficante would appear to have been acting to secure a prior standing agreement with the Castro regime concerning his continuing control over the Havana terminus of the 'French Connection' heroin pipeline.[93] The transversal flows of pipelines, it would appear, induces a parallel iterability of identities.

ANTI-CASTRO CUBANS

Organizationally, this body of suspects may be somewhat artificially divided into two groups: (i) the political: The Revolutionary Junta in Exile (JURE), The Cuban Student Revolutionary Directorate (DRE[94]), The Movement For the Recovery of the Revolution (MRR), The Cuban Revolutionary Council (CRC), The Sierra Junta (JGCE), UNIDAD (a coalition of 27 independent anti-Castro groups) and; (ii) the para-military: Operation 40, The November 30 Movement, Commandos L, and Alpha/66.

In my opinion, Alpha/66 is of particular importance, not least because 'its operational bases were located in the New Orleans-Dallas corridor', the parapolitical

---

93 Kurtz, 205-6 and 216; Scott, *Deep Politics and the Death of JFK*, 171-81. 'Santo Trafficante was indeed the mole in the [exile] assassination plots, reporting back to Fidel Castro. This was confirmed by other participants such as Sam Giancana...and Johnny Roselli. Referring to Trafficante, Giancana allegedly said, "Frankly, he's a rat."' Russo, 446.

94 The DRE, code-named AMSPELL by the CIA, was under the direct supervision of David Atlee Phillips and was responsible for radicalizing Cuban opposition against Castro, possibly as a means of generating popular support for a future intervention in Cuba. Morley, 128-9 and 170-7.

space(s) inhabited by Lee Harvey Oswald.[95] It was one of the most militant of the anti-Castro groups, and its members appeared to have anticipated, for whatever reason, a second amphibious invasion of Cuba sometime in early 1964 following JFK's re-election.[96] It also openly provoked JFK through staging its own autonomous operations against Cuba.

> Alpha/66 was the Cuban exile group which especially seemed to taunt President Kennedy. Not content to limit its assaults to attacks against Cuba and Castro's forces, it also went after foreign ships supplying Castro and conducted assassination raids on Russian troops to Cuba. Long before the missile crisis, when Kennedy's policy was to maintain separate U.S. policies toward Russia and Cuba, Alpha/66 seemed bent on provoking a direct conflict between Russia and the United States...At the height of the missile crisis, during the delicate negotiations to keep World War III from erupting, Alpha/66 continued its raids into Cuba and assaults on Castro's patrol boats...After the crisis, when Kennedy had issued his directive to halt the raids and shut down the exile training camps, Alpha/66 defied the ban by continuing to operate secretly, even attacking British merchant ships in Cuban waters. A lead editorial in the *[New York] Times* warned: 'No matter how much we may admire the anti-Castroism that motivates its actions, this group is nevertheless dangerously playing with the laws and the security of the United States.'[97]

---

95 Escalante, *JFK*, 31.

96 Kurtz, 179.

97 Fonzi, 121 and 122. Alpha/66 may very well have been a front for the more extreme CIA elements staffing and operating JM/WAVE; 'In the face of the often expressed Kennedy administration annoyance with the exile raiders and the officially announced crackdowns on their

Worse, Alpha/66 seems to have been implicated in some way with one of the most compelling incidents presaging JFK/DALLAS: 'Leon' Oswald's notorious meeting with Silvia Odio, an activist for the social democratic JURE, in Dallas on September 26 or 27 1963 is alleged to have taken place in the presence of two members —'Leopoldo' and 'Angelo/Angel'—of the Dallas chapter of Alpha/66.[98] Also of potential significance are Al-

---

activities...documents reveal that the Alpha/66 and Commandos L raids on Russian targets in Cuba...were known to JM/WAVE in advance and that no efforts were made to block them. A long time CIA asset, Alberto Fernandez, routinely reported on the movements and plans of independent raider groups including Alpha/66 and Commandos L.' Hancock, 103. It is worth noting that along with Alpha/66 the DRE also undertook a number of highly aggressive raids against Cuba in direct violation of Kennedy's wishes; the most spectacular of these attacks was the shelling of the Icar Hotel in Havana on August 24 1962. David Phillips had operational oversight of the DRE. Morley, 130-2.

98 Fonzi, 108-16; Kurtz, 167-8 and 190-1; Escalante, *JFK*, 83; Douglass, 158. Several days after the unexpected visit, Odio received a telephone call from one of the 'Mexican looking men' who told her that 'Leon' was an ex-Marine, "'an expert marksman and he would be a tremendous asset to anyone, except you never know how to take him. He could do anything, like getting underground in Cuba, like killing Castro. He says we Cubans don't have any guts, we should have shot Kennedy after the Bay of Pigs. He says we should do something like that.'" Hancock, 21. Soon after the visit, Odio wrote a letter to her father describing the uncanny encounter and telephone conversation—a letter that preceded Dealey Plaza by almost two months. Ibid, 22. Both of Odio's parents were familiar with Antonio Vecania, the founder and head of Alpha/66. Fonzi, 117-18. See below, this chapter. For Fonzi, 'If the incident did occur as Odio contended, understanding it was key to grasping the truth about Lee Harvey Oswald and the John F. Kennedy assassination. No theory of the assassination would stand without somehow accounting for it...That was the very point that the Warren Commission itself quickly recognized...On August 23rd, 1964, with the first drafts of the Warren Commission Report being written, Chief Counsel J. Lee Rankin wrote to J. Edgar Hoover: "It is a matter of some importance to the Commission that Mrs. Odio's allegations either be proved or disproved."' Fonzi, 114. An obvious problem with Odio's account is that, on the basis of the 'official story' formulated by the Warren Commission, Oswald was in Mexico City at this time. However, this problem disappears if we assume either that: (i) 'Leon' Oswald was actually an impersonator meant to

pha/66's extensive affiliation, along with the other extremist para-militaries, with a 'nomadic' community of anti-Castro Americans: mercenaries, gun runners, narcotics traffickers and contract CIA agents which included William-'Rip'-Robertson, Loran Eugene Hall (Lorenzo Pascillo), Roy Hargraves, Lawrence Howard, William Seymour, and Gerald Patrick Hemming, founder of the Intercontinental Penetration Force/IPF, a highly autonomous outfit of mercenary freebooters.[99] The wider community of Cuban anti-Castro activists in which Alpha/66 was embedded was similarly vast and,

cause Odio to misidentify the 'real' Oswald as the future assassin of the President, or (ii) that there were actually two separate persons called 'Oswald' being stage-managed by U.S. counter-intelligence, allowing 'Lee/Leon' to parapolitically inhabit two different spaces at the same time. See below, this chapter. Similarly, for Kaiser, Odio's visitation 'confirms that President Kennedy was assassinated by a conspiracy for which Lee Harvey Oswald was simply the trigger man. As it turns out, the visit links Oswald and his crime to an enormous network of mobsters, anti-Castro Cubans, and right-wing political activists.' Kaiser, *The Road to Dallas*, 2; see ibid, Chapter Twelve, generally. In the end, Odio's testimony was discounted by the FBI on psychiatric grounds; her psychiatrist Dr. Burton Einspruch advised James Hosty, the FBI agent investigating the case and a frequent 'contact' with Oswald in late 1963, that Odio suffered from '"grand hysteria, a condition [that] he found to be prevalent among Latin American women from the upper class."' Shenon, 214-15. If Odio's story is true, then 'Leon' may have been either Oswald himself (which would mean that he was being impersonated in Mexico City) or was the infamous 'second' Oswald, who has highly active in Dallas at this time. Peter Dale Scott strongly hints that the second Dallas Oswald was John Thomas Masen, a Dallas gun dealer and supporter of the far Right group The Minutemen. Not only was Masen stock-piling weapons to sell to anti-Castro Cubans, but he bore an uncannily strong physical resemblance to Oswald; even worse, he owned the only gun store in Dallas that carried ammunition for the Mannlicher-Carcano rifle, the weapon allegedly used by Oswald to kill Kennedy. A final note—the FBI file on Masen was assigned to Agent Hosty. Scott, *Deep Politics II*, 110-16.

99 Hinckle and Turner, 176.84. Kaiser tentatively identifies Odio's visitors Leopoldo and Angel as Loran Hall and Lawrence Howard. Kaiser, 2. Hall was suspected to have participated in Alpha/66 raids on Cuba. Kaiser, *The Road to Dallas*, 248.

not coincidentally, directly overlapped with Oswald's own contacts within both the pro- and anti-Castro underground.[100] Although I will take up this issue later, it is worth noting for now that three of the most important members of the Cuban diaspora—Frank Fiorni/Frank Sturgis, Eugenio Martinez, Bernard Barker—were all members of the future Nixon 'Plumbers' and were arrested during the Watergate break-in of June 17, 1972.

Arguably, the single most important of these usual suspects is Antonio Veciana, who founded Alpha/66 in mid-1962, apparently under the aegis of the CIA.[101]

> Alpha/66 emerged early in 1962, with Veciana its founder and chief spokesman. It received more press coverage than other militant exile groups because it appeared better organized, better equipped and consistently more successful in its guerilla attacks and sabotage operations...With strong management, clever use of propaganda, organizational and fund-raising skills, and expertise in weaponry and military operations, Alpha/66 soon rose to the forefront of Miami's numerous anti-Castro exile groups.[102]

Cuban intelligence was particularly interested in both Veciana and his organization as Escalante makes clear.

---

100 Almost too numerous to name, these include Sergo Arcacha Smith, Emilio Santana, Carlos Quiroga, Manuel Artime, Eddie Bayo, Orlando Bosch Avila, Eladio del valle Gutierrez, Sandalio Herminio Diaz Garcia, Manolito Rodriguez/Manuel Oscarberro, Ronaldo Masferrer, Antonio Cuesta, Carlos Prio Socarras, Manuel Ray, Paulino Sierra Martinez, Felipe Vidal Santiago, Antonio Varona, Hermonio Diaz Garcia. See Hancock, generally. Each had their own agenda, political and personal, and their radical proliferation evidences the highly nomadic and heterogeneous nature of the endlessly sub-dividing Dual State—at least on its clandestine frontier with the Cuba Project.

101 Fonzi, 117-71 and 391-6.

102 Ibid, 121 and 132.

We discovered that in September 1963 Veciana
was linked to two events closely related to the
Kennedy assassination. The first was the establishment of an Alpha 66 office in Dallas, headed
by Manuel Rodriguez Oscarberro, one of his men.
Located on Hollandale Street, it would appear to
be the same place in which "Oswald or a subject
very similar to him" was seen a few days before
the crime by the Dallas deputy sheriff according
to his testimony before the Warren Commission.[103] Vacenia also told Gaeton Fonzi [lead investigator for the House Select Committee on As-
sassinations] that a few days before the assassination he went to Dallas for a meeting with his CIA
case officer [Maurice Bishop]. On arrival, he
found the officer talking with a subject who was
not introduced to him, whom he later recognized
as "Oswald or somebody very like him," by
chance at the same time that the Cuban exile
Silvia Odio claimed to have received a visit from
Oswald with two counter-revolutionary activists
in Dallas.[104]

Although there is little doubt concerning the importance
of Veciana within the Cuban exile movement, controversy over the identity of Alpha/66's alleged CIA contact,
Maurice Bishop, remains. Both Escalante and Fonzi became convinced that Bishop was, in fact, David Atlee
Phillips, at that time the Agency's chief of Covert Action

---

103 See ibid, 118 for Fonzi commenting on an article about Silvia Odio by
Paul Hoch and George O'Toole that appeared in *The Saturday Evening
Post* in 1976: 'Alpha/66 had chapters all over the country...[and that]
one of the chapters [Veciana] visited was in Dallas at "3126 Hollandale."
Digging in the mounds of the Warren Commission files, Hoch had found
a report by a Dallas deputy sheriff saying that an informant told him that
a person resembling Oswald was seen associating with Cubans at '3128
Harlendale'.

104 Escalante, *JFK*, 168. The alleged meeting between Veciana, Bishop and
'Oswald' is discussed by Fonzi, 141-2.

in Mexico City.[105] I will discuss Phillips as Bishop in more detail later; of more immediate importance is that Bishop, like Alpha/66, were strongly committed to a full-scale U.S. military invasion of Cuba.

> Veciana claimed that 'Bishop' constantly pressured him to engage in actions against Cuba. In March 1963, Alpha 66 actually conducted a series of raids against Soviet ships in Cuban ports. Veciana stated that 'Bishop' had planned and ordered these raids in a desperate attempt to foment a confrontation between the United States and the USSR over Cuba, a confrontation that would, 'Bishop' believed, involve an American military invasion of the island.[106]

For the para-militaries, the Cuban Missile Crisis [107] provided the last window of opportunity for a direct U.S. attack of Cuba; 'The discovery of offensive missiles in Cuba provided precisely the pretext the United States would need to launch an invasion of Cuba. The opportunity was passed by.'[108] Ironically, it was precisely because of MONGOOSE, and the not unreasonable apprehension of American invasion that it created, that the Russians decided to install nuclear weapons in Cuba as a deterrent force.[109] Predictably, the JCS regarded the first and most attractive option being debated by the White House during the first phase of the crisis— airstrikes—as merely the initial phase of a full-scale operation that would necessarily culminate in the invasion

---

105 Escalante, *JFK*, 167.
106 Kurtz, 182.
107 Freedman, 161-245.
108 Ibid, 175.
109 Bohning, 112-13.

of Cuba.[110]

> The Joint Chiefs never deviated in their advocacy
> of a comprehensive military strike… [As late as
> Sunday, October 28] They still wanted an air
> strike followed soon after by an invasion.
> Kennedy was shocked. He commented that the
> 'first advice' he would give his successor was 'to
> watch the generals' and not to think that 'just be-
> cause they were military men their opinions on
> military matters were worth a damn.'[111]

Perhaps the tenor of the relationship between the pseu-
do-Yankee President and his Cowboy Generals was best
expressed by the Commandant of the Marine Corps
General David M. Shoup in conversation with Air Force
Chief of Staff General Curtis LeMay after their October
19 meeting with JKF.

> Somebody's got to keep them from doing the god-
> dam thing piecemeal. That's our problem. Go in
> there and friggin' around with the missiles. Go in
> there and friggin' around with the lift. You're
> screwed. You're screwed, screwed, screwed.
> Some goddam thing, some way, that they either
> do the son of a bitch and do it right, and quit frig-
> gin' around.[112]

In yet another example of the 'uncanny' that envelopes
JFK/DALLAS, the timing of the Missile Crisis coincided exactly with Phase IV of the original timetable of OP-
ERATION MONGOOSE, which called for 'Open revolt
and overthrow of the Communist regime' in the first half
of October 1962, to be followed in the second half by

---

110 Freedman, 177 and 447.
111 Ibid, 180 and 219.
112 Ibid, 186.

Phase V, the 'Establishment of [a] new government.'[113] Consistent with the MONGOOSE timetable, in February 1962 JFK authorized the JCS to draw up OPLAN-314-61, a series of contingency plans, accompanied by real-time military exercises, to prepare an American invasion of Cuba 'in the event that Castro or the counter-revolutionaries provided an acceptable pretext.'[114] (Ironically, it was OPLAN-314 that the JCS relied upon when pushing for a full-scale attack of Cuba during the Missile Crisis). On February 21, one day after the submission of OPLAN-314-61, the KGB formally advised Khrushchev that '"military specialists of the USA had revised an operational plan against Cuba... [to] be supported by military air assets in Florida and Texas... which, according to this information, is supported by President Kennedy."'[115] However, instead of 'resolving' the Crisis through invasion, JFK negotiated a pledge from Khrushchev to withdraw the missiles in exchange for a binding promise from the U.S. not to invade Cuba.

> The day after announcing the formal end of the crisis, on 20 November, [Kennedy] wrote to Khrushchev that 'there need be no fear of any invasion of Cuba while matters take their present favorable course.' Khrushchev chose to interpret the letter as saying that [Kennedy] had confirmed his commitment not to invade Cuba.[116]

---

113 Bohning, 90. Lansdale showed himself utterly prescient when submitting the first timetable on February 20 1962: '"a vital decision, still to be made, is on the use of open U.S. force to aid the Cuban people in winning their liberty. If conditions and assets permitting a revolt are achieved in Cuba, and if U.S. help is required to sustain this condition, will the U.S. respond promptly with military force to aid the Cuban revolt?"' Ibid.

114 Fursenko and Naftali, 149.

115 Ibid, 150.

116 Freedman, 223.

Although it is true that following the October Crisis, both JFK and his 'double' RFK had definitively decided against both U.S. military intervention in Cuba as well as covert action against Castro (including assassination) that could be directly attributable to the U.S., neither of the brothers were willing to suspend clandestine strategies altogether. Commenting on his own promise to Khrushchev, JFK pointedly remarked that "'an assurance covering invasion does not ban covert actions or economic blockade or tie our hands completely. We can't give the impression that Castro is home free.'"[117] What appears to have been put in place by the White House between November 1962 and November 1963 was an ultra-compartmentalized 'two track' approach to both Cuba and the Soviet Union. After effectively cancelling MONGOOSE in December 1962, JFK moved to create an entirely new anti-Castro covert operation, code-named AM/WORLD that was to be stationed offshore (primarily in Nicaragua and Costa Rica[118]) and to be manned and operated exclusively by Cubans.

> As 1963 progressed, the Kennedy administration was continuing its projects to either eliminate the Castro regime in Cuba (Track one) or to get the Russians off the island through some sort of agreement with Castro (Track two)...President Kennedy authorized thirteen new sabotage missions proposed by the Special Group on October 24 [1963] and gave final support for the AM/TRUNK project, a prospecting effort for

---

117 Bohning, 150.

118 According to Talbot this was, in fact, the primary objective of the operation; 'the brother's main concern was to contain the Cuban exile problem, and off-loading the militants to Central America had a certain political logic.' Talbot, 194. Talbot is in no doubt that the Kennedys were following a two-track approach to Castro at this time, with back-channel negotiations the preferred strategy. Ibid, 181, 190-4 and 227-8.

Cuban military officers who might be willing to support a coup against Castro. Robert Kennedy was involved not only with these CIA focused projects but also with the new autonomous group efforts...This independent CIA team, separated from JM/WAVE and with its own designation—AM/WORLD and its own facility...was moving the Kennedy Administration sponsored exiles offshore to start a major new and fully deniable effort against Castro. This effort was scheduled to mount several major seaborne attacks into Cuba before the end of 1963, to organize a provisional government that could assume control after a coup against Castro and ultimately lead to a new regime.[119]

AM/WORLD was headed by Manuel Artime, the founder and head of the MRR and who enjoyed extensive connections with Texan millionaires; the MRR, along with many other many of these anti-Castro private groups, were receiving extensive funding from petroleum interests (H.L. Hunt) and ranchers (Robert Kleberg, proprietor of the King Ranch).

Artime was given far more autonomy than had been previously associated with U.S. backed efforts; in return his charter was to operate totally outside the continental U.S. and to engage in a wide variety of public activities which would

---

119 Hancock, 200. See Escalante, *JFK*, 208: sometime during January to February 1963, RFK met with Manuel Artime 'to discuss training a force of exiled Cubans to invade Cuba. The plan would be directed at provoking an uprising in Cuba, coordinated with an exile landing at two points, Matanzas and Oriente (Near the Guantanamo naval enclave). The officers designated by the CIA for the plan were Howard Hunt and James McCord, both future Watergate "plumbers."' According to Waldron and Hartmann, the date of the uprising/invasion (unimaginatively code-named 'C-Day') had been set for 1 December. Waldron and Hartmann, 652.

make his U.S. sponsorship totally deniable.
Newly released CIA documents show that the Artime effort was highly compartmentalized and
isolated even from other 'secret war' operations
within the CIA.[120]

On the other hand, JFK sought to de-link the Soviet
Union from Cuba through the creation of the 'suspect'
back-channel; within the broader context of Détente I,
the U.S. would seek at least limited normalization with
both of its Communist antagonists; according to special
Presidential aide Arthur Schlesinger, 'the real concern
about Cuba in the last months of the Kennedy administration was the possibility of normalizing U.S.-Cuban relations.'[121] Of course, the 'price' paid by JFK for Détente
I would have been the cancellation of the invasion of
Cuba, which makes the evidence provided by Veciana in
his 1977 interview by the House Select Committee on
Assassination (HSCA) that much more meaningful.

According to Veciana, by the fall of 1962 his
mentor [Phillips/Bishop] was taking Alpha/66 and
its media exploits in a totally new direction. The
goal of the [Cuba] raids (now focused largely on
Russians and Russian installations) was very focused: *The purpose was to politically embarrass
Kennedy and to Force him to move against
Castro. As Bishop remarked, they had to put
Kennedy's back to the wall, forcing him to act
against Castro.*[122]

---

120 Hancock, 507.

121 Blight and Kornbluh, 112.

122 Hancock, 177. Emphasis in the original. Ex Comm meeting in the
   White House, 30 October 1962; in his notes, McNamara indicates that
   JFK "'stated that insofar as we had any control over the actions of Alpha
   66, we should try to keep them from doing something that might upset
   the deal with the Russians.'" Bohning, 153.

And this may very well be what may ultimately have led to the false-flag of Dallas; ironically, the extreme compartmentalization of AM/WORLD may have misled the para-militaries to misjudge the level of JFK's commitment to normalization.[123] Although not capable of engineering the strategy-of-tension by itself, the Cubans were connected to both intelligence and military operatives to provide an enormous from-ground-up push for an integrated spectacle.[124] In the words of Enrique Baloyra, a charter member of the DRE,

> There is a certain psychology involved in all this business, a psychology shared by groups like Alpha 66...The basic assumption these people make is that you cannot trust the Yankees, so you have

123 Conversely, if AM/WORLD really was nothing more than an expedient means of containing the 'problem' of the Cuban exiles, then anti-Castro extremists would have interpreted the embryonic efforts at normalization as a third and final betrayal by the brothers Kennedy. In April 1964, Felipe Santiago Vidal, a Cuban exile working in close association with the IPF was captured while on a penetration mission in Cuba. Fabian Escalante claims that during the interrogation prior to his execution Vidal claimed that 'he had been active in 1963 in informing Cuban exile groups [in Dallas] about Kennedy administration attempts to start a dialog with Cuba... [that] Kennedy was negotiating with Fidel Castro and shortly a deal would be cut to leave Castro in power, eject the Russians, and destroy the hopes of the exiles for a return to Cuba. John Kennedy was about to destroy "La Causa" forever.' Hancock, 79 and 89. It has been confirmed that both Ted Shackley and David Morales at JM/WAVE were aware of the back-channel with Havana. Ibid, 121.

124 This has been indirectly confirmed by Sam Halpern, a senior aide to Richard Helms, in discussion with investigative journalist Jeff Morley. Halpern relates that in May 1963 Desmond Fitzgerald attended a meeting of the NSC on the Cuba Project; at that meeting, National Security Advisor McGeorge Bundy, obliquely referring to AM/WORLD, remarked that '"We can give an impression of busy-ness in Cuba and we can make life difficult for Castro."' As Halpern remarked to Morley, '"I'll tell you one thing...I didn't know that word 'busy-ness.' It was never mentioned by [Fitzgerald] when he came back from that meeting, and it was a good thing he didn't because you may have had a *Seven Days in May* at that point."' Morley, 165-6.

to operate in the shadows and totally disconnect yourselves from any American agency. Their philosophy was: 'We are not going to follow what you tell us to do. What is sensible for you is not necessarily sensible for us.'[125]

LEE HARVEY OSWALD

'[The] anti-Castro people put Oswald together. Oswald didn't know who he was working for—he was just ignorant of who was really putting him together.'
—John D. Martino

Oswald is the quintessential para-political *nomad:* the (chaotic) bearer of multiple covert identities while moving across parallel clandestine spaces. It is virtually certain that Oswald was either a paid FBI informant/infiltrator and/or a CIA asset;[126] the crucial element still in dispute is whether he was the 'lone gunman' of the Warren Commission or the 'patsy' that he very publicly proclaimed himself to be—an action that very much violated the stereotypical notion of the Presidential assassin as self-aggrandizing ego-maniac. As liberal historian Lawrence Freedman has argued,

---

125 Bohning, 154.

126 In espionage parlance, Oswald might best be described as a 'dangle'; that is 'an individual who is circulated among potential intelligence targets strictly to see who responds to or contacts him, and to determine their connections.' Hancock, 91. In December 1962 the FBI initiated operation AM/SANTA in conjunction with the CIA in order to develop intelligence on Castro assets; the FBI was clearly 'using credible civilians having the *appearance and other attributes for the role of a pro-Castro revolutionary*, to penetrate pro-Castro organizations...' Ibid, 113. Emphasis in the original.

> Whether Kennedy was killed by a lone assassin or
> as a result of the complex plots involving the mob
> and Cuban exiles that are explained by conspiracy
> theorists, one way or another he was probably the
> victim of the Cuban issue in American politics.[127]

I will demonstrate that these are not mutually exclusive alternatives, as is evidenced by much recent work on JFK/DALLAS. David Kaiser situates Oswald within a 'vast' right-wing conspiratorial coalition of CIA officers and anti-Castro Cubans while fingering him as the lone 'trigger man'[128]; conversely, Russo embeds Oswald within a blow back pro-Castro assassination plot, a paid assassin but 'lone gunman' of the Cuban secret services.[129] My own purpose in this essay is to argue for a

---

127 Freedman, 243-44. This seems to have been Robert Kennedy's own early understanding of Dealey Plaza. In December 1963, in yet another striking example of Kennedy back-channelling, RFK dispatched family confidant William Walton to Moscow to deliver a private message to the Soviet government: (i) that RFK did not consider the assassination to have been a Russian plot and; (ii) that the Kennedy family 'believed that the former president had been the victim of a [domestic] right-wing conspiracy.' In Walton's own words, "'Dallas was the ideal location for such a crime...Perhaps there was only one assassin, but he did not act alone.'" Fursenko and Naftali, 344-6.

128 Kaiser, *The Road to Dallas*, 2.

129 Russo, generally. It is important to note that Russo fails to adequately consider an alternative reading that is clearly suggested by his own narrative: that the apparently pro-Castro 'recruiters' of Oswald were in fact anti-Castro double agents seeking to implicate Castro in JFK/DALLAS so as to precipitate a U.S. military invasion. To complicate matters even further, Oswald-as-spectacle raises the possibility of 'Leon' as a 'double patsy'. This scenario was laid out with remarkable precision by two of the staff attorneys of the Warren Commission, W. David Slausen and William Coleman. 'The evidence here could lead to anti-Castro involvement in the assassination on some sort of basis as this: Oswald could have become known to the Cubans as being strongly pro-Castro [with the possibility, of course, of Oswald as dangle]. He made no secret of his sympathies, so the anti-Castro Cubans must have realized that law enforcement authorities were also aware of Oswald's feelings and that, therefore, if he got into trouble, the public

minimalist theory of the assassination that is wholly explicable within the Debordean terms of the false-flag spectacle. It is, therefore, possible to show that very little would have been required for the integrated spectacle of Dealey Plaza to have been successfully staged, including the possibility of Oswald as the sole shooter.[130] Vitally, this goes to the persistent problem of speculation concerning the exact size of the conspiracy and the number of the conspirators; if both JFK and RFK were as badly alienated from their own government as some of the evidence shows,[131] then a very small number of middle or

---

would also learn of them...*It is possible that some sort of deception was used to encourage Oswald to kill the President*...The motive of this would, of course, be the expectation that after the President was killed, Oswald would be caught or at least his identity ascertained, the law enforcement authorities and the public would blame the assassination on the Castro government and a call for its forceful overthrow would be irresistible.'Hinckle and Turner, 269. Emphasis added. Hancock largely adopts this view, generally following the near-death 'confessions' of Cuban gambling syndicate associate John Martino; 'Oswald was approached and manipulated by anti-Castro exiles who represented themselves as pro-Castro operatives. At the time he was contacted, Oswald was being "run" in a counter-intelligence operation by a U.S. government agency, without doubt the FBI, but possibly a part of a joint agency operation [AM/SANTA].' Hancock, 16. The obvious problem with Martino as a source is that he first gained notoriety in 'conspiracy circles' in 1963 by claiming that Oswald had been recruited by Castro, a line of disinformation fully consistent with that taken by his very senior associate Johnny Roselli. Ibid, 12-13. For a recent attempt to recycle the Castro-Did-It theory, see Latell, in general. The author's career included a stint as a CIA desk analyst, a National Intelligence Agency Officer for Latin America in the early 1960s, and, from 1994-98, Director of the Centre for the Study of Intelligence. Much of the author's information concerning Oswald as a Cuban agent comes from the testimony of Florentino Aspilliga, a defector from the DGI. Latell, vi and xiii.

130 I should also point out that this scenario is also fully compatible with the 'accidental discharge' theory that has undergone a recent revival: that JFK's fatal head wound was the result of the accidental firing of a semi-automatic weapon by a Secret Serviceman—possibly Kennedy favorite Clint Hill—reacting in panic to the 'ambush' of Dealey Plaza.

131 See Talbot, generally.

even low-level operatives could have staged Dealey Plaza—what was essential is that no one within the diverse and over-lapping clandestine entities acted to serve as a braking mechanism upon the 'project'. Far more important than the exact mechanics of the assassination, then, is the political logic of the killing as public theatre coupled with the absolutely minimal operational requirements for its physical execution, rendering the notion of a 'conspiracy' to kill JFK genuinely plausible—or, at the very least, not inherently implausible. Section 5.03 of the U.S. Penal Code (1985) provides the following definition of criminal conspiracy.

1.3. Criminal Conspiracy

(1) Definition of Conspiracy. A person is guilty of conspiracy with another person or persons to commit a crime if the purpose of promoting or facilitating its commission he:

    (a) Agrees with such other person or persons that they or one or more of them will engage in conduct that constitutes such crime or an attempt or solicitation to commit such crime; or

    (b) Agrees to aid such person or persons in the planning or commission of such crime or of an attempt or solicitation to commit such crime.

(2) Scope of conspiratorial Relationship. If a person guilty of conspiracy, as defined by Subsection (1) of this Section, knows that a person with whom he conspires to commit a crime has conspired with another person or

persons to commit the same crime, he is guilty
of conspiring with such other person or persons, whether or not he knows their identity,
to commit such crime. [132]

Attention should also be paid to the Model Code's definition of culpability.

2.02 General Requirements of Culpability.

(1) Minimum Requirements of Culpability. Except as provided in Section 2.05, a person is not
guilty of an offence unless he acted purposely,
knowingly, recklessly or negligently, as the law
may require, with respect to each element of the
offense.

(2) Kinds of Culpability Defined.

(a) Purposely.

A person acts purposely with respect to a material
element of an offense when:

(i)   If the element involves the nature of his conduct or
        a result thereof, it is his conscious object to engage
        in conduct of the nature or to cause such a result;
        and

(ii)   If the element involves the attendant circumstances
        or he believes or hopes that they exist.

---

132 Denno, 35. The legal definition accords remarkably well with a
minimally acceptable philosophical definition: 'A *conspiracy* is a secret
plan on the part of a group to influence events partly by covert action.'
Pigden, 20.

(b) Knowingly.

A person acts knowingly with respect to a material element of an offense when:

(i)   If the element involves the nature of his conduct or the attendant circumstances, he is aware that his conduct is of that nature or that such circumstances exist; and

(ii)   If the element involves result of his conduct, he is aware that it is practically certain that his conduct will cause such a result.[133]

For the 'minimalist' conspiracy to be made out, therefore, only two things are truly necessary.

   (a)   Oswald was a (paid) FBI informant and/or CIA asset spying upon pro-Castro groups.

This is perhaps the most verifiable part of Lee's signature nomadic reality; 'Oswald functioned as a provocateur in New Orleans and was in contact with pro-Castro and anti-Castro Cuban exiles as well as double agents representing themselves as both.'[134] Oswald would have to have been a right-wing CIA 'mole' penetrating (and, ultimately, discrediting) the pro-Castro communities of both New Orleans and Dallas. This would not necessarily mean, however, that he was an intelligence asset at the time that he undertook his famous defection to the Soviet Union; he could have been a genuine dissenter, be-

---

133 Ibid, 7. The issue of culpability is important not so much for Oswald but for any confederates he may have had. Even if the conspiracy was of an extremely inchoate or informal manner, anyone who participated with Oswald in any way the issue of killing Kennedy would, *prima facie*, fall within the parameters of the legal definition of criminal conspiracy.

134 Hancock, 479.

came disillusioned, returned to the U.S., was then recruited as an informer, and then began acting out his fantasies of espionage. It is of great interest that *I Led Three Lives*, a television series about an FBI agent masquerading as a Communist spy, was Oswald's favorite television program as a youngster and reputedly had a tremendous psychological effect on him.

> Robert Oswald [Lee's eldest brother] remembers
> Lee watching [the show] intensely when he,
> Robert, left home to join the Marine Corps in
> 1952. 'My opinion of what he got out of "I Led
> Three Lives" and other programs of a similar
> nature [e.g. 'The Fugitive'] was the fact that he
> could put on a façade and pretend to be somebody
> he wasn't.' Robert would later consider the mean-
> ing for Lee. *It probably opened up a new world
> for him...[where] you could appear to be some-
> thing, then appear to be somebody else...To me,
> that was a training ground...If you're playing
> 'Cowboys and Indians,' you stop being the cow-
> boys and the Indians when you stop playing. But
> with Lee, with the 'I Led Three Lives' type show,
> he was still being somebody even though the
> show was over, the game was over. He still played
> another role.*[135]

Throughout his nomadic/clandestine migrations, Oswald may very well have been aided and encouraged in his private re-staging of the integrated spectacle by his various low-level controllers. There is no more supremely Debordean moment in the spectacle of JFK/DALLAS than this: Lee Harvey Oswald's solipsistic transformation of the virtual into the Real.[136]

---

135 Russo, 94. Italics in the original.

136 Although Robert Oswald's account has been questioned on numerous occasions, it was substantiated by Marguerite Oswald's—Lee's mother—

(b) Oswald was under the operational control of a CIA or military intelligence officer who was also a 'planner' of the assassination.

In the somewhat dramatic prose of Warren Hinckle and William Turner, 'Oswald was now in the most dangerous of worlds. He was acting out pro-Castro pantomimes under the command of a violently anti-Castro cabal domi-

---

own testimony to the Warren Commission on February 12 1964 (which, of course, does not necessarily prove anything). In any event, there is an undeniable element of 'high strangeness' in Oswald's relationship with culture, both high and popular. For example, his favorite opera was Tschaikovsky's adaptation of Alexander Pushkin's *The Queen of Spades*; Oswald attended several performances while in the Soviet Union. As the 'hip' reader might be aware, the *Queen of Hearts* playing card was the trigger-mechanism that controlled the homicidal actions of the 'Manchurian Candidate' Sergeant Raymond Shaw in both the eponymous novel and film. In addition to the John Frankenheimer film, two other movies that may have been viewed by Oswald close to the time of Dealey Plaza included *Suddenly* (1954 and, which like *The Manchurian Candidate*, starred Frank Sinatra), which concerned an alienated ex-serviceman who plots to assassinate the U.S. President (riding in the open air presidential limousine) using a long-range telescopic rifle, and *We Were Strangers* (1949, starring black-listed Communist 'fellow traveller' John Garfield) who unsuccessfully attempts to blow up the tyrannical President of Cuba Gerardo Machado—who was, in fact, overthrown in 1933. In her testimony to the Warren Commission Marguerite Oswald stated that 'Lee saw those films…I was with him when we watched them.' Albarelli, 62-3 and 65-6. Don DeLillo repeats this in his novel *LIBRA* at 370. Far more strange—and disturbing—than Oswald's relationship to cinema was John Kennedy's. Apparently, it was the President himself who pressed Frankenheimer, the director of *The Manchurian Candidate*, to undertake a film adaptation of the novel *Seven Days in May*, which outlined an abortive *coup d'etat* of the U.S. government by the Joint Chiefs of Staff. For discussion, see Talbot, 145-51. In Talbot's somewhat melodramatic prose, the 'fact that the president of the United States was driven to enlist the support of show business friends in his struggle with the military underscores how embattled he must have felt.' Ibid, 149. According to Kennedy courtier Arthur Schlesinger, '"Certainly we [sic] did not control the Joint Chiefs of Staff."' Ibid, 64. For JFK's estrangement from his generals, Chief of the Air Force Curtis LeMay in particular, see ibid, 66-70. Rumour has it that the fascistic leader of the military coup in *Seven Days in May*, General James Mattoon Scott, was based on LeMay. Ibid, 146. The cinematic nated by autonomous intelligence operatives and mob elements.'[137] In New Orleans, the list of probable CIA and/or FBI Oswald handlers would have included Guy Bannister, [138] David Ferrie,[139] and Clay Shaw.[140] In Dallas, the obvious CIA contact would have been with contract agent George de Mohrenschildt.[141] However, none of these individuals appear to have been senior enough to actually engage in both the planning and, even more

---

connection even extends to the assassination of Robert Kennedy; the Senator was staying at Frankenheimer's Malibu home when he was shot in the Ambassador Hotel in Los Angeles. Furthermore, Frankenheimer encountered RFK's assassin Sirhan Sirhan in the Ambassador: 'Ironically, Sirhan had brushed by Frankenheimer during Kennedy's victory speech, as the director stood watching Bobby on a TV monitor in the ballroom's archway. "It was *The Manchurian Candidate*," Frankenheimer later said. "I felt this shaking inside me."' Ibid, 372.

137 Hinckle and Turner, 236.

138 Kurtz, 158-61. Remarkably, Kurtz himself was a witness to the 'Communist pro-Cuban' Oswald's contact with the former head of the Chicago office of the FBI Bannister. "I myself saw Oswald and Bannister when they visited the campus of Louisiana State University in New Orleans...when Bannister condemned racial integration. I also saw them at a table in Mancuso's Restaurant, located in the same building as Bannister's office." Ibid, 159.

139 Ibid, 163; the probable recruiter of the teen-age Oswald in the Civil Air Patrol which may have constituted the very beginning of his 'double life'. Hinckle and Turner, 232-3.

140 Kurtz, 163-4. Shaw was the New Orleans contact for the Domestic Contact Division overseen by Tracey Barnes. Lane, 131. For both Shaw and Ferrie as CIA 'contacts' see Hinckle and Turner, 321. Ferrie was apparently employed as a contract agent of the CIA in the early 1960s, responsible for maintaining contact with the New Orleans community of anti-Castro Cubans. Stone and Sklar, 91. It has been established that at some time between 1955-6 the adolescent Oswald was a cadet member of the New Orleans branch of the Civilian Air Patrol headed by Ferrie. Albarelli, 70. There is a possibility that Ferrie either did or attempted to sexually molest Oswald. Ibid, 429-30.

141 Kurtz, 149-51. De Mohrenschildt committed suicide in 1977, several hours after investigator Gaeton Fonzi had made contact him on behalf of the House Select Committee on Assassinations (HCSA). Fonzi, 192. De Mohrenschildt's wife was apparently a good friend of several of the CIA's 'usual suspects': 'De Mohrenschildt's wife, Jeanne, also had a long

importantly, the implementation of counter-propaganda operations necessary for the successful performance of a false-flag event. This could only have been accomplished by positioning Oswald with the larger network of the Cuban paramilitaries that were themselves under the supervision of senior level CIA officers.

> [T]he only way individual militant Cuban exiles could act against JFK would be to place the apparent blame on Fidel Castro. No matter how hot their passion or how much support was offered, that was the only method that would allow them to actively target Kennedy without themselves dooming their cause. The use of a Castro-connected patsy was critical. Without a credible and maneuverable patsy, any attack on Kennedy would have been self-defeating. That patsy became visible to them in New Orleans in July of 1963. He became irresistible when they were informed that he was more than simply a naïve revolutionary sympathizer, but was in reality a low-level intelligence dangle who they could play at will.[142]

Accordingly,

> [O]ne of the major roles of the exiles in the conspiracy [was] managing and manipulating Lee Oswald. It was the exiles who contacted him, represented themselves as Castro agents, and continued contact with him up to the time of the assassination. The exiles were aware that Oswald was

---

history of working in intelligence and numbered among her friends and former operatives in the CIA Richard Helms, the agency's future director; James McCord, a close friend of Helms and the future Watergate burglar; Hunter Leake, an agent who worked at the agency's large New Orleans office; and David Atlee Phillips, the head of the CIA's Western Hemisphere Division.' Kurtz, 149-50.

142 Hancock, 368.

playing a role himself and that they had to maneuver him by continuing to represent themselves
as Castroites.[143]

Drawing upon my list of the 'usual suspects' from the
CIA, I find there to be two medium level case officers of
particular interest.

(1) TRACY BARNES

As Assistant Director of Plans to Richard Bissell for the
Bay of Pigs Barnes personally recruited many of the
CIA 'usual suspects' for the Cuba Project (E. Howard
Hunt, David Lee Phillips, and David Morales).[144]
Barnes' association with both Bissell and Mafia contact
Johnny Roselli placed Barnes 'at the center of virtually
every CIA assassination project of the early 1960s...'[145]
And, of the greatest significance, after Bissell's forcible
transfer to the Institute for Defense Analysis following
ZAPATA, Barnes was appointed head of the Domestic
Operations division of the CIA, the branch responsible
for the creation and operation of CIA 'front' companies,
and, apparently, exercising oversight of the Domestic
Contact Service, which handled the monitoring of infor-
mants and defectors; [146] 'in 1963, Domestic Operations

---

143 Ibid.

144 Ibid, 422.

145 Ibid, 424.

146 Ibid, 421-32. This branch was also responsible for the 201 files, which
were opened for every person considered by the Agency to be of
'"potential intelligence or counter-intelligence significance."' On
December 9 1960, a 201 was opened on Oswald, almost one year
following his (apparent) defection to the Soviet Union—an unusual time
lag. Stone and Sklar, 45. The file was controlled by Angleton's SGI.
Morley, 205. On November 9 1959, Oswald was put on the CIA 'Watch
List', which permitted operatives to read his mail; this program of postal

might well have been the starting point for Lee Oswald
being considered as an asset in specific CIA intelligence
collection projects ('dangles') such as the documented
1963 project targeting the FPCC [Fair Play for Cuba
Committee], first in the United States and then in Latin
America.'[147] If Oswald was indeed a CIA asset, which
seems almost certain, then the Domestic Contact Service
would have been the sub-division handling Oswald's
case file. In the estimation of Larry Hancock

> It is certainly possible that Oswald was used in a
> minor fashion for FPCC intelligence collection,
> something which grew into a much more aggress-
> ive propaganda program in New Orleans and then
> into an extension of that project in Mexico City.
> Such an extension would likely have been co-
> ordinated by the new Cuban Affairs officer, David
> Phillips, and monitored by Angleton's CI/SIG in-

interception was codenamed HT/LINGUAL and was administered by
Angleton's SGI group. John Newman has speculated that Oswald was a
'person of interest' to the CIA even prior to his infamous defection to the
USSR in November 1959 and that he might have been part of the
program run by the CIA's Russia division known as 'Soviet Realities'
(SR/6), which was dedicated to obtaining information about social and
economic conditions in Russia through the monitoring of 'defectors',
many of whom, of course, were not. Newman, *Oswald and the CIA*, 47-
59 and 168-98. As Simpich has put it, 'If there was anything of greater
value than a defector, it was a re-defector such as Oswald. Even if a re-
defector had nothing to do with intelligence, such a person was the
functional equivalent of a double agent.' James Angleton himself later
testified to the Church Committee in 1975 that 'the re-defection of
Oswald should have been "the highest priority for the intelligence
community."' Simpich, Preface, page one and two.

147 Ibid, 427. The FPCC was founded in April 1960 by pro-Castro
American journalist Robert Taber, who subsequently resigned his
presidency in February 1962. 'By this time the organization had become
a hopeless muddle of government informers, psychopaths, communists,
black militants, liberal social activists and socialists who carried with
them agendas that clashed with the group's modest objectives.' Albarelli,
302.

ternal security group.[148]

The possible role of Barnes, of course, also increases the likelihood of Angleton's own involvement, who emerges as the most interesting suspect at the most senior level of the CIA; 'the files maintained by the Special Investigations Group [SIG] were not part of the [CIA's] regular record-keeping system but were maintained in the archive controlled by Angleton. The program...sought to generate leads for new covert operations to be mounted by Angleton himself.' Apparently, Angleton had a fondness for off-the-books operations, establishing his own private '"command channels and communications"' that effectively 'bypassed CIA stations and flowed directly to his office in Washington.' Following Angleton's forced retirement in 1974, the CIA destroyed all of his files on the Kennedy assassination.[149]

(II) DAVID ATLEE PHILLIPS/MAURICE BISHOP

What makes Phillips a suspect of outstanding interest is that his entire career at the CIA was dedicated to the stage-managing (with uneven success) of extraordinarily elaborate clandestine spectacles. Next to Oswald himself, Phillips is the most Debordian character in my minimalist scenario. A life-long frustrated thespian ('Whenever possible during his Agency career, wherever he was stationed, Phillips would invariably start or join a little theater group'[150]), Phillips rose rapidly through the ranks of the Agency, establishing his 'reputation among his peers as *the* expert in the field' of counter-intelli-

---

148 Ibid.
149 Morley, 200-1.
150 Fonzi, 263.

gence, Psy-Ops, and propaganda.[151]

> His successes as an agent...were mainly in the
> area of propaganda, psychological warfare and
> counter-intelligence...Phillips was selected by the
> Agency to play an important role on overthrowing
> Jacobo Arbenz's leftist regime in Guatemala in
> 1954 [OPERATION PB/SUCCESS]. Phillip's
> task was to help set up a clandestine radio station
> in Mexico—the Voice of Liberation—sand, while
> pretending to be broadcasting from within
> Guatemala, orchestrate a crescendo of false re-
> ports about legions of rebels which didn't exist
> and major battles that never took place...In this,
> his first major assignment for the CIA, Phillips
> demonstrated a particular propensity for the mir-
> ror images so prevalent in counter-intelligence
> craft. For instance, part of the Voice of Libera-
> tion's mission was to generate disinformation that
> would foment a confusing array of rumors among
> the populace...Under such a propaganda barrage,
> the Arbenz government fled the country before
> many real bullets could fly. Phillips later termed
> the technique, which he would use again, 'the big
> lie.'[152]

PB/SUCCESS, when looked at in greater detail, carries with it two extremely discomforting implications for JFK/DALLAS. The first is that it illustrates the degree to which the spectacle is the inverted mirror-image of the 'situation', executed with a panache and brazenness that any true Situationist (or Orson Welles) could only impotently envy. An operation of enormous complexity,

---

151 Ibid. "Phillips was...told that he had the qualifications the Agency looked for in a propaganda specialist and his theatrical training thereafter concentrated on the techniques of propaganda and political action.' Ibid, 264.

152 Ibid, 264.

PB/SUCCESS was divided into two prongs: (i) a limited paramilitary infiltration of Guatemala by a small band of anti-Arbenz forces led by American puppet Carlos Castillo Armas supported by limited air raids by CIA owned World War II surplus aircraft;[153]and (ii) an entire network of black propaganda (or 'black ops') radio stations, based in the Dominican Republic, Managua, Honduras, and, most importantly, within the U.S. Embassy in Guatemala City itself.[154] Phillip's network ''The Voice of Liberation' effectively bridged the divide between conventional disinformation[155] to overt *simulation*, successfully manufacturing the mass illusion of an entire civil war that was not actually taking place[156] and an entire rebel army that did not really exist. [157]

> Frightened Guatemalans listening to the CIA radio broadcasts began fleeing from [Guatemala City], not wanting to be caught in the tremendous battle believed imminent for control of the capital. "Voice of Liberation" announcers actually appealed to the fleeing refugees to make way for the non-existent rebel columns. Few of the panicked

---

153 Schlesinger and Kinzer, 110. One of the major airfields for this 'phantom air force' was at Puerto Cabezas on the east coast of Nicaragua; during the Bay of Pigs, it was re-used as one of the major launching sites of air attacks against Cuba. Ibid, 114.

154 Ibid, 114.

155 'A typical broadcast assured listeners: "It is not true that the waters of Lake Atitlan have been poisoned."'' Ibid, 185.

156 'During a nighttime raid, the Americans played a tape recording of a bombing attack over loudspeakers set up on the [U.S.] Embassy roof that heightened the anxiety of the capital's residents.' Ibid, 183.

157 The Voice of Liberation: '"At our command post here in the jungle [the U.S. Embassy] we are unable to confirm or deny the report that Castillo Armas has an army of five thousand men."' Ibid, 185. These radiographic hallucinations were subsequently picked up and circulated globally by the international press corp. Ibid, 186. At no point did Armas have more than 400 men under his command.

> citizens stopped to wonder why, in their flight
> along the major highways, they never en-
> countered any advancing soldiers...With no one
> he could trust to give him accurate information,
> [President] Arbenz could no longer be certain that
> there wasn't at least some truth to the radio bullet-
> in.[158]

The second is that virtually all of the major operators of PB/SUCCESS—David Atlee Phillips, Tracy Barnes, E. Howard Hunt, 'Rip' Robertson—re-appear as key members of the 'usual suspects' for JFK/DALLAS.[159] Through and around Phillips was a semi-permanent 'unit', or 'crew' (if I can use this word) who were both closely linked with extremist reactionary political and paramilitary groups throughout Central America and the Caribbean and who were also proficient in Psy-Ops and counter-intelligence. In fact, this semi-nomadic unit (including other members such as David Harvey, Theodore Shackley and David Morales) transverses the shadow spaces of numerous black bag operations and may, in fact, have been in existence as early as the late 1940s: many of them appear to have made initial contact with each other while serving in the CIA station in Berlin.[160] Members of the unit also shared a fondness for basing their manifold command-and-control centers in Miami: headquarters for PB/SUCCESS was on the Opa-Locka Marine Air Force Base in Miami (consisting of a group of offices covertly secreted directly above a nursery school)[161] while JM/WAVE was based at the University

---

158 Ibid, 192.

159 And a few of them, such as Hunt, re-appeared a second time with NIXON/WATERGATE.

160 The Berlin Operating Base, or BOB. Hancock, 128 and 413-20. Other members included Henry Hecksher, who appears to have been the senior field officer for PB/SUCCESS. Ibid, 414.

161 Schlesinger and Kinzer, 110 and 113. Phillips and Hunt also

of Miami using the CIA front company Zenith Technical Enterprises Inc. as cover.

It is beyond dispute that for the CIA it 'was the "psychological actions" of the invasion force that were [truly] significant.'[162] As a result, in April, 1961, as part of ZAPATA, Phillips was appointed director of all propaganda/counter-intelligence operations for The Bay of Pigs.[163] This included the oversight of 'Radio Swan', a CIA broadcasting station located on Greater Swan Island, ninety-seven miles off the coast of Honduras, the very same 'black' radio station that had been used with such great success in PB/SUCCESS;[164] so successful, in fact, that the CIA attempted to duplicate Phillips' clandestine/Situationist success a third time under Lansdale.

> MONGOOSE's program of propaganda—consisting of radio and television broadcasting, balloon drops of leaflets, a distribution of photo-models

coordinated the 'Voice of Liberation' from Miami. Ibid, 114.

162 Blight and Kornbluh, 40. In fairness to the citizens of Guatemala City in 1954, belief in the spontaneous materialization of a rebel army was not, in itself, inherently implausible given national political conditions of that time. There was considerable political opposition to the Arbenz government among the traditional elites who had remained and were highly active within the country. This was in marked contrast to Cuba, where virtually the entirety of the pro-Batista establishment had either fled or were exiled to Miami—and where, not surprisingly, Phillip's spectacular theatre met with resounding failure. Coatsworth, xiv-xv and xix fn. 18.

163 Fonzi, 157.

164 Gleijeses, 6. During the Bay of Pigs, Radio Swan's greatest accomplishment was the unleashing of a cascade of weirdly beautiful Situationist images upon the resisting Cubans: "'Alert! Alert! Look well at the rainbow. The fish will rise soon. Chico is in the house. Visit him. The sky is blue...The fish will not take much time to rise. The fish is red.'" Rasenberger, 240. As with PB/SUCCESS these messages were intended to simulate the presence of an an organized counter-revolutionary force; this time, however, the un-real was actually the real —there was no domestic revolt against Castro.

and cartoon books by open mail, and dissemination of smuggled copies of *Time* magazine—[was]
integrated to the preparation of the population in
Cuba for regime change. Basic Madison Avenue
techniques, such as create musical and visual
symbols to express anti-regime sentiments,' were
a specialty of the U.S Information Agency, which
managed the *Voice of America*, and the technique
of adding 'new words to a favorite song' was a
staple of political subversion at least since *The
Beggar's Opera*. Thus, the transmission of anti-Castro sentiment was to function seamlessly in
everyday activities, capable of being passed person-to-person while augmenting less embodied
techniques such as painted slogans.[165]

Following the Bay of Pigs, Phillips served as the Chief
of Covert Action in Mexico City from late 1961 to the
autumn of 1963, coinciding with Oswald's alleged visitation to both the Soviet and Cuban Consulates.

How well Phillips did his work is revealed by the
fact that barely two years into his assignment—
just prior to Kennedy's assassination—he was
made Chief of Cuban Operations there. In both
jobs his main activities were in propaganda, dirty
tricks, and counter-intelligence, and his central focus was on maintaining a watch on Castro's intelligence agents, many of whom worked out of the
Cuban Embassy.[166]

On October 1, 1963 Phillips was promoted to chief of
Cuban operations in Mexico City; [167] as a result,
'Phillips' Cuban Project assignment [as with Barnes] led
him into activities involving domestic counter-intelli-

---

165 avis, 144.
166 Fonzi, 266.
167 Ibid, 429.

gence dangles against the FPCC and into the exile community of New Orleans.'[168]

ADDENDUM TO PHILLIPS:
ON THE 'LORDS OF MISRULE'

'You really have me consorting with a cast of sordid characters, don't you Mr. Garrison?'—Clay Bertrand/Shaw (Tommy Lee Jones), *JFK*

Consideration of the spectacle leads to consideration of the situation which, in turn, leads directly to the problem of *aesthetics*. If the spectacle is the inversion of the situation, then we must move from the tremulous beauty of poetry-in-the-street (*la Beaute est dans la Rue*) to the omnivorous obscenity of the clandestine. Upon further reflection Psy-Ops can be shown to bear an uncanny resemblance to Mikhail Bahktin's notion of the *carnivalesque*, or *mis-rule*, the inversion of conventional reality (political, moral, social, aesthetic) into its inverted double, the *grotesque*. When undertaking parapolitical research one is, in fact, uncomfortably aware of a nomadic environment—personalities, places, events—saturated with the 'fundamental attributes of the grotesque style', famously defined by Bahktin in his master work on Rabelais and the carnivalesque as 'exaggeration, hyperbolism, excessiveness.'[169] The grotesque, perhaps best defined as 'the ambivalently abnormal', is phenomenological in nature, grounded upon a *horror sensorium*: 'a fundamentally ambivalent thing...a violent clash of op-

---

168 Hancock, 177.
169 Bakhtin, 303. See ibidem, Chapter Five, 303-67.

posites...an appropriate expression of the problematical nature of existence.'[170] When treating the grotesque imaginary, as Bakhtin reminds us, we must always 'take into consideration the importance of cosmic terror, the fear of the immeasurable, the infinitely powerful.'[171] The inversion of the world is itself the onto-poetical ground of the grotesque, a world that is eternally teetering on the verge of a chaotic formlessness through the radical and uncontrollable proliferation of irreconcilable combinations, the perpetual construction of 'what we might call a double body'[172]: 'The grotesque body...is a body in the act of becoming. It is never finished, never completed; it is continually built, created, and builds and creates another body.'[173] Like its aesthetic Other, the sublime, the grotesque is quintessentially Modern, but with this crucial distinction: both modernism and the grotesque 'focus on the concepts of alienation, subjectivity, and absurdity, but the grotesque tends to focus on explicit representations of these ideas through disturbing imagery and actions, while modernism tends to focus on more implicit representations of these themes.'[174] In other words, the aesthetic paradigm of the grotesque requires the coming forth of a monster of some kind;[175] the 'grotesque alienation' that results arises from an en-

---

170 Thomson, 11.

171 Bakhtin, 335.

172 Ibid, 318.

173 Ibid, 317.

174 Martin, 47.

175 'Grotesque alienation is usually a result of external, physical change or action, communicated through imagery that may include violent acts, self-destructive behaviors [sic], deformity, transformation, monstrous creatures, and any number of other strange or disturbing scenes. However, the physically-based alienation depicted in such works is merely a catalyst or metaphor for the psychological alienation of one or more characters.' Ibid, 48-9.

hanced self-consciousness of the protagonist of being embedded within a pre-existent (un-constructed) estranged world, the dark numinous,[176] which neatly correlates with what I call the parapolitical landscape.

Undertaking the most ambitious analysis of the grotesque as a formal sub-category of the Modern, Wolfgang Kayser defines his subject-matter in such a way as to render most transparent the artistic and narrative similitudes between the grotesque and cosmic horror; 'The modern age questions the validity of the anthropological and the relevance of the scientific concepts underlying the syntheses of the nineteenth century. The various forms of the grotesque are the most obvious and pronounced contradictions of any kind of rationalism and any systematic use of thought.'[177] For Kayser, the grotesque consists of three signature themes. The first is 'the grotesque as the estranged world'; 'It is our world which has to be transformed. Suddenness and surprise are essential elements of the grotesque.'[178] The grotesque 'world', or landscape, as Bakhtin makes clear, is the aesthetic continuation by other means of the phenomenological primacy of the grotesque body.

> Thus the artistic logic of the grotesque image ignores the closed, smooth, and the impenetrable surface of the body and retains only its excrescences (sprouts, buds) and orifices, only that which leads beyond the body's limited space or

---

176 'In modernist grotesque alienation, there is no going back. The world is not alienated due to malignant influences that can be purged, as in the older [classical?] grotesque. In modernist grotesque alienation, the protagonist realizes that the world itself has always been alienating, and it is the illusion of stability that must be exposed, for the sake of intellectual integrity.' Ibid, 51.

177 Kayser, 188.

178 Ibid, 184.

> into the body's depths. Mountains and abysses, such is the relief of the grotesque body; or speaking in architectural terms, towers and subterranean passages[179]...This grotesque logic is also extended to images of nature and of objects in which depends (holes) and convexities are emphasized.[180]

The 'estranged world' of the grotesque, unifying both the high and the low, is, therefore, an artistic device deployed primarily in order to stage the mimetic rendition of the trauma-inducing encounter with the radically alien 'sublime'. Just like Peter Dale Scott's contemplation of the deep events of American history, the grotesque

> is primarily the expression of our failure to orient ourselves in the physical universe...We are so strongly affected and terrified because it is our world which ceases to be reliable, and we feel unable to live in this changed world[181] ...

> The grotesque instills fear of life rather than fear of death. Structurally, it presupposes that the categories which apply to our world view become inapplicable...the fusion of realms which we know to be separated, the abolition of the law of statics, the loss of identity, the distortion of 'natural' size and shape, the suspension of the category of objects, the destruction of personality, and the fragmentation of the historical order.[182]

Second is what Kayser denotes as 'the Grotesque as a Play with the Absurd', signified by the operational hege-

---

179 Ibid, 317-18.
180 Ibid, 318 fn. 6.
181 Ibid.
182 Ibid, 184-5.

mony of determinism (natural or otherwise) and the concomitant manipulation of reality by occult forces: 'the
unity of perspective in the grotesque consists in an
unimpassioned view of life on earth as an empty, meaningless puppet play or a caricatural marionette theatre.'[183] And third is the rather convoluted 'the Grotesque
as an Attempt to Invoke and Subdue the Demonic Aspects of the World', which may perhaps best be defined
in the following manner: 'In spite of all the helplessness
and horror inspired by the dark forces which lurk in and
behind our world and have the power to estrange it, the
truly artistic portrayal effects a secret liberation. The
darkness has been sighted, the ominous powers discovered, the incomprehensible forces challenged.'[184]

One of the most 'uncanny' aspects of JFK/DALLAS
is the fact that so many of the usual suspects were amateur or marginal artists or involved with that quintessential modern enterprise 'public relations': Phillips as
amateur thespian, Hunt as sub-par novelist, Lansdale as
Wall Street ad-man. Pursuing the Debordean logic of the
integrated spectacle to the highest level would involve
re-conceptualizing the usual suspects as signs of the
grotesque landscape, the quasi-competent 'lords of mis-
rule' of the post-Reality era of governance-by-spectacle.
Perhaps the most striking aspect of JFK/DALLAS and
the 'high strangeness' of the (possible) evidence generated within its wake is the half-smart/half-stupid nature of
bizarre occurrences and weird coincidences and conver-
gences; Don DeLillo employs this grotesque 'play with
the absurd' as the narrative foundation of his metaphysi-

---

183 Ibid, 186. For the intimate connections between the grotesque
and caricature, see Thomson, 38-40. Striking here is the utter
aptness of the marionette theatre as a signifier of the deep state.

184 Kayser, 188. See discussion of Oliver Stone's film *JFK* in Chapter
Five, below.

cal thriller *LIBRA*.[185] An outstanding example of this, one that almost certainly originated with Phillips and his grotesque post-Guatemala crew of Psy-Op pranksters, was the absurd (pseudo-demonic?) farce of B-26 no. 933. As part of ZAPATA, Mario Zuniga, an anti-Castro Cuban pilot, flew an American built B-26 bomber (no. 933) from the CIA base at Puertos Cubezas ('Happy Valley') in Nicauragua to Miami International Airport in the opening hours of the invasion of Cuba (Saturday, April 15). Zuniga's cover story was that he was a defector from the Cuban air force, claiming that there was a full-scale mutiny in the armed forces against Communist rule. A number of pilots, including Zuniga, had attacked Cuban military airfields before seeking asylum in the U.S..[186] As should have been predicted, Zuniga's story soon fell apart for the following 'someone-should-have-known' reasons: (i) Zuniga claimed a two hour flight time when Cuba was only 30 minutes away by air; (ii) the difficult to explain away presence of anti-dust tape covering barrels of the plane's machine-guns, which would have been removed if the guns had actually been fired; (iii) the nose of no. 933 was made of metal, while those of the B-26s in the Cuban air force were made of plexi-glass; and (iv) the machine guns were mounted on the nose of no. 933 while the B-26s of the Cuban air force were mounted under the wings.[187] I believe that it

---

185 See Chapter Four.

186 'At 6:00 am, Zuniga's statement claimed, he had taken off from San Antonio de los Banos and flown over to Libertad, where he and other pilots dropped bombs and strafed planes with machine guns, taking fire from ground artillery...As he returned to strafe his own airfield, at San Antonio, his co-conspirators attacked other Cuban airfields.' Rasenberger, 195.

187 Ibid, 194-5. To compound the absurdity even more, U.S. Ambassador Adlai Stevenson used photographs of Zuniga's plane to denounce the Cuban regime in the United Nations Security Council. As Phillips later wrote in his memoirs, *The Night Watch*: "'As I watched Stevenson

is important to keep these aesthetic digressions in mind when considering perhaps the single most Byzantine element in the Oswald 'drama': the shadowy movements of Oswald to and from Mexico City during September and October of 1963. It is also the piece of absurd theatre that offers the most compelling evidence of a higher-level degree of CIA manipulation of the assassin.

OSWALD IN MEXICO CITY

Mark Lane has recently reminded us of the centrality of the Mexico City CIA Station to the Agency's wider hemispheric operations.

> The newspapers were not bothersome in Mexico City and the police authorities had long since been co-opted by the use of several methods. Select mid-level officers were fed secret intelligence about minor or semi-major criminal activities permitting the favored to quickly 'solve' open cases through what appeared to be brilliant investigative work. They rose through the ranks knowing that they owed their careers to the CIA. Those open to bribery were easily recruited and the few important officials who were loyal to their own country were placed in situations, filmed sexual assignations as one device, so that their cooperation and silence was extorted. For those reasons the CIA chose Mexico City, rather than a city in the United States, to make plans that directly involved the United States.[188]

The ideal parapolitical ambience of Mexico City, there-

---

defend the deceitful scheme a chill moved through my body…What had we done? *Adlai Stevenson had been taken in by a hoax!*" Ibid, 205.

188 Lane, 194.

fore, would automatically provide any CIA covert operation the two most necessary requirements for success:
deniability and compartmentalization. And, if JFK/DAL-
LAS was indeed a false-flag spectacle with Oswald as
the pro-Castro gunman, then Mexico City would have
been the place to mount the required counter-intelligence
operation, with Phillips the thespian wannabe the man to
do it. Scott's argument on this point strikes me as conclusive.

> David Phillips does…seem a likely candidate to
> have co-ordinated the stories coming out of Mex-
> ico City and Miami. For in the second half of
> 1963 he was cross-posted to both stations, as
> chief of Cuban Operations in Mexico City, and as
> Chief of Psychological Operations (i.e., propa-
> ganda) in Miami. (In fact, it is possible that David
> Phillips held down three posts in 1963, and was
> doubling also as a member of the Special Affairs
> Staff Counterintelligence (SAC/CI) staff.)[189]

Oswald was reputedly in Mexico City from September
25 to October 3, 1963, making five separate visits to
both the Soviet and Cuban embassies in an attempt to
acquire a travel visa for both countries;[190] 'That meant
that *if* Oswald was in Mexico City and *if* he were involved in any intelligence activity, whether pro- or anti-
Castro, Phillips would have been either a player, or he
would have known about it.'[191] And what is so decidedly

189 Scott, *Deep Politics II*, 35.
190 Fonzi, 266.
191 Ibid, 279. What Oswald actually did during those six days is a puzzle.
In fact, part of the puzzle is whether or not it was the real Oswald in
Mexico City…in the end, the only 'proof' that the real Oswald was inside
the Cuban Consulate were his photograph and his signature on his visa
application. Ibid, 281. For Fonzi's compelling critique of the evidence for
Oswald's presence in Mexico City, see ibid, 278-97. A recurrent, but
tantalizing, sub-theme of the 'conspiracy literature' of JFK/DALLAS is

odd here is the memo of November 23, 1963 sent by J. Edgar Hoover to Chief of the Secret Services, James Rowley—a memo that constitutes one of the very few pieces of the paper-trail of JFK/DALLAS.

> The Central Intelligence Agency advised that on October 1, 1963, an extremely sensitive source had reported that an individual identifying himself

that U.S. intelligence had fabricated a 'second' or 'double' Oswald, who was activated at strategically crucial moments for counter-intelligence purposes; see Armstrong, 'Harvey and Lee', Parts I and II, generally. Pease identifies the ultimate 'control' over all counter-intelligence operations involving Oswald as James Jesus Angleton; Pease, 'Angleton', Parts I and II, generally. My personal preference would be to situate operational control at a lower level within the CIA hierarchy; hence, my preference for Tracy Barnes as a credible 'usual suspect'. The most sophisticated and extensive discussion of this issue is Scott, *Deep Politics II*, generally. The obvious problem with the theory is in identifying the precise moment and circumstances in which Oswald became on 'item of interest' to the intelligence agencies. Albarelli has tentatively suggested that the possible solution lies within Oswald's own early history of delinquency, the subject of the masterful first chapter of Don DeLillo's brilliant novel *LIBRA*. 'In April 1953, reportedly following additional school absences, Oswald was sent to Youth House, located on 12th Street between 1st and 2nd Avenues in Manhattan. Here he was placed under psychiatric observation for three weeks, from April 16 to May 7, 1953.' Oswald's forced stay at Youth House puts him uncomfortably close to a much more sinister institution, the Bordentown Reformatory. 'Boys sent to Youth House who were deemed incorrigible were routinely sent to the nearby Bordentown Reformatory in New Jersey, a home away from home for what were then commonly called "juvenile delinquents". There is no known evidence that Oswald went to Bordentown, but several physicians who worked at the reformatory also performed work at Youth House. The Bordentown facility is significant, because during World War II, and, from 1951 to 1964, it was the site of secret CIA and U.S. Army behavior-modification and mind-control experiments…which were intended to both trigger and study "a model psychosis characterized by visual and auditory hallucinations." Furthermore, during the Second World War, the Bordentown Reformatory was used by the OSS, precursor to the CIA, for truth-drug experiments.' Albarelli, 17-18; see also Marks, 201. Following JFK/DALLAS, on 9 December 1963 an article co-authored by Donald R. Flynn and Mike Pearl entitled 'N.Y. Psychiatric Report Cited Oswald Violence', appeared in the *New-York Journal-American*, opening with the as Lee Oswald contacted the Soviet Embassy in Mexico City inquiring as to any messages. Special Agents of this Bureau, who have conversed with Oswald in Dallas, Texas, observed photographs of the individual referred to above and have listened to a recording of his voice [The CIA had wire-tapped all of the telephone lines to the Russian Embassy] These special agents are of the opinion that the above-referred-to-individual was not Lee Harvey Oswald.[192]

_____

following sentence: "'A 10-year old psychiatric report on Lee Harvey Oswald emerged today as a startlingly accurate blueprint for precisely the kind of violence that erupted last November 22 in the assassination of John F. Kennedy.'" Ibid, 25. The psychiatrist who examined the juvenile Oswald and who authored the report, Dr. Renatus Hartogs, was linked to a number of other psychiatrists who were involved in the extensive CIA mind-control experimentation of the 1950s (including operations ARTICHOKE, BLUEBIRD, and, most importantly, MK/ULTRA): these contacts included, but were not limited to, Dr. D. Ewen Cameron, Dr. Harold A. Abramson and Dr. Milton Kurian. In 1965, Hartogs co-authored a book on Oswald suggestively entitled *The Two Assassins*, which argued—on fairly scant evidence— that Oswald fit the classic profile of the schizophrenic loner exactly. Ibid, 19-29. A possible additional factor at work here is that Oswald's half-brother John Pic was a corpsman in the U.S. Coast Guard and from April 1952 to February 1953 was assigned to the Coast Guard's Port Security Unit at Ellis Island. ' This security unit, an outgrowth of the Espionage Act of 1950, was charged with identifying, investigating, and ridding New York harbor, the Longshoreman's Union, and the maritime industry of communists and subversive elements.' Ibid, 13. See Marks for Abramson (61-2n, 64, 68, 79-83, 118, 120 and 169) and Cameron (131-9, 145, 148, 156, 159, 214).

192 Fonzi, 285. On the presence of Oswald's double in Mexico City at this time, see Newman, 'Oswald' generally; 'someone pretending to be Oswald made a series of telephone calls between September 28 and October 1, allegedly to and from the Cuban and Soviet Consulates in Mexico City.' Ibid, 218. See also Morley, 207-14 and 237. An added complication here was the testimony of Sylvia Tirado de Duran, the Cuban consular staff member who allegedly had an affair with Oswald during his stay in Mexico City. The taped conversation in question was reputedly a call that both Duran and Oswald made from within the Cuban Consulate to the Soviet Embassy on Saturday September 28, yet Duran told Mexican authorities that Oswald had not returned to the Consulate after Friday September 27. The CIA officer responsible for translating Duran's testimony in the original Mexican transcript was David Phillips;

The 'deep' significance of the confusion over the identity and movements of 'Oswald' was not lost on Fidel Castro, who made a remarkable series of comments to the U.S. Senate Assassinations Committee.

> 'You see, it was always very suspicious to me... that a person who later appeared to be involved in Kennedy's death would have requested a visa from Cuba. Because, I said to myself—what would have happened had by any chance that man come from Cuba—visited Cuba—gone back to the States and then appeared involved in Kennedy's death? That would really have been a provocation—a gigantic provocation...That is why it has always been something—a very obscure thing—something suspicious—because I interpreted it as a deliberate attempt to link Cuba with Kennedy's death.'[193]

In a similar manner, Escalante casts damning aspersions upon a series of obviously fake letters allegedly sent to Oswald from Cuba in the days immediately following

---

even though fluent in Spanish, Phillips 'mis-translated' Duran's remarks, changing "'He [Oswald] never called back'" to "'she [Duran] does not recall whether or not Oswald telephoned her at the Consulate number on Saturday." Ibid, 236-7. For more on Oswald and Duran, see below, this chapter. Simpich has argued that this tape is the single most important piece of evidence in JFK/DALLAS; the conspirators, probably members of William Harvey's Staff D (along with affiliates such as David Morales and Johnny Roselli) impersonated Oswald (and perhaps Duran as well) not only as part of their false-flag agenda, but also to convince CIA counter-intelligence chief James Angleton that the Mexico City wire-tapping operations had been penetrated by a Cuban double agent and that the obviously fake voices were an attempt to provide the Americans with disinformation. The plan was that Angleton would fall for the trap and launch a full-scale 'mole hunt', looking for possible Castroite double agents within the anti-Castro network, which would inadvertently provide effective cover for the JFK/DALLAS crew. See Simpich, Chapter Five and Scott, *Deep Politics II*, 117-30.

193 Fonzi, 284-5.

the assassination, clear signs, in his view, of an absurdly incompetent attempt at a 'frame'.[194]

> But perhaps the single most intriguing piece of evidence is provided by Alpha/66 director Anthony Veciana, who claimed that on February 1, 1964, in an apparent attempt to make the Oswald frame-up 'stick', he was approached by his ubiquitous CIA controller Maurice Bishop and asked to provide additional cover for Oswald's activities in Mexico City.

> At the time, there were newspaper stories about Oswald having met with a Cuban couple in Mexico City. Veciana recalls these stories reported that the wife spoke excellent English. Bishop said that he knew that Veciana had a cousin, Guillermo Ruiz, in Castro's intelligence service[195] who then happened to be stationed in Mexico City. Ruiz's wife, coincidentally, spoke excellent English. Bishop asked Veciana to try to get in touch with Ruiz and offer him a large amount of money if Ruiz would say that it was he and his wife who had met Oswald.[196]

The vital question at this point is, of course, was Maurice Bishop the cover name for David Phillips? The classic, and most extensive, statement of the case for Phillip-as-Bishop, is the one offered by Gaeton Fonzi in his

---

194 Escalante, *JFK*, 134-45; Hinkle and Turner, 262-3. The alleged authors of the epistles included 'Pedro Charles', 'Miguel Galvan Lopez' (who conveniently identified himself as 'Ex-Captain of the Rebel Army') and 'Mario del Rosario Molina'. Escalante, *JFK*, 135-7. The clumsiness of the fabrications readily puts one in mind of ZAPATA's farcical B-26 no. 933. See above.

195 Fonzi does not appear to make much of this rather remarkable fact.

196 Fonzi, 143.

monumental *The Last Investigation*.[197] However, not all conspiracy investigators are convinced. Scott, for one, finds Veciana unreliable and the character of Bishop a 'red herring';[198] nonetheless, Scott clearly assigns Phillips ultimate responsibility for the 'double' Oswald scenario that appears to have been enacted in Mexico City,[199] so that even if Oswald (and Veciana) was not being handled by Phillips as Bishop, he was still being manipulated by Phillips via counter-intelligence operations being run out of the Mexico City Station. The story becomes even more complicated—but equally more seductive—if I take into account Veciana's second post-JFK/DALLAS anecdote concerning Bishop. In 1967 Phillips was promoted to Chief of the Cuban Operations Group of the CIA's Western Hemisphere Division, responsible for all Agency anti-Communist actions run throughout Central and South America. According to Veciana, in 1971 Bishop, with the assistance of anti-Castro Cuban personnel, organized an aborted assassination attempt against Castro while on a State visit to Chile, one that bore an uncanny resemblance to 'typical' JFK/DALLAS conspiracy narratives.

> '[Bishop] told me,' Veciana says, 'that it was an opportunity to make it appear that the anti-Castro Cubans killed Castro without American involvement'...According to Veciana....[the conspirators] planted phony documents so that if the two who were going to assassinate Castro were caught and killed, the trail would lead to the Russian

---

197 Ibid, 261-97, 304-37, and 364; see also, Hancock, 179-81. Ross Crozier, the CIA case officer who handled the DRE for Phillips from 1960-62, initially claimed that Phillips used that alias but later admitted to making an error. Morley, 185.

198 Personal communication with the author, June 27, 2013.

199 See Scott, *Deep Politics II*, generally.

agents in Caracas. It was an elaborate scheme. False surveillance reports were slipped into the files of the Venezuelan secret police to indicate that the Cuban assassins had been seen meeting with the Russian agents...Also in the files were fake passports, diaries and notes which would be planted in one of the assassin's hotel rooms to prove his contacts with the agents. But the most damaging evidence they concocted was a photograph showing what appeared to be one of the assassins leaning into a car window talking with one of the agents. The photo was actually of another Cuban who closely resembled the assassin. As instructed, this double stopped the Russian agent's car as he left his home one morning, leaned in and asked him for a match. A telephoto shot was taken of this encounter.[200]

If this story is true, the implications for JFK/DALLAS as a spectacular deep event are obvious: both of the assassins, who really were the actual shooters, had a complex web of disinformation and black propaganda woven around them without their apparent knowledge or participation. Even more intriguing is the reason why the plot failed—both assassins pulled out at the last moment, having 'developed a sub-plot based on the assumption that the shooters would be immediately caught and killed.'[201] An additional germane fact, although not conclusive in itself, is that from 1971 to 1973, Phillips was responsible for conducting all covert, or 'Track II' actions against the Allende government in Chile, culminating in the *coup d'etat* of September 11, 1973 and the (apparent) murder of President Allende.[202] Because of his spectacular success with Track II, Phillips was pro-

---

200 Fonzi, 137-8.
201 Ibid, 137.
202 Ibid, 339 and 340.

moted to Director of the Western Hemisphere Division of the CIA in June, 1973.

Juxtaposing Phillips with Oswald and (tentatively) identifying Phillips as Bishop, allows me to arrive at two conclusions about JFK/DALLAS. The first is that Phillips/Bishop is an exemplary example of the criminal sovereign. Indeed, Phillips appears to have been very much a 'Cowboy' within the Yankee paragon of the Agency; apart from the fact that 'Cowboy' is CIA parlance for an experienced covert operator, Phillips was a literal Cowboy as well as a figurative one, having been born in Fort Worth, Texas, far from the spawning-grounds of the Eastern Establishment.[203] He also, along with many of the other officers involved with the Cuba Project, very much fit the 'character profile' of a criminal sovereign—provided, of course, that I am actually able to assume the existence of such a thing. Fonzi himself was in no doubt concerning Phillip's personal proclivity for spectacular power.

> One retired CIA officer, who still prefers anonymity, was chief of collections in covert action when Phillips was on the Cuban desk. 'There wasn't a period when I could sign off on a cable from him,' he said. 'I usually had to send them back for some glaring technical errors. He was an incredibly sloppy officer, but he had a keen sense of public relations. Phillips was a grandstander. He was one of those guys who wanted to run countries in his own free-wheeling style. We had a lot of guys like that. Howard Hunt was another fellow cut precisely from the same cloth as Dave Phillips.[204] They were romantic adventurers. They couldn't possibly subject themselves to the kind of dry,

---

203 Ibid, 263.
204 On Phillip's and Hunt's exceptionally close friendship, see ibid, 307-8.

> arid, dispassionate anonymity you have to have if
> you're going to be a good espionage. Phillips was
> the supreme adventurer, one of a crowd of grand-
> standers who got into this goddamn CIA and once
> they got in they found out that in America, the
> grandstanding country, they could actually play to
> the galleries. And they've got away with it...One
> of the problems with the Central Intelligence
> Agency...is that it operates with two sets of books
> [*Yankee and Cowboy?*] It allows men like David
> Phillips, who [it] could not endure otherwise, to
> get into positions where they can't be dropped off
> the line...Now once you reach that certain point,
> you can do almost no wrong because you've got
> too much guilty knowledge inside your head.'[205]

My second conclusion is that the concept of Dealey Plaza as an open-air stage for the theatre of the false-flag is proven by the person of Phillips himself. It is not merely the case that Phillips happened to be a conspirator who engineered a deep event as a false-flag; rather, the truth of Dealey Plaza as the central component of a strategy-of-tension operation would actively require the presence of Phillips, or someone very much like him, operating within and through the counter-intelligence divisions of either the CIA or some parts of the myriad networks of military intelligence.[206] Further, the Dallas

---

205 Ibid, 329-30.

206 I have suspected for quite a while, but have so far been unable to prove, the 'background' role of military intelligence, including the Defense Intelligence Agency/DIA, within JFK/DALLAS. I feel it likely that many of the 'usual suspects' from the CIA may very well have constructed within the media as cut-outs for DIA operatives. It is also possible that military intelligence may solve the 'problem' of Maurice Bishop: that Veciana was mis-led into thinking that his contact officer was with the CIA and not with the DIA and/or Army Intelligence. Apparently, 'Maurice Bishop' was an alias used by a number of different CIA case officers. Albarelli, 441-2. To the best of my knowledge, Bill Simpich's recently published on-line book, *State Secret*, does the best job

spectacle as counter-intelligence operation obviates the need to positively establish that Oswald was *not* 'the lone gunman' of the Warren Commission; both the operational, and legal, definition of conspiracy can be established even if Oswald was the sole shooter.

> The Dallas script did not position Lee Oswald as a lone nut acting entirely on his own initiative. The plot was intended to present the assassination as a conspiracy, one that would lead directly to Fidel Castro and a Castro intelligence organization operating within the United States. The plotters spent considerable effort associating Lee Oswald with purported Castro agents and positioning him as being paid by Castro in the killing of President Kennedy. This script did not present Oswald as a devout Castro activist and revolutionary—as might have been anticipated from the New Orleans FPCC activities of Oswald—but rather as a nut or an unstable gun for hire. That was the characterization presented to Sylvia Odio [on September 26 or 27, 1963]. Oswald was presented as someone *dangerous, emotional, and unpredictable*.[207]

What matters was the clandestine network operating around him.

> The plotters were presenting Oswald as a paid Castro agent associating with Castro operatives. They had one sacrificial patsy but no shortage of shooters; beyond any other consideration they had to ensure that John Kennedy died. Their original concept seems to have included multiple officials as targets, perhaps explaining the shots to Gov-

---

in discussing the participation of military intelligence services in the Cuba Project. See Simpich, generally.

207 Hancock, 219.

ernor [John] Connally. There was no reason for
them to limit the number of shots or shooters.[208]

On the basis of my 'minimalist' conspiracy scenario,
then, premised upon the public staging of the false-flag,
the 'enormous network of mobsters, anti-Castro Cubans,
and right-wing political activists' that Kaiser outlines
can be restricted to the following key suspects: David
Atlee Phillips, Tracy Barnes, Antonio Veciana, George
de Mohrenschildt, Guy Bannister, and, in the not im-
probable (but as yet unproven) recruitment of one or
more supplemental—or even substitute shooters—for
Oswald, David Morales. And if we are able to not im-
plausibly expand the covert parapolitical parameters of
JFK/DALLAS to include multiple shooters, then Oswald's 'network' would include the Cuban snipers Eladio del valle Gutierrez, Sandalio Herminio Diaz Garcia
and Nestor Izquierdo. In order to make out a conspiracy
it is not necessary, therefore, to refute any of the Os-
wald-shot-the-President forensic evidence; I need merely to re-contextualize it.

ADDENDUM TO OSWALD IN MEXICO CITY: PHILO-COMMUNISTS TWISTING THE NIGHT AWAY[209]

It is necessary, however, to discuss in some detail one of
the most troubling aspects of Oswald's supposed trip to
Mexico City. In the second half of 1969, Charles
William Thomas, an official of the U.S. Embassy in
Mexico City throughout the 1960s who was also a CIA
'plant' within the State Department,[210] submitted a series

208 Ibid, 298; see also ibid, 219-20.
209 For much of what follows, see chapters Eight and Ten in Albarelli.
210 Albarelli, 353. Thomas committed suicide in April 1971. Ibid, 359. For

of reports ("Investigation of Lee Harvey Oswald in Mexico"), along with extensive attached memoranda, to Secretary of State William Rogers. The core of these reports concerned Elena Garro de Paz, the former wife of the poet Octavio Paz and an important writer in her own right, who claimed on several occasions to have seen Oswald, along with two unidentified 'gringos', at a twist party in Mexico City sometime in 'late September' 1963.[211] The party was allegedly held at the home of Garro's cousin Ruben Duran, who was married to Sylvia Tirado de Duran, a receptionist at the Cuban Consulate in Mexico City and (allegedly) Oswald's 'mistress' during his visit.[212] According to Garro, 'most of the guests at the party were communists or philo-communists,' in-

---

Scott in general, see Shenon, 1-10, 505-8 and 527-31.

211 Ibid, 347. As Morley puts it, the 'chain of communication was elaborate'—and suspicious: Garro told her friend the Costa Rican poet Eunice Odio who told a CIA asset codenamed TICHBORN who told the director of covert action for the CIA station in Mexico City, who then told station chief Winston Scott. Morley, 336. Scott then received independent verification of the story from June Cobb, a CIA informant and a 'friend received independent confirmation of Garro's story from June Cobb; Cobb was a highly valued CIA asset who specialized in 'penetration operations' against the Fair Play for Cuba Committee (Oswald's 'old outfit') through seduction. Her main sponsor within the CIA was David Phillips. Ibid, 240 and 176. For Cobb's history as a CIA asset, see Albarelli, 377-425; for Eunice Odio, see ibid, 413-16.

212 Ibid, 274. Duran only confessed to a sexual tryst with Oswald following the application of 'enhanced interrogation techniques' by Mexican police following her arrest on November 23 1963. Shenon, 521. Interestingly, Duran has always described Oswald as both short and blond, while Oswald was fairly tall (5'9") and brown haired. Ibid, 552. The original transcript of Duran's interrogation clearly refutes her relationship with Oswald as well as his presence in the Cuban Consulate on Saturday 28 September, Newman, *Oswald and the CIA*, 405-13. As John Newman uncategorically concludes: 'The CIA and the Mexican government were the source of this bogus story.' Ibid, 408. Also of note was that Duran's 'description of Oswald as blond and short was mysteriously ignored by the Warren Commission.' Ibid, 413; see ibid, 405-13.

cluding the Cuban Consul Eusebio Azcue, General Clark Flores of the Mexican Olympic Committee, the pro-Castro writer Emilio Carballido, and Sylvia Duran herself, along with the three Americans.[213]

> At the party, the man she [Garro] assumes was Oswald[214] wore a black sweater [maybe the same black sweater he wore in Dallas when he was shot by Jack Ruby]. He tended to be silent and stared a lot at the floor. Of his two young American companions, one was very tall and slender and had long blond hair which hung across his forehead. He had a gaunt face and a rather long, protruding chin...The other was also rather tall and had short, light brown hair, but had no real distinguishing characteristics...All three were obviously Americans and did not dance or mix with the other people. The three were evidently friends, because she [Garro] saw them by chance the next day walking down the street [Insurgentes Avenue] together.[215]

Elsewhere in his report on Garro's story, Thomas states that Garro also claimed that on another occasion, sometime either before or after the late September twist party with 'Oswald', she attended *another* party that included Carballidio, Azcue, and a tantalizingly unidentified 'Latin American man with red hair.'[216]

---

213 Albarelli, 274.

214 Or, perhaps, the ubiquitous second Oswald?

215 Ibid, 353.

216 One of the minor mysteries of JFK/DALLAS is that reports of a 'negro' with frizzy red hair appear periodically throughout the saga. He figures prominently in a bizarre incident involving Gilberto Alvardo, a CIA asset and an informant for the CIA-backed Nicaraguan Intelligence Service. On November 25, Alvardo contacted the U.S. Embassy in Mexico City claiming that he had personally witnessed Oswald inside the Cuban Embassy receiving a payment of U.S. $6500 from a negro with red hair. Contaminating any possible value of this story was the fact that

Reputedly, Carballidio and Azcue

> *along with a few others, got into a heated discussion on that* [undated] *occasion about President Kennedy, and they came to the conclusion that the only solution was to kill him.*[217]

This remarkable outburst of un-diplomatic language, occurring in the presence of numerous witnesses, bears more than a passing similarity to Oswald's own equally spectacular announcement: during his visit to the Cuban Embassy on September 27 Oswald allegedly shrieked out his intent to murder JFK because, apparently, Kennedy's trade embargo with Cuba was preventing Oswald from obtaining a visa to travel to Havana.[218] Complicating things even further, Thomas claimed that Garro 'said that Carballido is known as a Castro agent in Mexi-

---

Alvardo falsely identified himself as a radical leftist and a member of a pro-Castro Nicaraguan guerrilla outfit, the Frente de Liberacion Nacional (FLN). Morley, 220-29. Alvardo's most enthusiastic supporter was David Phillips. Ibid, 219.

217 Albarelli, 354. Emphasis in the original.

218 There is enormous controversy over this alleged event. 'The ultimate source of the information …was, remarkably enough, Fidel Castro himself. The Cuban dictator's words had been relayed to the FBI from a "confidential" bureau informant…According to the informant, Castro had repeatedly been overheard in Havana talking about what his diplomats in Mexico City had known about Oswald. "Our people in Mexico gave us the details in a full report of how he acted when he came to Mexico," Castro was quoted as saying… "Oswald stormed into the Embassy, demanded the visa, and, when it was refused him, headed out saying 'I'm going to kill Kennedy for this,'" Castro was quoted as saying.' Shenon, 382. As Simpich has pointed out, not the least striking element of this story is that Oswald apparently went to the Cuban Embassy to demand a visa when he should have gone to the Consulate; the fact that no Embassy staff member pointed this out to him speaks volumes. Simpich, Chapter Five, pages twenty to twenty-one, traces the genealogy of disinformational weirdness. See also, Scott, *Deep Politics II*, 90-109; 'Paradoxically, one can argue that the greater the number of falsehoods in the story, the greater the potential evidentiary importance.' Ibid, 95.

co. He has been to Red China, the Soviet Union, and many times to Cuba.'[219] Garro never recanted her story; during Robert Kennedy's visit to Mexico City in November 1964, Garro 'was among those trying to pass information about Oswald to Kennedy during his stay.'[220]

This bizarre event does have to be dealt with for, if true, it presents compelling prima facie evidence that Oswald was either recruited as an assassin by representatives of the Cuban government in Mexico City, or, at the very least, was operating under the influence of these Cuban diplomats and pro-Castro Mexicans in the mistaken assumption that killing Kennedy would result in his being granted a visa to Cuba—a scenario which, as a point of law, does meet the definition of criminal conspiracy.[221] The evidence, however, indicates that Garro's story is either bogus or, more ominously, the result of yet another covert act of disinformation. The U.S. Embassy's Legal Attache and FBI liaison Nathan Ferris conducted the preliminary investigation of Garro's claims after she approached the U.S. Embassy soon after Dealey Plaza and rejected her story, noting that '"someone who was at the [first] party had stated that there were no Americans there.'"[222] In 1977, Thomas Mann, the U.S. Ambassador to Mexico in 1963, approached staff members of the HSCA and informed them that Secretary of State Dean Rusk had personally ordered him to

---

219 Albarelli, 354.

220 Talbot, 301.

221 See Section 5.03 (1) (a) of the U.S. Penal Code (1985): a criminal conspirator 'Agrees with such other person or persons that they or one or more of them will engage in conduct that constitutes such crime or an attempt or solicitation to commit such crime.'

222 Albarelli, 350. The general consensus among JFK/DALLAS investigators is that the FBI report effectively discredited Garro's story. Personal communication with Peter Dale Scott.

terminate any investigation in Mexico City that would "'confirm or refute rumors of Cuban involvement in the assassination'"; he also speculated at that time that Silvia Duran was a CIA asset.[223] Oscar Contreras, a law student at Mexico City's National Autonomous University in 1963, claimed to have met with Oswald on campus and agreed to help him obtain a Cuban visa[224]; however, in June 2013, in conversation with investigative journalist Philip Shenon, Contreras claimed to have later seen Oswald at a distance during a reception in the Cuban Embassy but did not approach him, 'because of warnings from Cuban friends that he might be some sort of CIA plant.'[225] (This fits well with Hancock's own estimation of the affair: 'Oswald's own activities in Mexico City can best be interpreted as an extension of his FPCC propaganda role with possible enhancement as a test of whether he could establish himself in an anti-American role with the Cuban Embassy.'[226]) Finally, Thomas himself makes clear in his own report to Rogers that 'some of the people appearing in the Elena Garro scenario may well be agents of the CIA.'[227] In the alternative, even if we were to accept the story as true, there is still considerable internal evidence of a CIA frame of Oswald, consistent with the false-flag. It is definitely possible that Emilio Carballido was a CIA double-agent: following JFK/DALLAS, Carballido, spent approximately one year in Cuba and, when he returned to the U.S. in September 1965 via Mexico, although he was a known Leftist, [228] 'he got a job teaching at Rutgers University

223 Shenon, 543-44.

224 Ibid, 522-3.

225 Ibid, 554.

226 Hancock, 121.

227 Albarelli, 352.

228 'Emilio Carballido, according to CIA and FBI files generated in 1966,

through Dr. Jose Vasquez Amaral, who was formerly with the Rockefeller Foundation', a known CIA affiliate and 'front'.[229] If Carballido was a mole, this could provide evidence for an alternative theory that occasionally appears within the conspiracy literature: that the Marxist Oswald was recruited by anti-Castro double agents posing as pro-Castro operatives; in a less complicated narrative, however, he could simply be one of the CIA sources for the frame. Of particular interest, therefore, is the utterly uncanny history of a strong candidate for the (possibly non-fictitious) second American at the twist party for whom Garro provided a 'near perfect description': Thomas Eli Davis III.[230] Davis appears to have been both a CIA asset[231] and an informant for the Federal Bureau of Narcotics (FBN).[232] He also seems to have participated in at least some of Jack Ruby's gun-running shipments to Cuba.[233] In May 1963 in Downey California, Davis attempted to recruit an outfit of American 'soldier-of-fortune types' for a mercenary expedition to Haiti by placing an advertisement in the Los Angeles Times.[234] Significantly, Davis' (unspectacular) recruiting efforts took place simultaneously with the far more suc-

---

entered the U.S. on September 21, 1965. A 1966 FBI document reports that Carballido had a number of ties that the Bureau viewed as "Marxist" and "Communist", said information forwarded confidentially to the U.S. State Department.' Ibid, 354.

229 Ibid.

230 Ibid, 353.

231 Albarelli speculates that Davis may have been subjected to MK/ULTRA mind-control experiments at the CIA front Lafayette Clinic during his internment there from July 16 to October 1 1958. Ibid, 314-15. A preoccupation with MK/ULTRA is one of the signature characteristics of Albarelli's work.

232 Ibid, 323.

233 Hancock, 526.

234 Albarelli, 321.

cessful efforts of anti-Castro paramilitary Loran Hall.

> Hall, surely not coincidentally, was also recruiting
> for what was most likely the same operation. In-
> deed, there is serious speculation, according to
> one former CIA operative, that Davis' Los
> Angeles operation was deliberately slip-shod and
> high-profile by design so as to throw off FBI in-
> vestigators from Hall's concurrent recruitment
> activities. Said the same official, who declined to
> be named in this book, 'It is a common ploy with
> the CIA. Sometimes there can be 3 or 4 opera-
> tions in play at one time but only one is actually
> fully planned and intended to go forward. It is
> similar to sophisticated drug traffickers sending
> out three or four large shipments of drugs with the
> objective that only one shipment will actually
> make it to its intended destination.'[235]

It should come as perhaps no surprise that George de
Mohrenschildt conducted a series of Haitian-based oil
and geological business ventures, some of which 'according to at least two former U.S. State Department officials, involved the technical, in-country [Haiti] services
of Thomas Eli Davis III, [as well as] two or three other
American soldier-of-fortune types who were in and out
of Haiti, Guatemala, Panama, and the Dominican Re-

---

235 Ibid, 325. We can also link both Davis and Hall with that nameless
black guy with red hair. After Oswald's death, the address '1318 ½
Garfield, Norman Oklahoma' was found in his address book. Apparently
both Davis and Hall lived briefly in Norman Oklahoma prior to the
assassination. As for the residents of 1318 ½ itself, they consisted of
several white teenagers along with one African youth. Albarelli writes:
'Additionally, and very intriguing is that at least two elderly residents of
the…neighbourhood, not wanting to "get involved in any way with
anything to do with that Oswald character," reported that the "Black man'
that lived with the group at the address "stood out some" because "he had
reddish hair."' Ibid, 88.

public on a regular basis...'[236]

In other words, not three left-wing defectors at the twist party but three right-wing infiltrators.

In the end there are three ways to interpret Oswald's bizarre journey through the grotesque parapolitical landscape of Mexico City: (i) that the entire story was a wholesale fabrication of the CIA that doubled as both a key component of the false-flag operation as well as one part of a wider cover up most likely coordinated by either David Lee Phillips and/or CIA station chief Winston Scott (see below); (ii) Oswald was in Mexico City (with or without two gringo companions), but deliberately acted in an irrational and highly theatrical manner whether under operational control or not; or (iii) that Oswald himself was never in Mexico City but one or more imposters were (with or without two gringo companions) who were under orders to engage in a series of spectacular performances. In all three scenarios the presence of clandestine agency is undeniable.

OSWALD-AS-NOMAD

Of Oswald, the central nomadic actor of the spectacle of JFK/DALLAS, only three things may be said with certainty. The first is that he was clearly a 'person of interest' to U.S. intelligence agencies (CIA, FBI, DIA) and was probably actively employed by them, either as a (paid) informant for the FBI and/or a (paid) 'asset' by the CIA or DIA (dangle, provocateur, infiltrator, fake de-

---

236 Ibid, 343. The reader might be interested to know that Davis 'died in September 1973 in an abandoned Texas quarry while allegedly attempting to steal copper. He was electrocuted when he cut through a high power line.' Ibid, 319.

fector, cut-out).[237] The second is that there was a genuinely strange covert operation/event of some unspeci-
fied kind involving Oswald(s) in Mexico City (20
September to 3 October 1963), providing direct evidence
that either Oswald's person (direct participation) and/or
identity (indirect participation; the 'second Oswald')
was manipulated on multiple occasions by either the
CIA and/or military intelligence. The third is that he was
involved in some manner with the very public assassination of JFK in Dallas on November 22 1963. Determin-
ing the nature of the spectacle of Dealey Plaza
ultimately hinges on the maddeningly nebulous third
certainty. As Dallas Police Chief Jesse Curry said "We
don't have any proof that Oswald fired the rifle...No one
has been able to put him in that building [the Texas
Book Depository] with a rifle in his hand."[238] The problem for the 'conspiracy theorist' is that there is absolutely nothing that puts the Mannlicher-Carcano into
anybody else's hands—an evidentiary obstacle that has
proven insurmountable over the years. There is currently
no direct evidence that would allow us to insert the CIA
or military intelligence into Dealey Plaza. One and Two
can be proven and placed together to form a plausible
and discernible 'deep background' to the spectacle; the
difficulty is that the move from One and Two to Three
still requires a deductive inference or conjectural leap of
some kind; there is no direct evidence that any of this
formed part of an assassination conspiracy. 'Oswald',
real or fake, could have been embedded within a pletho-
ra of anti-Castro espionage activities none of which bore
any direct connection to Dealey Plaza; here, a wholly

---

237 The fusion of CIA and FBI anti-Cuban counter-intelligence operations
   in December 1962 with AM/SANTA makes bright-line distinctions here
   essentially useless.

238 As quoted in Summers, *Not in Your Lifetime*, 98.

synchronous convergence among separate CIA operations involving a fake defection to Cuba by an Agen-
cy-run 'Oswald' and the presidential execution in Dallas
emerges as an undeniable possibility. Much of what has
become known in common parlance as 'the cover-up'[239]
may have been more about *deniability* rather than suppression; the systematic concealment or destruction of
evidence of *knowledge* of Oswald by national security
agencies in reaction to a massive lapse of national security (the system-wide failure to detect and monitor an
objective threat to the Chief Executive), coupled with
the need to maintain the integrity of intelligence and
counter-intelligence operations, both domestic and foreign (e.g., Mexico City) in the face of judicial or Congressional investigation. Any 'conspiracy' would have
been strictly 'off-the-books' meaning that there would be
comparatively little that would need to be covered-up;
the conspirators (if any) may very well have counted on
the automatic implementation of a thoroughgoing 'damage control' operation in the event of such a catastrophic
breach of security protocols. And it is within this shadow
space of 'trade craft' we can postulate any given number
of scenarios, including the extraordinarily simple:
Phillips, having previously secured the 'deep background' of Oswald as pro-Castroite, contacts De
Mohrenschildt to instruct Oswald to shoot at the President[240] which 'the patsy' understood as one phase of a

---

239 See below.

240 Technically, it would not even have been necessary to kill JFK: any
kind of homicidal attack by a Castro agent would have been sufficient to
raise the false-flag. Kennedy's throat wound (presumably Oswald's
second shot), which, if not fatal, would have been permanently
debilitating, rendering the 'iconic' head-shot, whether administered by
Oswald, a second gunman, or a panicked Secret Service agent,
superfluous.

fake Cuban defection operation.[241]

In the end we are back to the methodological centre-piece of understanding Dallas-as-Spectacle: Occam's Razor and the implausible accumulation of improbabili-ties. In my opinion the most intellectually honest way to confront the logical dilemma inescapably posed by cir-cumstantial evidence is to invoke the counter-intuitive: out of approximately 160 million U.S. citizens what are the exact odds that the man who shot the President is the same person who was either the actor in or the subject of a Byzantine intelligence operation in Mexico City two months prior to the execution? Ultimately what matters most is the accumulative circumstantial evidence of Os-wald as a low-level clandestine actor that, when taken in its entirety, works to drastically reduce the implausibility of Dealey Plaza as the spectacle of the false-flag.

Both the beginning and the end of Oswald lie within the nomadic space(s) he inhabited and the thresholds that he traversed.

THE COVER-UP/PHASE II

'What may have been promoted as a bril-liant counter intelligence operation against the Cubans may have become a huge prob-lem for the CIA on November 22.'—Larry Hancock

If Dealey Plaza is understood as a false-flag spectacle—

---

241 Or, if Oswald's Marxist credentials were genuine, as a heroic act on behalf of the Cuban people, one which provided him with the necessary credentials to seek asylum in Havana—at least in the considered opinion of De Mohrenschildt and/or any other fake pro-Castroites Oswald may have been in contact with.

in effect, the importation of OPERATIONS NORTH-WOODS into domestic space—then it becomes necessary to divide JFK/DALLAS into two distinct components. 'Phase I' was the actual political murder itself, preceded by the 'frame-up' of Oswald via the CIA-affiliated segments of the anti-Castro para-militaries.[242] 'Phase II' was what in common parlance is known as the 'cover-up' but might be better understood as 'damage control.' For the most outstanding fact of JFK/DALLAS, the successful execution aside, was that it utterly failed in its purpose: the integrated convergence of public opinion around a military invasion of Cuba. In place of this was offered a spectacle of a very different but equally integrative kind: Oswald as 'the lone gunman', tantamount to the substitution of the Enemy-from-Without by the Enemy-from-Within. Therefore, along with other parapolitical scholars such as Scott, I can postulate a two-phase operation, but one in which the two components are in active opposition.[243]

---

242 See Scott, *Deep Politics II*. For Scott, it is clear 'that a number of the "phase one" stories linking Oswald to Cuba did come from a single milieu of anti-Castro Cubans in Miami close to, and in some cases supported by, the CIA's JM/WAVE station there.' Ibid, 35.

243 It needs to be mentioned here that many conspiracy theorists, such as Mark Lane, interpret Phase I and II as inter-linked sequences of a single covert plan; for whatever reason, JFK was assassinated by elements within the national security services and Oswald was framed as a Cuban and/or Soviet agent precisely so that the political and media Establishment would cover up the crime on behalf of the perpetrators by committing themselves to the politically far safer media image of Oswald as 'lone gunman'. In other words, the 'evidence' of Oswald's Cuban links was a form of clandestine political blackmail that threatened World War III; the non-covert but equally spectacular agencies of both the Government and the media would therefore be *forced* to both deny the presence of a conspiracy to kill the President and to insist upon Oswald's identity as a loner. Lane, generally. For me, the obvious difficulty with this interpretation is, apart from the staggering level of political and military risk that it would have involved, is that it is far too complicated, involving far too many actors. Employing Occam's Razor again, I feel

On November 23, 1963 the newly sworn-in President Lyndon Johnson[244] held two separate meetings with the Director of the CIA, John McCone, concerning reports of several alleged meetings between Oswald and suspected KGB assassination specialist Valery Kostikov in Mexico City the previous September; 'Undoubtedly, McCone alarmed Johnson by voicing CIA suspicions of the Soviets employing Oswald to assassinate Kennedy, possibly in retaliation for Kennedy's humiliation of the Soviet premier, Nikita Khrushchev, during the Cuban missile crisis of October 1962.'[245] Whatever effect the frame-up may have had on Johnson was quickly nullified by a series of memos and (taped) conversations between the President and both the Director of the FBI, J. Edgar Hoover, and the Deputy Attorney-General Nicholas Katzenbach. In the decisive memo from Hoover to Johnson, dated November 24, 1963, the FBI chief makes it clear that 'The thing that I am concerned about, and so is Mr. Katzenbach, is having something issued so we can convince the Public that Oswald is the real criminal.'[246] Similarly, in a memo from Katzenbach[247] to Bill Moyers, special assistant to LBJ, he for-

---

that the optimal theory to pursue is that of an operational de-linkage between Phase I and Phase II, while insisting that both phases display the logic of the spectacle. And this, in turn, requires understanding the assassination as a false-flag operation directed against Cuba.

244 A concise chronology of President's Johnson damage control efforts immediately following Dealey Plaza is provided by Hancock, 323-34.

245 Kurtz, 169.

246 Oglesby, *Who Killed JFK?*, 12.

247 Katzenbach's own opinion about Dealey Plaza expressed in personal discussion with Talbot is interesting: 'Today, Katzenbach even suggests that Oswald may have been backed by others. "I'm as certain as one can be there was no other gun shot," he told me, characterizing as "silliness" views to the contrary. "But it's not silliness to speculate that somebody was behind Oswald... I'd almost bet on [anti-Castro] Cubans. If I had the choice, if it had to be one of the three," he said, referring to the CIA, the

mally declares that

> 1. The public must be satisfied that Oswald was the assassin; that he did not have confederates who are still at large; and that the evidence was such that he would have been convicted at trial.

> 2. Speculation about Oswald's motivation ought to be cut off, and we should have some basis for rebutting [the] thought that this was a Communist conspiracy or (as the Iron Curtain press is saying) a right-wing conspiracy to blame it on the Communists. Unfortunately the facts on Oswald seem about too pat—too obvious (Marxist, Cuba, Russian wife, etc.) The Dallas police have put out statements on the Communist conspiracy theory, and it was they who were in charge when he was shot and thus silenced.[248]

In a striking covert move that directly anticipates Nixon's behavior ten years later during the Watergate scandal, Johnson deploys the FBI to clandestinely 'over-

---

Mafia, and Cuban exiles, "I'd say the Cubans probably had the worst judgment."'. Cited in Talbot, 290.

248 Hinckle and Turner, 263 and Robert Hennelly and Jerry Policoff in Stone and Sklar, 485-6. In the words of revisionist historian James K. Galbraith, "'Once you hear the conversations that Johnson had with [future Commission members Earl] Warren and [Senator Richard Russell], you recognize that the commission was not set up for the truth about the assassination...Nonetheless, it had a very high purpose, which was to protect Johnson from the far right, from being stampeded into nuclear war. This is the haunting risk that keeps Johnson wake nights throughout his presidency."' Cited in Talbot, 285. On Johnson's efforts on suppressing any possible connection between Oswald and either the Soviet KGB or Cuban DGI, see Morley, 215-31. In a television interview given just prior to his death in 1970, Senator Russell publicly declared that he "'never believed that Lee Harvey Oswald assassinated President Kennedy without at least some encouragement from others...And that's what a majority of the committee wanted to find. I think that someone else worked with him on the planning.'" Cited in ibid, 282.

ride' the CIA in its estimation of Oswald's 'Cuban connection'. On December 9, 1963, the FBI unilaterally (and improperly) released its own investigation of the Dallas shooting to the public, concluding Oswald to have acted alone;[249] this 'pre-emptive' maneuver via media spectacle effectively bound the Warren Commission to the FBI's conclusions in advance and forced an integrating convergence of public authority.[250]

> When confronted with this report, the CIA abruptly curtailed its own internal investigation and carefully followed both J. Edgar Hoover's and Lyndon Johnson's strong desire to adhere to the lone assassin interpretation. Both deputy director Richard Helms and director of counter-intelligence James Jesus Angleton made sure that no evidence damaging to the lone assassin-no conspiracy thesis would surface, especially evidence that might implicate the Central Intelligence Agency, or anyone associated with it. Helms, Angleton, and other leading CIA figures clearly preferred to blame the assassination on a 'lone nut' than to allow a thorough investigation into matters their agency preferred to keep under the rug.[251]

---

249 Kurtz, 21.

250 Hinckle and Turner, 264-5. As Talbot has remarked, without 'an investigative unit of its own, the Warren Commission was utterly dependent on the information provided by Hoover at the FBI and Helms and Angleton at the CIA.' Talbot, 276. Anecdotal evidence strongly suggests that the dominant personality of the Commission was none other than Allen Dulles. Ibid, 274.

251 Kurtz, 171-2. Within Mexico City, most of the Phase II cover up work was undertaken by the head of the CIA station Winston Scott, who received a letter of commendation from the chief of Western Hemisphere division,, J.C. King: "'your analyses were major factors in the clarification of the case, blanking out the really ominous spectre of foreign backing."' Morley, 232. There is little doubt that Scott's Phase II work doubled as a cover up for the whole series of CIA anti-Castro

The paper-trail of both the memos and the oral testimony point to the 'cover-up' as inhabiting the same parapolitical contours as the original strategy-of-tension component of Phase I.

> Masking the myriad purported links between Oswald and the pro-Castro community, the 'lone gunman' was the creation of official damage control, not an element of the conspiracy... Among the difficulties in understanding the Kennedy conspiracy, perhaps the most challenging is reconciling the many elements that appear to be contradictory. This has been made even more difficult for those who have viewed the 'cover-up' as an extension of the conspiracy. That difficulty disappears if we first view the conspiracy to frame Oswald as a Castro (or both Cuban and Soviet associated) conspirator, a plan that came totally unraveled when Oswald was taken into custody. And second, we see that the so-called 'cover-up' was an independent, largely unplanned and highly reactive effort to ensure that a Lee Oswald would [take] the fall all by himself—as a lone nut.[252]

---

operations in Mexico City, including LIENVOY and LIFEAT, that any investigation into Oswald would have threatened to expose.

252 Hancock, 298 and 311. Another reason why I reject Lane's overly elaborate theory of the cover-up is that it requires an absurdly uneconomical expenditure of effort. If the CIA wanted to disassociate itself from Oswald after the fact, then it would have been far simpler, and more convincing, to have framed him as an a-political paranoid or schizophrenic misfit, more along the lines of a Sirhan Sirhan or an Arthur Bremer, rather than as a pseudo-intellectual pro-Castro provocateur. Oswald's 'displays' of neo-Marxist activism are simply too public to be meant for anything other than popular consumption as spectacle. Perhaps the most infamous example of this was Oswald's 'street fight' with anti-Castro Cubans while handing out FPCC leaflets on Canal Street in New Orleans on August 9, 1963; this was followed up several days later by his equally infamous appearance on a local television show. The anti-Castro Cubans whom Oswald engaged with were all members of the DRE; in his report, the police officer who arrested Oswald after the fight wrote

The entire rationale of Phase II was to pre-emptively neutralize the spectacular power evidenced in the false-flag of Dallas: the integration of the public will to invade Cuba in retaliation for the Communist provocation of murdering JFK. The parapolitical logic of Johnson and all of the other operatives of Phase II mirrors perfectly both the operational and political logic of the strategy-of-tension; opposite in effect but identical in kind.[253]

> One thing is crystal clear. Based on the records releases of the 1990s, fear was a factor in many of the activities that followed the assassination. President Johnson used fear in the creation of the Warren Commission; he personally gave Earl Warren the responsibility to validate the FBI report, which presented Oswald as the lone assassin. That FBI report, itself generated after no more than a few days of investigation, was leaked to the media even before the report itself was completely finalized. Johnson himself, with the assistance of his personal political aide Clifford Carter, had contacted and ordered the Dallas Police and the Dallas District Attorney not to file conspiracy charges against Lee Oswald. In addition, Johnson officially took the murder investigation and major pieces of evidence away from Dallas and apparently ordered them into the possession of the FBI prior to midnight on the evening of the murder.[254]

The cross-purpose operating between Phase I and Phase II signifying the multiple divergences between the assas-

---

that Oswald "'seemed to have set them up, so to speak, to create an incident, but when the incident occurred he remained absolutely peaceful and gentle.'" The chief spokesman for the DRE in New Orleans, Carlos Bringuier, felt that Oswald was a 'plant' of either the CIA or FBI. Morley, 171-2.

253 Ibid, 295-305.

254 Ibid, 275.

sination and the cover-up is itself prima facie evidence of the dualistic nature of the American State: the strategy-of-tension that was to result from the assassination phase undertaken by some sort of network of CIA/anti-Castro Cubans was covertly neutralized through the pre-emptive damage control phase executed by both the White House and the FBI through the ironic creation of a rival 'spectacle' of their own, the Warren Commission. From a purely *judicial* perspective, of course, the findings of the Warren Commission, even if factually accurate, or legally worthless, as a 'properly' constituted and empanelled independent body of inquiry cannot be, under law, pre-committed to any finding of fact. Similar concerns may also be expressed concerning the autopsy of JFK, which appears to have been performed in total violation of prescribed forensic procedure. Not only was the body improperly removed from Dallas, the scene of the crime, [255] but the post-mortem in Washington appears to have been directed to arrive at a pre-ordained conclusion; at Bethesda Naval Hospital, Admiral George Buckley, JFK's personal physician, 'briefed the doctors with the information that *"the police had captured the guy who did this and all we need is the bullet."*' [256] If, however, the clandestine modus operandi of Phase I was coun-

---

255 'Less than an hour after the president was declared dead, the Secret Service removed his body from Parkland Hospital. The Dallas County Medical Examiner, Earl Rose, tried to block the doorway, resisting its removal until an autopsy was performed. (And, legally, he was quite right to do so—in 1963, it was not a federal crime to murder a president, and so the federal authorities had no right to make off with the evidence.) But the Secret Service simply shifted him out of the way and left for Love Field.' Oglesby, *Who Killed JFK?*, 40.

256 Hancock, 301. Emphasis in the original. See also DiEugenio, 288-309. Although enormously controversial, perhaps the most legally significant outcome of Jim Garrison's prosecution of Clay Shaw was the District Prosecutor's exposure of deliberate and repeated violations of forensic propriety. See both Garrison and DiEugenio.

ter-intelligence, then that of Phase II was disinformation. And, as Debord reminds us, disinformation is a vital part of the integrated spectacle, neutralizing the dissenter through the strategic deployment of partial truths and selective counter-claims and counter-factuals. The covert magic of disinformation is that the signaling of its presence operates solely through slanderous imputation; 'In a world that *really* has been stood on its head, truth is the moment of falsehood.' In this way, the 'conspiracy nut', such as Jim Garrison or Mark Lane can be undermined through the enormity of the potential for political subversion in the event of the validation of their claims, this with the threshold of counter-intuition having been raised considerably by the elaborate theatre of the spectacular(ly) Dual State.[257]

> [Disinformation is] openly employed by particular powers, or, consequently, by people who hold fragments of economic or political authority, in order to maintain what is established; and always in a *counter-offensive* role. Whatever can oppose a single official truth must necessarily be disinformation emanating from hostile or at least rival powers, and would have been intentionally and malevolently falsified...Unlike the straightforward lie, disinformation must inevitably contain a degree of truth but one deliberately manipulated by an artful enemy. That is what makes it so attractive to the defenders of the dominant society. The power which speaks of disinformation does not believe itself to be absolutely faultless, but knows that it can attribute to any precise criticism the excessive insignificance which characterizes disinformation; with the result that it will never have to admit to any particular fault. In essence,

---

257 For the orchestrated campaign to discredit Lane by CIA 'plants' in the mass media, see Lane, 71-154 ; for Garrison, see DiEugenio, 157-66.

> disinformation would be a travesty of truth. Whoever disseminates it is culpable, whoever believes it is stupid.[258]

Paradoxically, once understood as a failed exercise in the raising of the false-flag, the political murder of JFK becomes, in terms of the coldly cynical logic of spectacular power, a remarkably trivial thing: it was a 'fake' event that yielded an integration of *inaction*. What is far from trivial, however, and of far greater interest, are the cascades of much wider parapolitical occurrences flowing directly from the successful integration-of-no-thing. For it appears that the integrity of the spectacle required a radical resolution of Civil War II that would culminate in the even more pressing need for another deep event: the only way that Johnson could guarantee the preservation of the media image of the lone gunman was by preempting future Cowboy action through the offering up of a substitute theater of war for Cuba. It cannot be a coincidence that Johnson's de facto termination of the Cuba Project[259]—which is precisely what the Warren Commission represented—coincided with the initial beginnings of what was to become the full-scale U.S. military intervention on Vietnam. As Esterline insightfully remarked, "'one recognized the inevitability that the total U.S. involvement in Vietnam precluded anything being done in terms of Castro. Since the missile crisis, there didn't seem to be anything new and different that would warrant any diversion from Vietnam.'"[260]

In truth, the groundwork for a parapolitical 'swap' of Vietnam for Cuba had already been prepared fairly early in JFK's term. On April 20, 1961, the day after the sur-

---

258 Debord, *Comments*, 45.
259 Talbot, 271 and 285.
260 Bohning, 254.

render of the Cuban amphibious force at the Bay of Pigs (Brigade 2506), JFK issued two executive orders to Secretary of Defense Robert McNamara. The first called for the immediate development of plans to remove Castro with U.S. military force, subject to the vital caveat that this request *"should not be interpreted as an indication that U.S. military action against Cuba is probable"*;[261] these plans ultimately culminated in MONGOOSE. The second directive created a Presidential Task Force on Vietnam chaired by Deputy Secretary of Defense Roswell L. Gilpatric that was to immediately formulate 'A Program of Action to Prevent Communist Domination of South Vietnam.'[262] These elements of linkage and equivalence were strongly buttressed on April 24, 1961 with McNamara's receipt of a memo from Deputy Director of the NSC Walter Rostow entitled 'Notes on Cuba Policy', who, in even stronger terms than JFK established a new orthodoxy of geo-strategic thought.

There is building up a sense of frustration and a perception that we are up against a game [sic] that we can't handle...There is one area where success against Communist techniques is conceivable and where success is desperately required in the Free World interest. That area is Vietnam...a clean-cut success in Vietnam would do much to hold the line in Asia while permitting us—and

---

261 Bohning, 70-1. Emphasis added.

262 Rasenberger, 316-17. Although the subject of extensive historical debate, for consummate Kennedy insider, speech-writer Ted Sorensen, Vietnam did not loom large in the President's thinking: "'Vietnam was *not* central to the foreign policy of the Kennedy presidency...Berlin was, Cuba, the Soviet Union—but not Vietnam. Vietnam was a low-level insurrection at that point.'" Cited in Talbot, 215. According to Talbot, Vietnam only began to acquire serious status in the autumn of 1963 with the beginning of the political crisis in Saigon that culminated in the assassination of South Vietnamese President Ngo Dinh Diem on 1 November. Ibid, 217-18.

the world—to learn how to deal with indirect aggression.[263]

Herein 'clean-cut success' clearly signified the Cowboy-friendly policy of military intervention; accordingly, on April 27, 1961 Gilpatric's Task Force submitted its Program to the President who instantly authorized the deployment of an additional 400 'anti-guerilla troops' (i.e., counter-insurgency forces) in South Vietnam.[264] Simply put, if the clandestine script of JFK/DALLAS called for the integrating invasion of Cuba, then it was an abject failure. However, the (largely) successful disinformation strategy of Phase II raises the possibility that a vague yet discernible secondary goal—a 'subliminal' Track II—was, in fact, achieved: the installation of a red-blooded Cowboy in the Presidency in place of a half-assed Yankee.[265] The spectacular swapping of Johnson for Kennedy and the subsequent 'Cowboy-izing' of the war in Vietnam served as the short-term resolution of the civil war of simulacra, albeit at the cost of the by now waning Yankee Establishment.[266]

A comparative reading of two of the most important

---

263 Ibid, 337.

264 Ibid. 337.

265 'Kennedy, despite his Irish Catholicism, was an Establishment figure... [his] introduction to the Establishment arose from his support of Britain, in opposition to his father, in the critical days at the American Embassy in London in 1938-1940. His acceptance into the English Establishment opened its American branch as well. The former was indicated by a number of events, such as sister Kathleen's marriage to the Marquis of Hartington and the shifting of Caroline's nursery school from the White House to the British Embassy after her father's assassination...Another indication of this connection was the large number of Oxford-trained men appointed to office by President Kennedy.' Quigley, 1245.

266 Although, as I discuss in Chapter Three, there is some evidence that Johnson was a reluctant militarist, prompting the need for another staging of the integrated spectacle in the Gulf of Tonkin.

national security documents of this time provides some compelling circumstantial evidence for my Debordean hypothesis. The first document, prepared for JFK, was National Security Action Memorandum (NSAM) 263 of October 1963.

> **At a meeting on October 5, 1963**, the President considered the recommendations contained in the report of Secretary [Robert] McNamara and General [Maxwell] Taylor on their mission to South Vietnam.
>
> **The President approved the military recommendations contained in Section I B (1-3) of the report,** but directed that no formal announcement be made of the implementation of plans to withdraw 1,000 U.S. military personnel by the end of 1963.
>
> o   It remains the central object of the United States in South Vietnam to assist the people and Government of that country to win their contest against the externally directed and supported Communist conspiracy. The test of all decisions and U.S. actions in this area should be the effectiveness of their contributions to this purpose.
>
> o   The objectives of the United States with respect to the withdrawal of U.S. military personnel remain **as stated in the White House statement of October 2, 1963**.[Emphasis added]

NSAM 263 has to be read and understood in light of a meeting of the National Security Council (NSC) on the evening of October 2 which was convened specially by JFK to discuss the McNamara-Taylor Report. What ensued was, as McNamara said, 'heated debate about our recommendation that the Defense Department announce plans to withdraw U.S. military forces by the end of 1965, starting with the withdrawal of 1,000 men by the end of the year...once discussions began, we battled over the recommendations.'[267] In fact, the so-called McNamara-Taylor Report may have been drafted by the Kennedy brothers themselves. While on their fact-finding mission to Vietnam, McNamara and Taylor would cable their daily summations to Marine General Victor Krulak (special assistant for counterinsurgency and special activities for the JCS from February 1962 to January 1964) at the Pentagon who would deliver them regularly to the White House. Both John and Robert Kennedy would dictate the final version of the text directly to Krulak, who would then return to the Pentagon. 'When the secretaries finished typing up the report in Krulak's office, it was then bound in a leather cover, flown to Hawaii, and placed in the hands of McNamara and Taylor on their way back from Vietnam. They read the report on their flight to Washington, and presented it to Kennedy at the White House on the morning of October 2.'[268] The military implication of the conclusion of

---

267 Douglass, 187.

268 Douglass, 187. It should be noted that the source of Douglass' account is L. Fletcher Prouty who was referred to by Oliver Stone in an outburst of hyperbole remarkable even by his standards as an anti-conspiracy whistle-blower of such stature as one whose '"name will go down in history." Cited in Chomsky, 140. For a decisive critique of Prouty as a reliable source for 'inside' Washington, see Robert Sam Anson in Stone and Sklar, 208-29.Of course, if McNamara was not the true co-author of the Report, then this would go a long way towards explaining the apparently inexplicable: McNamara's sudden transformation into a 'hawk' following Dealey Plaza. See Chapter Three. Porter unpersuasively attempts to argue that McNamara's outbursts of 'dovishness' during the Kennedy administration were due mainly to a truly exceptional sense of personal loyalty to JFK; 'In McNamara and Taylor, Kennedy had two top national security advisers whom he trusted to come back with the policy

NSAM 263 now becomes clearer.

[Section] 1: CONCLUSIONS AND RECOM-MENDATIONS

B. Recommendations:
We recommend that:

- o A program be established to train Vietnamese so that *essential functions now performed by U.S. military personnel can be carried out by Vietnamese by the end of 1965. It should be possible to withdraw the bulk of U.S. personnel by that time.* [269]

- o In accordance with the program to train pro-gressively *Vietnam to take over military func-tions*, the Defense Department should announce in the very near future presently prepared plans to withdraw 1000 U.S. military personnel by the end of 1963. This action should be ex-plained in low key as an initial step in the long-term program to replace U.S. personnel with trained Vietnamese without impairment of the war effort.[270]

While NSAM 263 does not by itself offer definitive proof that JFK intended to gradually withdraw from Vietnam,[271] it does provide unambiguous 'evidence of

---

recommendations he needed, because of their personal ties to the Kennedy family.' Porter, 168 and 173.

269 'Unequivocally, the goal was withdrawal *after victory*, by 1965.' Chomsky, 129. In truth, 'the sticky question lay in deciding when, if ever, the ARVN [the South Vietnamese army] had reached that elusive performance level.' Jones, *Death of a Generation*, 384.

270 Emphases added.

271 'No issue in the interpretation of US policy on the road to war in Vietnam has stirred as much controversy as the role of John F. Kennedy.'

absence' of the political will in the Kennedy administration to authorize full-scale military intervention at that time.[272] The second document is draft version of NSAM 273, which was presented to Johnson for his signature on November 26, 1963; however, this draft was actually prepared on November 21.

Porter, 141. The interpretation offered by Logevall impresses me as the most judicious: 'Kennedy was ambivalent [about Vietnam], more so than many of his top aides. He also was more resistant than most to making an unequivocal American pledge to preserve an independent, non-communist South Vietnam, and he repeatedly made clear his opposition to using American ground troops in the war. He wanted out of the war and probably said so privately to like-minded people. But this says little about his actual intentions in the autumn of 1963.' Logevall, 69. Whether JFK was the co-author or not, the McNamara-Taylor report 'had accomplished the major task set for them by Kennedy: to produce a consensus paper and bring back from Saigon a plan he could call a policy. Upon landing back in Washington on 2 October, McNamara went straight to the White House, where Kennedy approved the recommendations and ordered the gradual implementation of a "selective pressures" policy. "As of tonight, we have a policy," he told those present.' Ibid, 55. According to presidential speechwriter and consummate Kennedy insider Ted Sorensen, JFK thought that the Vietnam imbroglio was going to be '"this nation's severest test of endurance and patience…He was simply going to weather it out, a nasty and untidy mess to which there was no other acceptable solution…"'. Sorensen cited by Leslie H. Gelb in Stone and Sklar, 392. Perhaps the simplest way of reconciling opposing academic viewpoints is to understand JFK's (limited) prevarications over Vietnam as just one more example of a preference for two-track approaches; Porter provides compelling detail about JFK's signature use of back-channel diplomacy in attempting to resolve the Laos 'crisis' of March-May 1961 ; ibid, 143-52. He also somewhat less convincingly presents evidence of JFK sporadically attempting to establish a back-channel with Hanoi via New Delhi throughout 1962-3 which were effectively sabotaged by the Assistant Secretary of State for Far Eastern Affairs W. Averell Harriman; ibid 153-65.

272 As Porter rightly reminds us, Kennedy 'never made a formal decision against military intervention in either Laos or Vietnam…Instead, he spoke on the record only of conditions for agreeing to military intervention that were in fact so stringent as to make it impossible.' Porter, 142-3. However, there is strong evidence to suggest that the real

The President has reviewed the discussions of
South Vietnam which occurred in Honolulu, and
has discussed the matter further with [U.S. Ambassador to South Vietnam Henry Cabot] Lodge.
He directs that the following guidance be issued
to all concerned:

> It remains the central object of the United
> States in South Vietnam to assist the people
> and Government of that country to win
> their contest against the externally directed
> and supported Communist conspiracy. The
> test of all decisions and U.S. actions in this
> area should be the effectiveness of their
> contribution to this purpose.

> The objectives of the United States with re-
> spect to the withdrawal of U.S. military
> personnel remain as stated in the White

---

reason for the 'secret' withdrawal plan was to signal to senior South
Vietnamese generals the U.S. desire for 'regime change' in Saigon. The
exact wording of NSAM 263 'posed a major dilemma. It sought to
achieve the [McNamara-Taylor] mission's central objective of a phased
withdrawal...In reality, however, this step was the one most coveted by
the generals as a quiet signal of US interest in a coup.' For McNamara,
the withdrawal strategy 'would either "push us toward a reconciliation
with [President] Diem or toward a coup to overthrow Diem"' Jones,
Death of a Generation, 379 and 383. As co-conspirator General Tran Van
Don remarked to his CIA contact Lucien Conein in a meeting on October
28, four days before the *coup d'etat*, '"The only way to win [the war]
before the Americans leave in 1965 was to change the present regime."'
Ibid, 400. See generally Jones, *Death of a Generation*, Chapter 16. In
slightly less cynical terms, Logevall sees NSAM 263 as a more limited
attempt to pressure Diem to undertake the political and agrarian reforms
understood by Washington to be necessary for the preservation of the
South Vietnamese regime. Logevall, 54-5. 'As for the one-thousand-man
withdrawal plan, it must be understood as being primarily a device to put
pressure on Diem, as appearing at a time of general military optimism (or
at least non-pessimism) in the war, as being wholly conditional upon
battlefield success, and as designed to neutralize growing domestic
American concerns and counter the appearance that Washington was
taking over the war effort.' Ibid, 69.

House statement of October 2, 1963.

There are two important differences between NSAM 263 and the draft version of 273: (i) all reference to Section I B has been removed from the later document, and (ii) the reference to the President in NSAM 273, drafted the day before JFK's murder, is to Johnson, not Kennedy; it was the Vice-President, not the President, who had attended the Honolulu Conference.

> The record confirms that the first and only President to ever review the discussions conducted at the Honolulu Conference and further discuss them with Ambassador Lodge in Washington was LBJ. How do we know with certainty? JFK never survived Dallas. He never returned to Washington to meet with Lodge or anyone else. He returned to Washington in a casket. The only person to whom this DRAFT document could therefore refer by implication is LBJ. Although he was not yet president at the time it was written—LBJ is the one who met with Ambassador Lodge in Washington and is the one who signed the final version of NSAM 273 on the 26th.[273]

As Scott has pointed out, the subject of the Honolulu meeting was OPLAN-34, which had been approved by General Taylor and the JCS at a meeting at the Pentagon on November 20. But it had not been shown to McNamara and it was never seen by Kennedy. Calling for a substantive escalation in the deployment of U.S. armed forces in South Vietnam—in a marked deviation from JFK's signature strategy of covert operations and counter-insurgency—'the 34-A Operations led in August 1964 to the first bombing of North Vietnam with U.S. planes, something which 'President Kennedy for two

---

273 Burnham, 2.

and one half years had resisted.'[274] And the deep event that provided the necessary linkage between the implementation of OPLAN-34 and the U.S. invasion of South Vietnam was yet another spectacle.

---

274 Scott, '9/11', 25; Kaiser, *American Tragedy*, 211. Although Scott does not raise this point explicitly, his discussion of NSAM 273 clearly implies that certain members of the Cabinet, such as Secretary of State Dean Rusk, had foreknowledge of Dealey Plaza. If so, then it would strongly imply that either active planning or passive knowledge of JFK/DALLAS was present at the most senior levels of the CIA; in my opinion, the most likely candidate for the 'master mind' of the spectacle would have been James Jesus Angleton, the Director of Counter-Intelligence and the officer exercising executive oversight over both Barnes and Phillips.

[Dallas: November 22, 1963. Lyndon B. Johnson swearing in the oath of presidential office aboard US Air Force One (at Love Field Airport two hours & eight minutes after JFK's assassination) accompanied by Jackie Kennedy (still wearing blood stained suit.) Photograph by Cecil W. Stoughton, White House Press Office]

3 | False Flag II: LBJ & the Gulf of Tonkin

*'Cuba and Vietnam bracket Frontier
Camelot as the ends of a coffin.'*
—Carl Oglesby

I n Oglesby's schema, the geo-strategic transition from
Atlanticism to Pacificism served as the primary flash-
point between the Yankee and Cowboy factions, the primary indicator of a wider shift in the U.S. political economy away from the East and traditional industrial
capitalism and towards the West and the newly coalesc-
ing 'military industrial complex'.

> Precisely according to their material interests and
> their historical perspectives, Yankee conscious-
> ness affirmed the priority of the Atlantic basin
> while Cowboy consciousness affirmed the prior-
> ity of the Pacific Rim. [Prior to Vietnam] these
> images had been harmonized in the conduct of a
> two-front, two-ocean, two-theater war, a great At-
> lantic and Pacific effort joined and supported
> equally by all descendants of Civil War foes. This
> World War II coalition endured in the strategy of
> two-front Cold War in which Red Russia traded
> places with Nazi Germany and Red China with
> Fascist Japan, a friend for a foe and a foe for a

friend.[1]

Unlike in the UK, which had been replaced as Hegemon by the U.S. after 1945, the American political system was not able to successfully maintain the war coalition indefinitely; in Great Britain, the monolithic nature of the ruling class permitted imperialism to act as a unifying force that thwarted regionalism,[2] whereas in America, the entrenched regional autonomy of two qualitatively different political elites inevitably gave way to internecine struggle. Ironically, it had been the sudden acquisition of a vast 'hinterland' following the U.S.-Mexican War (1846-48) that set the stage for the 'irrepressible conflict' of the War Between the States; the outbreak of secessionist warfare itself is *prima facie* evidence of the radical, and potentially subversive, independence of Southern/Cowboy elites. In the future, therefore, any attempt to make permanent the ascendancy of Pacificism would require the successful staging of an integrated spectacle.

In his Introduction to *Tonkin Gulf and the Escalation of the Vietnam War*, the standard history of the Gulf of Tonkin Incident, Edwin Moise relates an unintentionally revealing anecdote.

> There was one point on which all of the Vietnamese [I interviewed] advocated a viewpoint I could not accept. All said they believed that the United States had planned, ahead of time, the sequence of events that culminated with the airstrikes [against North Vietnam; DRV] of August 5, carried out in retaliation for the supposed incident of the previous night. This had been the view

---

1 Oglesby, *Yankee-Cowboy War*, 160.

2 On imperialism as the political lubricant of the British political system, see Nairn, *The Enchanted Glass*, generally, and Nairn, *Pariah*, 32-60.

in Hanoi right from the start; an article in the November 1964 issue of the DRV Navy Journal *Hai Quan* (Navy) said: 'After fabricating the 'second Tonkin Gulf incident,' the Americans used it as a pretext to retaliate. But actually, all their plots were arranged beforehand.' *This was precisely what I would have believed had I been in the place of the Vietnamese. I am convinced, on the basis of my own research on the way Washington handled the affair, that these events had not been planned, and that the report of the second incident [August 4] had not been a deliberate fabrication. The first time I tried to explain this to the historians in Hanoi, however, I felt embarrassed. I was quite sure that President Johnson had been making an honest mistake when he bombed the DRV in 'retaliation' for an action the DRV had not committed, but I was acutely aware of how preposterous this tale must have sounded to my audience.*[3]

Ironically, Moise's attitude mirrors none other than that of Secretary of Defense McNamara.

I find it inconceivable that anyone even remotely familiar with our society and system of Government could suspect the existence of a conspiracy which would have included almost, if not all, the entire chain of military command in the Pacific, the Chairman of the Joint Chiefs of Staff, the Joint Chiefs, the Secretary of Defense and his chief assistants, the Secretary of State, and the President of the United States.[4]

Moise (along with McNamara) evidences no understanding of the spectacular power of the false-flag. It is useful to sharply contrast his attitude with that of James G.

---

3 Moise, xiv-xv. Emphasis added.
4 Bamford, 300.

Hershberg on Cuba concerning the potential for Cuba to serve as an integrated spectacle.

> A review of Pentagon planning makes it clear that for a small circle of high civilian and military officials, the idea that the United States might deliberately provoke events in Cuba that could serve as a pretext for U.S. intervention represented a possible course of action, frequently invoked, rather than an unthinkable libel that had emerged from the paranoid fantasies of Havana and Moscow.[5]

It is useful to recall at this juncture the centrality of 'maritime incidents' to the parapolitical imaginary of the Pentagon planners of OPERATION NORTHWOODS.

> A 'Remember the Maine' incident could be arranged in several forms:
>
> a. We could blow up a U.S. ship in Guantanamo Bay and blame Cuba.[6]
>
> b. We could blow up a drone (unmanned) vessel anywhere in the Cuban waters. We could arrange to cause such incident in the vicinity of Havana or Santiago as a spectacular result of Cuban attack from the air or sea, or both. The presence of Cuban planes or ships merely investigating the intent of the vessel could be fairly compelling evidence that the ship was under attack. The nearness to Havana or Santiago would add credibility especially to those people that might have heard the blast or seen the fire. The U.S. could follow up with an air/sea rescue operation covered by U.S.

---

5 Hershberg, 163.

6 This appears to have been what RFK was referencing on October 16, 1962 during the Missile Crisis.

fighters to 'evacuate' remaining members of the non-existent crew. Casualty lists in U.S. newspapers would cause a helpful wave of national indignation.[7]

As one might expect by now, OPLAN-34A (as incorporated into the draft version of NSAM 273) explicitly 'required the intelligence community to provide detailed intelligence about the [South Vietnamese/RVN] commando targets, the North's coastal defenses and related surveillance systems.'[8] And under Section 7, we find 'With respect to action against North Vietnam, there should be a detailed plan for the development of additional Government of Vietnam resources, especially for sea-going activity, and such planning should indicate the time and investment necessary to achieve a wholly new level of effectiveness in the field of action.'[9]

From the time of the implementation of NSAM 273 on November 26, 1963, all U.S. Navy signals intelligence (SIGINT[10]) operations were conducted in strict compliance with OPLAN-34A. Colloquially, these operations were known as 'Desoto missions', their objective being to determine the extent of North Vietnam's maritime penetration of the South and to evaluate effectiveness of North Vietnamese coastal defenses;[11] at the same time, these missions were to double as a highly public means of asserting 'American freedom of navigation in international waters.'[12] At all times, Desoto missions

7 Davis, 140.

8 Schuster, 30.

9 Ibid.

10 See Hanyok generally.

11 Bamford, 292-99; Moise, 51; Hanyok, 4-12.

12 At that time, North Vietnam was unilaterally claiming a five nautical mile territorial limit; Schuster, 30; Moise, 55.

were to be strictly coordinated with independent but concurrent South Vietnamese commando raids against the North; on several occasions U.S. naval actions were curtailed in order to prevent interference with the South Vietnamese operations. In other words, the DeSoto missions were enveloped by the clandestine disinformation of plausible denial; by early 1964,

> Covert [South Vietnamese] maritime operations were in full swing, and some of the missions succeeded in blowing up small installations along the coast, leading General Westmoreland to conclude that any close connection between 34A and Desoto would destroy the thin veneer of deniability surrounding the operations. In the end, the [U.S.] Navy agreed, and in concert with [Westmoreland], took steps to ensure that '34A operations will be adjusted to prevent interference' with Desoto patrols.[13]

The first Desoto mission was conducted by the USS *Craig* in March, 1964; 'The North Vietnamese did not react, probably because no South Vietnamese commando operations were underway at that time.'[14] However, for some 'mysterious' reason, the second Desoto mission, to be undertaken by the USS *Maddox*, 'was not canceled even though it was scheduled to start at the same time that a late July commando mission was being launched. Consequently, while *Maddox* was in the patrol area, a South Vietnamese commando raid was underway southwest of its position.'[15] The obvious question that arises is: was the *Maddox* Desoto mission of August 1964 in-

---

13 Andrade and Conroy, page 2 of 7.

14 Schuster, 31.

15 Ibid. The 34A mission in question took place on the night of 4-5 August. Hanyok, 30.

tended to induce a North Vietnamese attack? Admittedly it is 'difficult to imagine that the North Vietnamese could come to any other conclusion that the 34A and Desoto missions were all part of the same operation.'[16] Former Under-Secretary of State George Ball is un-equivocal on this point.

> At the time there's no question that many of the people who were associated with the [Vietnam] war were looking for any excuse to initiate bomb-ing...The 'DeSoto' patrols, the sending of a des-troyer up the Tonkin Gulf was primarily for pro-vocation...I think there was a feeling that if the destroyer got into some trouble, that it would provide the provocation we needed.[17]

The dilemma in its entirety is perhaps best expressed by Vietnam War historian Fredrik Logevall.

> This all leads to one very large question: Did U.S. leaders engineer the crisis in the Tonkin Gulf? Did they, in other words, deliberately seek to pro-voke a North Vietnamese reaction in order to se-cure a casus belli? The provocative nature of the Oplan 34-A and Desoto patrols is beyond dispute, but provocation can be deliberate or incidental, intended or unintended. Was it deliberate in this case? Certainly with respect to the alleged second attack, on 4 August, a good case can be made that it was deliberate...Concludes historian John Pra-dos: 'A two-destroyer force [ordered] to sail in close proximity to the North Vietnamese coast for

---

16 Andrade and Conroy, 3 of 7; also Hanyok, 29-30.It is interesting to note, therefore, that when discussing 'the U.S. decision to have the 34A raids and the DeSoto patrol taking place at the same time, William Bundy [the Deputy Secretary of State for Far Eastern Affairs] said, "Rational minds could not readily have foreseen that Hanoi might confuse them."'Moise, 67.

17 Bamford, 301.

ninety-six hours? Rationalize as you may, it was taunting Hanoi to do so.'[18]

To complicate things even further, the *Maddox* was in fact misidentified by the North Vietnamese as an operational vessel in support of a South Vietnamese commando raid on Hon Me and Hon Nieu Islands on July 30, 1964.[19]

> The North Vietnamese Ministry of Foreign Affairs made all this clear in September [1964] when it published a 'Memorandum Regarding the U.S. War Acts Against the Democratic Republic of Vietnam in the First Days of August 1964.' Hanoi pointed out what Washington denied: 'On July 30, 1964...U.S. and South Vietnamese warships intruded into the territorial waters of the Democratic Republic of Vietnam and simultaneously shelled: Hon Nieu Island, 4 kilometers off the coast of Thank Hoa Province [and] Hon Me Island, 12 kilometers off the coast of Thank Hoa Province.' It also outlined the *Maddox's* path along the coast on 2 August and the 34A attacks on Vinh Son the following day.[20]

On August 2, North Vietnamese patrol boats launched an unsuccessful attack on the *Maddox*; [21] On August 4, although both vessels reported being under 'enemy' torpedo attack, neither the *USS Maddox* or the *USS Turner Joy* were targeted by the North Vietnamese coastal pa-

---

18 Logevall, 199-200.

19 Moise, 67.

20 Andrade and Conroy, 4 of 7.

21 'The three [RVN] torpedo boats continued through the American barrage and launched their torpedoes at 1516. All missed, probably because the North Vietnamese had fired too soon. One 12.7mm machine gun bullet hit *Maddox* before the boats broke off and started to withdraw.' Schuster, 32.

trols; instead, errors with SIGNIT 'led U.S destroyers to open fire on spurious radar contacts, misinterpret their own propeller noises as incoming torpedoes, and ultimately report an attack that never occurred.'[22] Discernible in both incidents is the logic of the false-flag; after the failed Vietnamese attack of August 2, the 'non-event' of August 4 was retroactively seized upon by U.S. military intelligence and re-presented as the 'real thing'. According to Ray S. Cline, CIA Deputy Director for Intelligence in 1964,

> What in effect happened…is that somebody from the Pentagon, I suppose it was McNamara, had taken over raw Sigint and [had] shown the President what they thought was evidence of a second attack on a [U.S.] naval vessel. And it was just what Johnson was looking for…Everybody was demanding the Sigint; they wanted it quick, they didn't want anybody to take any time to analyze.[23]

SIGINT served as the basis for LBJ's (apparent) belief in the reality of the August 4 torpedo attack and has been exhaustively analyzed by cryptology expert Robert J. Hanyok, who identified three fatal flaws with the intelligence: (i) more than 90% of all signals were omitted from both the post-attack summary report and the final report submitted in October 1964 which relied upon only *six* transmissions;[24] (ii) there are unmistakable signs of the misleading editing of intercepts; [25] (iii) there was a misleading translation and re-editing of several North

---

22 Ibid, 33.

23 Bamford, 299.

24 Hanyok, 49.

25 'The SIGINT was not manufactured. Instead, it consisted of fragments of legitimate intercept lifted out of its context and inserted into summary reports to support the contention of a pre-meditated North Vietnamese attack on 4 August.' Ibid, 3.

Vietnamese after-action reports that appeared to be indicating an imminent torpedo attack, but were, in fact, referring in a rather confused manner to the August 2 incident.[26] Read in its entirety, Hanyok's conclusion is inescapable:

> Beginning with the period of the crisis in early August, into the days of the immediate aftermath, and continuing into October 1964, SIGINT information was presented in such a manner as to preclude responsible decision-makers in the Johnson administration from having the complete and objective narrative of events of 4 August 1964. Instead, only SIGINT that supported the claim that the communists had attacked the two destroyers was given to administration officials.[27]

Yet, like Moise, Hanyok dare not call this 'conspiracy'.

> This mishandling of the SIGINT was not done in a manner that can be construed as conspiratorial, that is, with manufactured evidence and collusion at all levels.[28] Rather, the objective of these individuals was to support the Navy's claim that the Desoto patrol had been deliberately attacked by the North Vietnamese.[29]

Highly selective intelligence analysis, or 'cherry-picking',[30] is, in fact, wholly consistent with deliberations

---

26 Ibid, 33-7.

27 Ibid, 3.

28 In fact, neither are required for a conspiracy: disinformation coupled with an intent to deceive by merely some of the parties involved are all that is necessary.

29 Ibid, 3.

30 This is essentially Hanyok's understanding of the event: 'While the [intelligence assessment] initially issued on the 4 August incident may be contentious, thin, and mistaken, what was issued in the Gulf of Tonkin

within both the Pentagon and the National Security Council that had been taking place ever since the implementation of NSAM 273. In contrast to Hanyok, Gareth Porter's interpretation of the Tonkin Gulf incident reflects a far more sophisticated understanding of parapolitical logic;[31] for him, 'Lyndon Johnson's decisions for war were the result of a continuing struggle between Johnson and his principal advisors—and particularly Robert S. McNamara—over escalation of the war.'[32] It is an historical cliché of the LBJ administration that Johnson's actions in Vietnam were governed by an over-arching fear of being politically out-flanked by the Republican right: aggressive Cold War containment and expanded intervention in Vietnam were acts of political expediency offered in exchange for the domestic implementation of the progressive Great Society agenda. As a result, by late 1964 'Johnson's advisors knew that Johnson was not going to agree to start the bombing [of North Vietnam] while he was campaigning for the presidency.'[33] At a meeting between Johnson and the JCS on March 4 1964 the President pointedly remarked: '"[W]e haven't got any Congress that will go with us, and we haven't got any mothers that will go with us in a war...

---

summaries beginning late on 4 August was deliberately skewed to support the notion that there had been an attack...That the NSA personnel believed that the attack happened and rationalized the contradictory evidence away is probably all that is necessary to know in order to understand what was done." Ibid, 49.

31 See generally Porter, Chapter Six.

32 Porter, 181. The 'S' in McNamara's name stands for 'Strange'.

33 Ibid, 191. A political calculation that is not terribly difficult to understand by the JCS, Johnson's perceived status as a Cowboy notwithstanding. An additional factor at work here, however, may have been growing concerns over the political stability of the post-Diem regime of General Nguyen Khanh; a surge in U.S. military support may have been felt necessary to stabilize South Vietnam. Hanyok, 9 and Porter, 185-8.

I've got to win an election." Two weeks later White House aide Michael Forrestal advised [NSC Advisor] McGeorge Bundy that the JCS believed that Johnson was avoiding the "correct decisions" on Vietnam in order to assure his election.'[34] According to Porter, the 'most serious pressure for military action in the Gulf came not from the Republicans but from Johnson's own national security team.'[35]

It is very important, therefore, to reconstruct carefully the chronology of parapolitical events from March to August 1964, focusing in particular upon the actions of the Department of Defense's ever enigmatic Secretary McNamara. Porter highlights one incident that is particularly disturbing in its implications.

> In mid-May, for the first time in Johnson's presidency, Johnson's principal advisers—McNamara, Rusk, McGeorge Bundy, CIA Director John McCone and Taylor—constituted themselves as the Executive Committee of the NSC, or 'ExComm'. The political significance of that decision can hardly be overestimated. The ExComm had been convened in the Kennedy administration only at Kennedy's direction during the Cuban Missile Crisis and then in late August 1963 over the political crisis in Saigon, and in both cases, the president had attended almost all of the meetings of the group. Johnson's five principal advisors, however, used it as a mechanism to develop a strategy for getting him to escalate the war. Those meetings produced the first intense pressures from the national security bureaucracy on Johnson to make a commitment to the use of direct US military force

---

34 Porter, 189. Perhaps disingenuously, in early April Johnson claimed to long-time Kennedy insider Richard Goodwin that "'They're trying to get me in a war over there'". Ibid.

35 Porter, 193.

against North Vietnam.[36]

At a June 10 1964 joint meeting of the JCS and the NSC, McNamara opined "'that in the event of a dramatic event in Southeast Asia we would go promptly for a Congressional resolution'" for greater military intervention in Vietnam.[37] Although at that time still formally engaged in contingency planning for future possible interventions in Indochina, CINCPAC (the U.S. military command in the Pacific) 'had decided by August 2 [1964] that the planning for an expansion of the war would need to be completed by November 1. The date implies that CINCPAC wanted to be ready to carry out such plans promptly after the presidential election, if this turned out to be necessary.'[38] Accordingly, when the

---

36 Ibid, 190. With no apparent show of irony, McNamara himself had by this time turned against OPLAN 34A, which he had such a central role in creating; after returning from another inspection trip to South Vietnam in March 1964 he openly referred to the plan as "'a program so limited that it is unlikely to have any significant effect.'" Hanyok, 9.

37 Moise, 30. It is important to note that one of the primary objectives of the (apparently) self-appointed ExComm headed by McNamara was to develop a draft of a future congressional resolution widening U.S. military intervention in Indochina. The operative provision of one draft prepared in mid-June did not, in fact, call for congressional approval at all but merely asserted the unilateral intent of the Executive to directly attack Hanoi, stating that the U.S. "'is determined to prevent by whatever means may be necessary, including the use of arms, the Communist regime in North Vietnam, with the aid and support of the Communist regime in China, from extending, by force or threat of force, its aggressive or subversive activities against any non-Communist nations in Southeast Asia.'" This draft was ultimately rejected on the grounds that it would have committed Johnson to a much more ambitious military program than he was willing to accept at that time. Porter, 192. See also Hanyok on this: 'President Johnson demurred, fearing that it would ruin the image of moderation he had been cultivating for the presidential election in November. The draft resolution was quietly shelved *until another opportunity came along*.' Hanyok, 46. Emphasis added.

38 Moise, 42. 'It seemed very likely that the administration would have to escalate the war soon after the election; indeed, President Johnson had [National Security Advisor] McGeorge Bundy ask Ray Cline, the CIA's

SIGINT began to flow into Washington on August 4, 'McNamara was clearly determined that the administration should take full advantage of any second naval incident in the Tonkin Gulf to bomb the North.'[39] At a pivotal lunch session between McNamara and Johnson on August 4, the President agreed with the Secretary's recommendation for an 'execute order' for air strikes against the North Vietnamese PT boat and fuel depot in Vinh, the time being set was for 7:00 pm Washington time.[40] At 4:08 pm EST that same day, McNamara telephoned the chief of CINCPAC Admiral Ulysses S. Sharp, 'not to launch...an investigation but to see if he could get a statement from him that the attack had definitely taken place.'[41] Porter relates that

> Sharp...recommended that McNamara 'hold this execute'..."until we have a definite indication that this [the torpedo attack] happened," adding that he thought he could have a "definite indication" within an hour...McNamara rejected Sharp's proposal. "If you get your definite information in two hours," said McNamara, "we can still proceed with the execute and it seems to me we ought to go ahead on that basis; get the pilots briefed, get the planes armed, get everything

---

Deputy Director for Intelligence, whether the United States could afford to wait that long. Would Vietnam already be irretrievably lost? Cline's evaluation was that it would just barely be possible to put off a major increase in the U.S. effort until after the election; "you're going to have your back to the wall."' Ibid. 45.

39 Porter, 193. As Hanyok somewhat laconically remarks, "That there might have been a lot of pressure on the NSA people to produce "proof" is quite likely. Regarding that charged period, Ray Cline, the former CIA deputy director, recalled that "Everybody was demanding the sigint... they wanted it quick, they didn't want anybody to take any time to analyse it."' Hanyok, 38.

40 Porter, 194.

41 Ibid.

lined up to go. *Continue the execute order in effect, but between now and 6 o'clock get a definite fix and you call me directly.* "[42]

As Porter correctly notes, this incident is even more unsettling than the anomalous meetings of ExComm.

> It was the responsibility of the president—not that of the secretary of defense—to decide to go ahead with an order for the bombing of a foreign country when new information made it unclear whether US ships had been attacked or not. Yet the president's log conversations for August 4 show that McNamara did not call Johnson following that crucial conversation with Sharp. Instead, he proceeded with his own plan to issue the execute order. At 4:49 pm, according to the Pentagon's subsequent chronology, the strike execute message was transmitted from the Pentagon to CINCPAC headquarters in Hawaii for re-transmission to the Seventh Fleet. One minute after that message had been sent, the president's phone log indicates that he called McNamara from the mansion. Again, that call was not recorded,[43] but the subsequent phone conversations between McNamara and Johnson show that McNamara still did not alert Johnson to the latest developments.[44]

Porter also makes much of Johnson's request on August 7 for 'a full accounting of communications between

---

42 Ibid, 195. 'McNamara did not want to delay the execute order, because he would then have to explain the delay to Johnson, which might well have led to the cancellation of the strike pending a full investigation. Instead, McNamara insisted on proceeding with the strike execute order even before the earlier reports of torpedo attacks on U.S. vessels had been verified.' Ibid, 195.

43 McNamara had two other telephone conversations with Johnson earlier in the day, both unrecorded—at 3:44 pm and 3:51 pm, both immediately prior to the critical telephone call to Admiral Sharp. Ibid, 194.

44 Ibid, 195-6.

CINCPAC and DOD on August 4-5—suggesting a suspicion that he had not been fully informed about what McNamara knew...Johnson's intense interest in getting the full facts on what had happened and what McNamara had known suggests that Johnson felt he had been kept in the dark.'[45] Porter is, therefore, ultimately able to conclude that the 'real target' of ExComm's machinations 'was Lyndon Johnson himself.'[46]

It is of more than passing interest to note how Porter'-s somewhat revisionist reading of LBJ's culpability neatly parallels the wider literature about JFK's withdrawal plans: both Chief Executives intuitively sought restraint and both were ultimately undone by the conspiratorial 'evil courtiers' of the NSC and JCS—a standard motif of western political discourse that extends at least as far back as the rediscovery during the Renaissance of Tacitus' account of the reign of the Roman Emperor Tiberius. However, just as with JFK, an alternative reading of LBJ is possible—namely that he had set up a two-track approach within his own administration.[47] Johnson having used McNamara as a surrogate is as consistent with the historical evidence of Johnson as doubting Cowboy. It is inherently implausible for ExComm to have convened without either presidential knowledge or approval; it is fully possible, however, that LBJ did not attend those sessions, especially if he was using McNamara as a ventriloquist's dummy to project his own hawkish voice—a striking example, if true, of plausible

---

45 Ibid, 198. In September, LBJ indefinitely suspended both OPLAN-34 and the Desoto patrols. Ibid, 200.

46 Ibid, 192.

47 Porter himself should not be adverse to this possibility; in establishing his case for JFK's desire to withdraw from Vietnam altogether, he describes the President's deft exploitation of 'multiple levels of deception' as a 'triumph of Machiavellian manoeuvring'. Ibid, 177-8.

denial within the White House itself.[48] The Gulf of Tonkin incident presented LBJ with a golden opportunity for staging his own integrated spectacle: assuming a public stance of reluctant warrior, Johnson could appear to be both reasonable and ferocious at the same time, completely outmaneuvering his Republican rival Barry Goldwater on both counts. Additionally, there are at least a few indications that the pressure being applied to the NSA concerning the SIGINT was actually coming from LBJ himself. As Hanyok writes

> Yet, despite doubts [about August 4], people in the intelligence and defense communities kept their silence. As much as anything else, it was an awareness that President Johnson would brook no uncertainty that could undermine his position. Faced with this attitude [CIA deputy director] Ray Cline was quoted as saying: '...we knew it was bum dope that we were getting from the Seventh Fleet, but we were told only to give the facts with no elaboration on the nature of the evidence. Everyone knew how volatile LBJ was. He did not like to deal with uncertainties.'[49]

Last, and not least, is an anecdote that directly recalls Kevin Spacey's 'Francis Underwood' from *House of Cards*; according to George Ball, in meetings with McNamara after August 4, Johnson would refer 'in a "*sort of kidding way*"...to his own doubts that the [torpedo]

---

48 Similarly, LBJ's request on August 7 can be as easily understood as an exercise in 'covering his tracks' as an attempt to uncover the truth; it may also have doubled as useful political blackmail to be used against McNamara in the event of dissension. As Porter comments on McNamara's memoirs, 'Consciously or unconsciously, McNamara has remembered what he needed to shift his responsibility for going to war over Vietnam from his own shoulders to those of Lyndon Johnson.' Porter, 180.

49 Hanyok, 39.

attack had actually taken place.'[50]

On any interpretation, however, the explicit deference shown to overtly political factors in the recommendations of CINCPAC clearly indicates a sensitivity for the need to forge a political consensus; if a Cowboy-style of intervention was being planned for Vietnam—in lieu of Cuba having been removed as a target—then the JCS, as a parapolitical entity within the U.S. Dual State, would have been fully aware of the need to circumvent Yankee intransigence, which Johnson himself was publicly manipulating for electoral gain. It was very much the clearly simulated nature of the (non-) event in the Gulf of Tonkin on August 4 that is precisely the basis of the historical (and parapolitical) status of the 'Incident' as a deep event: 'If President Johnson had had to make do with genuine incidents, none of which involved so brazen a challenge to the United States, public enthusiasm for retaliatory strikes would have been weaker, and he could not have gotten his resolution through Congress with so little debate or by so overwhelming a vote.'[51] Furthermore, Washington's 'framing' of the Tonkin Gulf incidents were in strict compliance with the parapolitical logic of OPERATION NORTHWOODS; in the absence of substantive combat on August 2 (which would have included the possible loss of American lives), the non-attack of August 4 was re-staged as a spectacle, proof of North Vietnam's status (instead of Cuba) as an 'international menace'. The Gulf of Tonkin Resolution, passed virtually unanimously by the U.S. Congress on August 10, 1964, served as both the successful performance of the NORTHWOODS script as well as the final stage in the implementation of NSAM 273. The Resolution reads

---

50 Porter, 200. Emphasis added.

51 Moise, 254.

> Whereas naval units of the Communist regime in
> Vietnam, in violation of the principles of the
> Charter of the United Nations and of international
> law, have deliberately and repeatedly attacked
> United States naval vessels lawfully present in in-
> ternational waters, and have already created a ser-
> ious threat to international peace…the Congress
> approves and supports the determination of the
> President, as Commander and Chief, to take all
> necessary measures to repel any armed attack
> against the forces of the United States and to pre-
> vent any further aggression…Consonant with the
> Constitution of the United States and the Charter
> of the United Nations and in accordance with its
> obligations under the Southeast Asia Collective
> Defense Treaty, the United States is, therefore,
> prepared, as the President determines, to take all
> necessary steps, including the use of armed force,
> to assist any member or protocol state of the
> Southeast Asia Collective Defense Treaty request-
> ing assistance in defense of its freedom.[52]

Not surprisingly, the passage of the Resolution did nothing to abate the U.S. intelligence community's appetite
for false-flag stagecraft. On September 8, 1964, less than
one month after the Tonkin Resolution, Johnson received an exceptionally forward looking memo authored
by Assistant Secretary of State for Far Eastern Affairs
William Bundy, entitled 'Courses of Action for South
Vietnam'.

> The main further question is the extent to which
> we should add elements to the above actions that
> would tend deliberately to provoke a DRV reac-
> tion, and subsequent retaliation by us. Example of
> actions to be considered would be running U.S.
> naval patrols increasingly close to the North Viet-

---

52 Schuster, 28.

namese coast and/or associating them with 34A operations. We believe that such deliberately provocative elements should not be added in the immediate future while the [RVN] is still struggling to its feet. By early October, however, we may recommend such actions depending on [RVN] progress and Communist reaction in the meantime, especially to U.S. naval patrols.[53]

As Debord reminds us, 'The spectacle is continually rediscovering its own basic assumptions—and each time in a more concrete manner.'[54] JFK/DALLAS, was a remarkably abstract, or reified, spectacle—the integrative function of the successfully pre-empted Phase I was appropriated by the authors of Phase II and strategically redeployed as a media offensive of disinformation, securing the opaqueness of the Dual State. With the double fiction of both (para-) political unity and cognitive transparency endlessly circulating throughout the capillaries of the post-Oswald mass media, the Dual State was now in a position to attempt the badly overdue suspension of Civil War II through an even more audacious clandestine action—the successful staging of the false-flag targeting an 'enemy' combatant that possessed the irresistible virtues of inhabiting the geo-strategic 'prime real estate' of the Pacific while remaining a geo-politically safe theater of (future) operations. The U.S. phase of the Vietnam War(s), 1965 to 1973, was not merely the product of a spectacle; it was the spawning ground of an effusion of new and ever greater demonstrations of spectacular power, 'the first televised war.'

53 Reprinted in *The Pentagon Papers*, 359.
54 Debord, *Society*, 22.

[Philadelphia: June 30, 1968 | Nixon campaigning, by Oliver Atkins.]

4 | False Flag III: Nixon/Watergate

'Conspiratorial play is a universal of power politics, and where there is no limit to power, there is no limit to conspiracy.'
—Carl Oglesby

'I don't have—I can't conceive of what that caper was all about, I really can't conceive it.'—Richard Helms

That compendium of parapolitical occurrences conventionally known as 'The Watergate Scandal' is complete simulacrum. The 'third rate burglary attempt' was actually a fiction; that is, a parapolitical 'comedy of errors', which, just like JFK/DALLAS and LBJ/TONKIN, signifies precisely nothing, revealing itself as a perfect spectacle. Although generally understood in the popular consciousness as an autonomous event, I will show that Watergate (or, following clandestine parlance once again, NIXON/WATERGATE) in fact forms part of a parapolitical continuum, incorporating a series of doubled events governed by the covert application of spectacular power. Just as Johnson effectively swapped Vietnam for Cuba, so did Nixon (a covert Yan-

kee masquerading as a Cowboy) swap Vietnam for De-
tente II—the second, and vastly more successful exercise in triangulated multilateralism first attempted by
JFK and which provoked an analogous clandestine response.

It is not widely known that the grandest historical ambition of the Nixon administration was the cessation of
Civil War II and the re-unification of the warring elites
through an all-inclusive neo-Cowboy realignment of the
national political culture: 'The New American
Majority'.[1] As History would have it, however, that
(para-) political honor was to be reserved for Ronald
Reagan; it was on the Gipper's watch, and not Tricky
Dick's, that the U.S. was launched upon its unalterable
trajectory towards the 'suicidal' State of Pure War.[2] But
upon ascending the Presidency in 1969, Nixon's more
immediate—and indispensable—task was the final resolution of the dilemma of Vietnam. 1968, the year of the
Tet Offensive, Johnson's decision to not seek re-election,
and the riots of the Chicago Convention, marked the moment of the de facto U.S. decision to withdraw from Indochina, driven by the war induced systemic crisis
within the Capitalist World-Economy; specifically, the
U.S.-based gold-outflow crisis and the structural en-
trenchment of the global inflationary spiral. 'The larger
economic system of the Western world as a whole was
suffering from another great malaise which in some way
or another was connected to the Vietnam War.'[3] The
American war in Southeast Asia, and 'the mounting in-
flation that ensued, undermined the international system
built up since 1947, and in particular weakened the posi-

---

1 Haldeman, 323.
2 See Wilson, 'Speed/Pure War/Power Crime' generally.
3 Oglesby, *Yankee-Cowboy War*, 159.

tion of the United States, the linchpin of the system...[4] [so that after 1967] the rules and institutional bases of the old structure began to disintegrate.'[5] The political challenge was to devise a way of withdrawing from Vietnam in such a manner that the U.S. centric nature of global 'rules and institutional bases' could be maintained. In order to accomplish this, given the pronounced shift towards the Cowboy faction under Johnson, it was necessary for Nixon to successfully play a complex game of dual representations on two different levels simultaneously. Firstly, President, Nixon's impeccable Cowboy credentials ('Only Nixon can go to China'), signified primarily by his open animosity against the Yankee 'Eastern Establishment,' was deployed as the camouflage for a covert quasi-Yankee agenda of withdrawal from the Pacific and a (relative) shift backwards towards Atlanticism. Secondly, Nixon deployed as his surrogate double his decidedly Yankee National Security Adviser Henry Kissinger[6] to implement Détente I while covertly hidden behind the cut-out of the 'official' Secretary of State William Rogers.

> Both Nixon and Kissinger saw the government bureaucrats as roadblocks to be circumvented. To Nixon, Congress was under the thumbs of the Democrats; the Department of State and the Central Intelligence Agency were havens for the Eastern Establishment liberals who hated him; and the military [the JCS] was full of doctrinaire, inflexible anti-communists. To circumvent them all, Nixon determined to use an agency first estab-

---

4 Geoffrey Barraclough, cited in ibid, 161.

5 C. Fred Bergsten, cited in ibid, 161.

6 'Kissinger had no background in Chinese affairs; his interests lay in European and Soviet relations.' Haldeman, 91. In Kisinger's own words: 'I am not interested in anything south of the Pyrenees.'

lished in 1947 that had lain dormant in the
Kennedy and Johnson years but was under the
complete control of the White House—the National Security Council. For a man who loved
secrecy, it was perfect. While the statutory members of the NSC were officers of the cabinet, the
national security adviser and his staff were presidential appointees who did not have to be confirmed by Congress. The NSC was chartered as a
clearinghouse for information from State, the
Pentagon, and the intelligence community flowing to the White House, and it could take action
quickly.[7]

Nixon's much touted 'Secret Plan' for 'ending'(= 'winning') the war in Vietnam was nothing more than an extraordinarily byzantine 'exit strategy', governed by the
parallel considerations of the gold-flow crisis and the necessity of securing détente with both the Soviet Union
and the People's Republic of China, the two primary
sponsors of North Vietnam. Pivotal to the secret plan
was the successful negotiation of a series of triangulated
set(s) of accords: the comparative 'loss' of Vietnam
would not constitute an absolute loss within the binary
logic (zero-sum game) of the Cold War if Détente II
could be realized; simultaneously, the presentation of détente as a multilateralist fait accompli would domestically undercut both the military and ideological opposition
to the exit strategy. The carefully orchestrated exit, of
course, would require the following: (i) a carefully
phased withdrawal from Vietnam, accompanied by a
frenzied intensification of the war effort (the bombing of
Hanoi) and the infliction of the maximum degree of destruction upon the physical infrastructure of Vietnam,
reaching its apogee in the secret bombing of both Laos

---

7 Colodny and Gettlin, 6-7.

and Cambodia;[8] (ii) the U.S. securing the 'normalization' of relations with China (most importantly for the
investment opportunities this represented, a central component of the Cowboy Asia-First strategy and the Nixon
affiliated 'China Lobby') along with a new era of stabi-
lization with the USSR (consistent with the Atlanticist
orientation of the Yankee faction), and; (iii) deploying
Détente II as the foundation for a new neo-Yankee foreign policy consensus by making irreversible a post-
Vietnam geo-strategic shift away from the Asia-Pacific
back towards a new North Atlantic-European coalition.
However, in order to physically implement the 'Secret
Plan', the indispensable key to success was the successful creation and operation of a 'private', 'secret', or
'para-government' within the White House itself as a
means of obviating both the Yankee and Cowboy elites.
And this, in turn, made necessary a series of unprecedented covert actions by the Chief Executive himself.

This grandly parapolitical interpretation of the Nixon
administration renders far more intelligible an important
but generally under-appreciated event of Nixon's tenure:
the failure to implement what is known as Huston Plan.
Formulated in 1970 and named after a junior White
House staffer (Tom Charles Huston), the plan was an attempt to amalgamate the domestic counter-intelligence
programs of all the major intelligence agencies (CIA,
DIA, NSA, FBI) into a single elite committee in order to
provide Nixon 'with one informed body of opinion on

---

8 This constitutes another, if generally overlooked, form of linkage
between Vietnam and Cuba: the bombing campaign against Hanoi and
the open-ended trade embargo against Havana were both intended to
inflict so much economic and physical hardship as to render their
respective systems of Marxist-Leninism unviable as models for regional
development.

domestic political intelligence.'[9] Also underappreciated is the fact the Huston Plan for the intelligence services neatly prefigured Nixon's later (and equally unrealized) plans for the radical centralization of the entirety of the federal bureaucracy through the creation of a 'Super-Cabinet'; under this plan, four traditional Cabinet posts (State, Defense, Justice and Treasury) would be retained, while all of the others, and their associated independent agencies, would be brought under the direct control of a new set of cabinet officials responsible for four policy domains: Economic Affairs, Human Resources, National Resources, and Community Development. 'In effect, this would accomplish two goals: stream-line all of the dozens of helter-skelter and redundant independent agencies into four departments that were manageable; and concentrate them so that all departments of the executive branch of government would be controlled by the White House.'[10] The enactment of the Huston Plan was effectively blocked by the bureaucratic intransigence of Hoover,[11] causing Nixon to feel compelled to create his own private domestic counter-intelligence force. The President, in his signature 'Gangster-ese', made clear to White House special counsel Charles W. Colson his desire to create an entire series of clandestine measures to prevent media leaks within the Executive branch.

> I don't give a damn how it is done, do whatever has to be done to stop these leaks and prevent further unauthorized disclosures; I don't want to be told why it can't be done. The government cannot survive, it cannot function, if anyone can run out

---

9 Kutler, 98; cf., Ibid, 96-101.

10Haldeman, 168.

11Theoharis and Cox, 470-77 and Gentry, 652-8.

and leak whatever documents he wants to…I
want to know who is behind this and I want the
most complete investigation that can be conducted…I don't want excuses, I want results. I want
it done, whatever the cost.[12]

Although the paragon of cold-blooded careerism, there
is little doubt that Hoover acted out of an overriding impulse to pre-empt a parapolitical catastrophe when
thwarting Nixon over the Huston Plan.

Yet to Hoover the act [of undermining the Huston
Plan] was not only rational but necessary. If the
extreme [domestic counter-intelligence] options
in the final report [of the intelligence heads] were
adopted, and implemented, and the wholesale
bugging, tapping, mail opening, and break-ins became known—as almost invariably they would
be, when attempted by amateurs—the Nixon administration could easily self-destruct. By cutting
off liaison, Hoover hoped to distance the FBI, and
his own reputation, from the inevitable holo-
caust.[13]

There is no doubt that there is a direct clandestine 'connection' between the failure of the Huston Plan and Colson's creation of a secret White House counter-
intelligence unit, euphemistically known as 'the
Plumbers', who proved to be the ultimate instigators of
NIXON/WATERGATE—the notorious slush fund at the
heart of the Watergate scandal ('follow the money') was
created primarily to finance the off-the-books operations
of the para-intelligence system.

Although the Huston Plan was officially aban-

12Kutler, 108.
13Gentry, 655.

doned, its measures were used in a variety of
forms, the most extreme being the creation of the
Special Investigative Unit, more familiarly known
as the 'Plumbers'. Ostensibly established to determine the source of new leaks from inside the
Administration, the Plumbers graduated to 'black
bag jobs' and illegal entries. The linkage between
the official scuttling of the Huston Plan and the
Plumbers is curiously mixed. Some argued—most
notably [FBI Deputy Director for Domestic Intel-
ligence] William Sullivan—that killing the plan
led to the creation of the Plumbers, to mounting
similar enterprises, and thus, to Watergate. [John]
Ehlrichman said that the inability of the White
House to get rid of Hoover necessitated finding
'other ways of doing things.' Huston heatedly
denied that his plan offered a model for the
Plumbers and other Watergate-related enterprises,
yet conceded that if Hoover had gone along with
the plan, the Administration would have never
had to do its own 'black-bag jobs.'[14]

The Plumbers, then, were more than a 'simple' extension
of Nixon's para-government; they were a semi-au-
tonomous covert entity that was in direct competition
with the myriad CIA and FBI domestic counter-intelligence operations that were being run simultaneously
and, very often, within the same political spaces. And all
of this during the most acutely sensitive, and dangerous,
parapolitical moment for Nixon: the simultaneous alienation of both the Yankee and Cowboy factions. The
Cowboys were alienated by the retreat from full Pacificism; the Yankees were alienated through their marginal-
ization within the executive foreign and military policy
decision-making processes. And both effects ultimately
flowed from the systemically clandestine nature of

14 Kutler, 102; for the creation and early history of the Plumbers, see ibid,
102-25.

Nixonian governance. Kissinger himself has made this clear.

> Nixon feared and shrank from imposing [overt] discipline. But he was determined to achieve his purposes; he thus encouraged procedures unlikely to be recommended in textbooks on public administration that, crab-like, worked privily around existing structures. It was demoralizing for the bureaucracy, which, cut out of the process, reacted by accentuating the independence and self-will that had caused Nixon to bypass it in the first place.[15]

But prospectively even more dangerous, as Hoover might have intuited, was the easily foreseeable reaction of the Cowboys, especially those of the JCS; in the words of Admiral Thomas Moorer (Chief of Naval Operations, 1967-70 and Chief of the JCS, 1970-74): "The dislike of Kissinger came down to one word: détente—détente with the Soviet Union."[16]

In sharp contrast to the 'pure' Cowboy Johnson, from whose historical record on Vietnam we can infer that he never met a General that he did not like, it is Nixon's hopelessly entangled relationship with the Department of Defense itself that provides the key to understanding the extraordinarily convoluted para-political dynamics of the NIXON/WATERGATE.

> Nixon's relationships with the senior military officers of the nation were the most complex of those within the upper echelon [of government]. It was impossible to carry out the war in Southeast Asia without cooperation from the Pentagon, and such matters [central to the overall success of the

---

15 Colodny and Gettlin, 9.
16 Hougan, 76.

'Secret Plan'] as the secret bombing of Cambodia
and the war against North Vietnamese cities required the support of the Joint Chiefs of Staff. But
Kissinger courted individual service chiefs and
encouraged them to report directly to him rather
than to Secretary [of Defense Melvin] Laird. He
also, on behalf of the President, requested that the
JCS set up a 'backchannel' through which he and
Nixon, could transmit private messages within the
government and abroad. Such backchannels were
normally operated for the government by the CIA
and the National Security Agency (NSA), but
Nixon wanted to circumvent those intelligence
agencies. Using special codes, teletypes, and secure terminals located at the Pentagon and the
White House Situation Room, the President and
his National Security Advisor could send and re-
ceive messages to selected American officials and
members of foreign governments around the
world without alerting the rest of the United
States government.[17]

The supreme danger of this heavy reliance upon backchannels', as with the earlier case of JFK, of course, was
that it left the White House unusually dependent upon,
and therefore vulnerable to, that very military complex
whose Cowboy agenda the Executive was covertly attempting to terminate. Presidential Domestic Affairs special adviser John Ehrlichman once remarked upon the
tangible 'invisible presence' of the Armed Forces within
the Nixon administration.

Reflecting on those events…Ehrlichman says he
now realizes how vulnerable the White House
was to military surveillance. 'All the cars that we
rode in at the White House were driven by military drivers…All of the telephone calls that we

---

17 Colodny and Gettlin, 8.

made in and out of our homes, in and out of Camp
David, were through a military switchboard. It
was a little bit like the purloined letter. It was
there so plainly nobody noticed it most of the
time. We talked in the cars, we talked on our
phones, we talked from Camp David, and thought
nothing about it. This was part of the warp of the
place, that you had military listening or in a position to listen to everything.'[18]

An obviously Debordean question comes to mind: if
JFK's murder was the JCS's attempt to pre-empt Détente
I, then would this explain the strikingly, almost patho-
logically, paranoid behavior of both Nixon and Kissinger
as they, in full knowledge of the clandestine nature of
the earlier false-flag, attempted a parallel 'back-run'
around the same military intelligence establishment that
proved itself capable of killing its own Chief Executive?
And an even more wonderfully ironic Debordean insight: even if the Warren Commission was correct in its
conclusions, would not Nixon's own history of clandestine proclivities lend him to (misinterpret) the public
event of Dealey Plaza as an exercise in spectacular power (counter-intelligence plus disinformation), causing
him to fall within a parapolitical trap entirely of his own
making? Just as with JFK/DALLAS, NIXON/WATER-
GATE erupted as a parapolitical counter-action in the
form of a false-flag spectacle, this time as a bloodless
'constitutional crisis' provoked, crucially, by the enemy-
from-within; here, the moment of Schmitt's 'decision' is
constitutional in nature, not Executive (unlike JFK and
Tonkin), but no less of an 'emergency' by that fact alone.

---

18 Ibid, 67-8.

'THIS IS A COMEDY OF ERRORS (=DOUBLES)'

By God, [Nixon's] *got some former CIA men working for him that I'd kick out of my office. Someday, that bunch will serve him up a fine mess.'*—J. Edgar Hoover

Jim Hougan, the author of *Secret Agenda: Watergate, Deep Throat and the CIA* (1984), the greatest parapolitical account of NIXON/WATERGATE[19], provides us with an interesting anecdote; 'In a conversation with President Nixon, John Dean would one day wonder: "How did it all start? Where did it start? It started with an instruction to me from Bob Haldeman to see if we couldn't set up a perfectly legitimate campaign intelligence operation over at the Re-Election Committee."[20] Following Hougan I have constructed a 'minimalist' theory of the spectacle of NIXON/WATERGATE that, in many decisive respects, parallels the one that I have formulated for JFK/DALLAS. Just as with Oswald-Phillips/Barnes, it consists of only two components; it is the 'deep background' that is complex.

(i) G. Gordon Liddy, the ostensible leader of the Plumber's espionage team that broke into Democratic Party Headquarters in the Watergate Hotel, was in actuality a dupe of his subordinates, E. Howard Hunt and James McCord.

(ii) Hunt and McCord were secretly working for

---

19 During my work with the Watergate literature, I have not been able to determine that Hougan has ever been made the subject of the same sort of disinformation campaign suffered by many of the JFK/DALLAS researchers.

20 Hougan, 96.

the CIA while using the White House as a
cover for domestic intelligence operations
that (in Hunt's case) included spying upon
the Nixon administration.[21]

The exact nature of the motive of the stage-managed
break-in on June 17, 1972 is not of central importance;
for Hougan the 'real' targets of the bugging operation
were the clients of the prostitutes in the Columbia Plaza
Apartments for purposes of political blackmail,[22] while
for Don Fulsom the objective of the burglars was to acquire information as to the content of suspected conversations between the DNC Chairman, Larry O'Brien and
sometime Nixon supporter Howard Hughes, who had
been supplying bribes to the President in exchange for
legal favors.[23] What really matters here is that: (i) both
Hunt and McCord were active CIA operatives for the
whole of their time in the White House; (ii) that the CIA
had consciously decided to destabilize the Nixon presidency; and (iii) that both Hunt and/or McCord deliber-

---

21 Ibid, xvii. An interesting fact about McCord was that he also served as a
lieutenant-colonel in a special military reserve unit based in Washington
DC that was attached to the highly obscure Office of Emergency
Preparedness; 'the unit's assignment was to draw up lists of radicals and
to help develop contingency plans for censorship of the news media and
US mail in time of war.' Bernstein and Woodward, 23.

22 Ibid, xviii.

23 Fulsom, 160-1. It was the strong suspicion of the White House that
O'Brien was a covert political lobbyist for Hughes, whose global empire
of corporations had been effectively folded into a parallel network of CIA
'front' companies. By the early 1970s, 'the Hughes organization was
servicing the CIA on a world-wide basis, becoming the largest private
contractor employed by this agency. No job was too big or too small.
Hughes Aircraft and the Hughes Tool Company were used as a
"paymaster-type front" for undercover agents wherever they might be.
Payments would usually be made in cash, Hughes-person to CIA-person,
but at times cheques were drawn for CIA personnel on Hughes payroll
accounts. Hughes would be reimbursed to the penny and mill by the
CIA.' Hinckle and Turner, 333.

ately sabotaged the Watergate break-in as the means of doing so, a view shared by no less than the White House Chief of Staff H.R. Haldeman: 'the CIA monitored the burglars throughout...the break-in was probably deliberately sabotaged.'[24] And it is very unlikely to have been an accident that the Watergate represents the re-emergence of the doubled 'two Eduardos' of ZAPATA: E. Howard Hunt and James McCord, both of whom appear to have been CIA 'moles' planted within the White House.[25]

Beginning in the late fall of 1969, CIA officer Hunt began 'pestering' Colson for employment within the new Nixon Administration.[26] As though to prove his status as a former CIA operative, Hunt formally retired from the Agency in 1970 and began (in yet another slyly Debordean touch) working for the Washington-based public relations firm the Robert R. Mullen Company, which was itself a 'front' corporation for central intelligence.[27] As Hougan points out

> The circumstances of Hunt's retirement from the CIA are important. If it can be shown that his departure was merely an operational convenience, useful for purposes of deniability and, perhaps, infiltration, then it would appear that the CIA— and not the White House—was Hunt's real principal throughout the Watergate affair. And there is much to suggest this.[28]

24 Haldeman, 317.

25 For Hunt as CIA 'mole', see Hougan, 3-9; for McCord, see ibid, 9-26.

26 Ibid, 3.

27 Ibid, 6.

28 Ibid, 7. According to Hougan, 'when it came time for Hunt to undertake a series of questionable intelligence operations [e.g., breaking into the offices of Daniel Ellsberg's psychiatrist, Dr. Lewis J. Fielding; Hougan, Chapter Three], ostensibly on behalf of the White House, it was the CIA

As I have discussed, both Hunt and McCord were active in the Bay of Pigs operation, and, therefore, had known each other from at least April, 1961; both, had shared code-name 'Eduardo', and both, therefore, were highly familiar with the Operation MONGOOSE and Alpha/66 anti-Castro Cuban units. In April 1971 Hunt, once more under the moniker 'Eduardo', travelled to Miami, ostensibly for a ten-year re-union celebration of ZAPATA with local Cuban operatives; in fact, it was a mission to re-activate key anti-Castro agents who later became members of the Plumbers and, therefore, the burglars of the Watergate: Frank Sturgis, Bernard Barker, and Eugenio Martinez.

> As Martinez makes clear…in his memoir about the April 1971 visit, Hunt's purpose was recruitment. "What is Manolo doing?…What is Roman doing?"…He said that he wanted to meet with the old people. It was a good sign. We did not think he had come to Miami for nothing.' It was in this way, then, that Hunt obtained his agents for secret operations that, as it happened, were as yet undreamed of by the Nixon administration, which would supposedly conceive of, and sponsor, them. As…Charles Colson put it in an interview with this writer: 'Hunt's visit to Barker [in April 1971] was, pure and simple, a get-ready-for-action call. You'd have to be an idiot to think otherwise.' Leaning forward in his chair with a look of anger

---

that provided him with the extensive 'technical support' that the missions required. In a similar way, Hunt relied upon veteran CIA contract agents to help carry out these operations, and even applied to the CIA's External Employment Assistance Branch (EEAB) for help in locating men skilled at lock-picking, electronic sweeps and entry operations. He used the agency to conduct computer name traces as required, and had a sterile telephone installed in the White House to ensure the secrecy of his regular telephone conversations with unidentified officials of the CIA… Hunt's retirement from the CIA was dubious in the extreme.' Ibid, 8-9.

> and perplexity, Colson added: 'But there wasn't
> any action anticipated. Not then. The Pentagon
> Papers hadn't been published. The Plumbers were
> months away. So, you tell me: how did Hunt
> know [in April] that he'd need the Cubans?'[29]

It is also important to keep in mind that, as of April 1971, Martinez was still formally working for the CIA; 'A veteran of Operation MONGOOSE, Martinez was actually still employed by the Agency at the time of the break-in, receiving a retainer of $100 a month for reporting on the Cuban exile community in Miami.'[30] This rather inconvenient truth was assigned the greatest importance by Haldeman in his post-NIXON/WATERGATE memoirs: 'The CIA was connected to the Watergate matter in innumerable ways; indeed, *at least* one of the burglars, Martinez, was still on the CIA payroll on June 17, 1972—and almost certainly reporting to his CIA case officer[31] about the proposed break-in *even before it happened*. The first lawyer in the police precinct when the burglars were brought in the night of June 17 was reportedly a CIA-connected attorney,[32] there to represent men who had allegedly retired from the agency and had no connection with it.'[33] For Hougan, then, what all these 'clandestine contacts add up to is the clear implication that the CIA was Howard Hunt's real principal during this time of employment at the White House. Once this is understood, the possibility suggests itself that several of Hunt's White House operations, publicly described as failures, were actually success-

---

29 Hougan, 29.
30 Powers, 289.
31 Robert Ritchie; Hougan, 220.
32 Douglas Caddy. Hinckle and Turner, 361.
33 Haldeman, 34.

ful.'[34] Thus, within the mass media, Hunt would,

> By virtue of this immaculate incompetence, come
> to be seen as a kind of clown—a spook whose op-
> erations inevitably backfired. Thus, the press—
> while condemning those who dismissed the Wa-
> tergate break-in as a mere 'caper' or 'third-rate
> burglary'—would nevertheless be quick to pro-
> nounce the burglars 'bunglers'. Just as the Nixon
> forces wished that we would dismiss the break-in
> with a laugh, so did liberal Democrats and the
> press intend that we should dismiss the burglars
> with a grin. This was so, in large part, because
> Nixon's enemies wished to make a morality play
> of the affair. Necessarily, this entailed a simple
> story with the President at its center. Close scru-
> tiny of the burglars (and of the burglaries them-
> selves) was to be avoided because such scrutiny
> raised questions about their loyalty to President
> Nixon. This, in turn, obscured the issue of presid-
> ential guilt and, in doing so, threatened Nixon's
> ouster. In a sense, therefore, the Democrats and
> the press were as much opponents of a full invest-
> igation of the Watergate affair as was the White
> House itself. Both sides had reason to fear the
> truth.[35]

And just as with JFK/DALLAS, we have an implicit division of labor (and intent) between the spectacle itself
and the media representation ('the cover-up') of the

---

34 Hougan, 55. Commenting upon the Senate Watergate Committee's
minority staff findings of CIA involvement in the burglary, Minority
Counsel Fred Thompson remarked, "'the question was becoming one of
whether the CIA had been a *participant* or a benign *observer* of the
break-in or, in view of the bungling of the burglary and the mysterious
circumstances surrounding it, whether CIA operatives had perhaps
sabotaged the break-in to weaken the White House and strengthen the
Agency in its struggle for survival.'" Haldeman, 135.

35 Hougan, 55.

event, Phase I ('the burglary') and Phase II ('the story'). The vital difference, however, is that unlike with the earlier false-flag, both phases of NIXON/WATERGATE were thoroughly integrated and coordinated, constituting a far more integrated, and integrating, exercise of the strategy-of-tension, this representing the thorough convergence of Cowboy and Yankee interests.

NIXON/WATERGATE AS INTEGRATED SPECTACLE

> *'Our recent history is a forgery, the by-product of secret agents acting on secret agendas of their own.'* –Jim Hougan

> *'A strange and basically stupid sequence then unfolded.'*—H.R. Haldeman

In his *Comments on the Society of the Spectacle*, Debord makes much of Nixon and Watergate, although in a manner that the orthodox North American liberal would find scandalous: the successful stage-managing of the constitutional *coup d'etat* at the heart of the NIXON/WATERGATE spectacle signifies not the apotheosis of the transparently democratic public State but its termination.

> The widespread talk of a 'legal state' only dates from the moment when the modern, so-called democratic state generally ceased to be one...
> Never before has censorship been so perfect...
> People often cite the United States as an exception because there Nixon eventually came to grief with a series of denials whose clumsiness was too cynical: but this entirely local exception, for which there were some historical causes, clearly no longer holds true, since Reagan has recently

been able to do the same thing with impunity.[36]

Even more than either with JFK/DALLAS or LBJ/TONKIN, NIXON/WATERGATE was played out through the media capillaries of the integrated spectacle; 'The generic term "Watergate" eventually became synonymous with media leaks.'[37] It was the sheer saturation of the media coverage that invested the spectacle with power while, paradoxically, enabling the clandestine nature of the deep event to hide in plain sight; 'For nearly two years the country had been blitzed by the minutiae of Watergate and force-fed the images of increasingly uninteresting men. Was there anybody left who did not consider himself a reluctant expert on the topic? Probably not.'[38] For it was precisely through the mass conscription of the mas population into the ranks of the 'experts' that the integrative function of the spectacle was allowed to establish itself as 'common sense'.

> Of all the media that helped develop and popularize [the orthodox] version, none was of greater importance to the story than Watergate's 'hometown newspaper,' the *Washington Post*...the *Post* was uniquely well equipped to cover and influence this particular story. It was the newspaper that the scandal's principals read each morning at the breakfast table, and, as such, it contributed directly to shaping the debate within both the capital and the Capitol...The *Post*, moreover, was a newspaper whose senior editors and reporters belonged to that part of the Washington establishment which is immune to changes of political ad-

---

36 Debord, *Comments*, 70 and 22. The reference to Reagan relates to the Iran-Contra Affair (or 'Iran-Gate').

37 Kutler, 190.

38 Hougan, xvi.

ministration...[39]

In truth the *Post* 'did not truly reveal the story of the initial break in and subsequent cover-up. Rather, it reported the results from ongoing investigations being conducted by the federal prosecutors, and a grand jury in the summer/fall of 1972.'[40] Instead, that newspaper's primary function lay with the publication of '"eye-popping stories, preceding disclosures by law enforcement...that built momentum and drew in the rest of the press at a time when Watergate might otherwise have faded from public view."'[41] Throughout NIXON/WATERGATE there appears to have been at work a very precise mechanism of timed disclosures and strategically calculated leaks,[42] the mass media at all times operating in prefect synchronization with the FBI and the Department of Justice.

> Contrary to the widely held perception that the
> *Washington Post* 'uncovered' Watergate, the
> newspaper essentially tracked the progress of the
> FBI's investigation, with a time delay ranging
> from weeks to days, and published elements of
> the prosecutor's case well in advance of the trial.
> Keeping the story in the news was meaningful
> and important, of course, especially when that
> newspaper was the *Post*. Owing to its prize read-

---

39 Ibid, 261-2.

40 Ibid, fn. 7, 203. 'From the outset, local Washington reporting, especially in the *Post*, closely tracked the FBI's work, relying primarily on raw Bureau reports.' Kutler, 190

41 Nixon lawyer Leonard Garment, cited in Holland, 3.

42 In Haldeman's opinion, even with the compounding errors of judgment of the White House during the infamous 'cover-up', 'it took a series of almost incredible "breaks," happening at precisely the right times, to escalate a war with the [Washington] power blocs into a Presidential catastrophe [that] even [Nixon's] enemies could not envision.' Haldeman, 188.

ership, it had an influence that far outstripped its circulation. Every important official in Washington and every reporter based there read the *Post*, which meant the newspaper was an elite publication in that it helped define the news coming out of Washington…Perhaps most significantly, the Nixon administration reacted initially to the *Post*'s stories by denying and dissembling, creating an epic credibility gap with the media and eventually the public from which the White House never recovered.[43]

So integrating was the spectacle (-as-media) that even the nominally independent judiciary had no other realistic political option than to serve as the hapless pawn of Phase II; for all intents and purposes Watergate Judge John Sirica was 'co-opted' by the *Post*.

Sirica… read [*The Post*] on his way to court each day, with the result that its questions often became his questions[44]… As the *Washingtonian*, a liberal magazine, described Sirica's conduct of the trial: he 'badgered, accused and castigated witnesses, prosecutors and defense lawyers. He read transcripts and confidential bench conferences to the jury. He used the threat of lengthy sentences to force defendants into abandoning their constitutional rights. He turned the trial into an inquisition, and justice into a charade.'[45]

In this light, the significance (and timing) of James Mc-Cord's notorious (and unsolicited) letter of confession to Judge Sirica—claiming that the CIA was being framed by the White House as being behind the break-in—at the very moment that the prosecution of the burglars had ef-

---

43 Holland, 3.
44 Hougan, 262.
45 Ibid, 262-3.

fectively stalled, becomes that much greater.[46]

> The impact of McCord's March 19 [1973] letter
> to Sirica is lost on no one. That letter is what
> kicked Nixon over the precipice by conclusively
> identifying the Watergate Operation with the
> White House...[McCord] was the first to say (1)
> that John Mitchell was implicated; (2) that
> CRREP [Committee to Re-elect the President]
> money was used to hush up the Plumbers [pre-
> dominantly Hunt]; (3) that the White House was
> trying to hide behind the CIA and at the same
> time put the CIA in its pocket; (4) that Nixon was
> the master of the White House cover-up opera-
> tion.[47]

No less did the trial of the Watergate burglars itself become a spectacle-within-a-spectacle, both a cause and an
effect of the integrative function. This is precisely what
we should suspect, given the *Post*'s not inconsiderable
ties with the CIA. Central to this parapolitical network
was Robert Bennett, Hunt's supervisor at the Robert R.
Mullen Company, a CIA company that had extensive involvement with the JM/WAVE affiliated broadcasting
station Radio Free Cuba, set up in the immediate after-
math of the Bay of Pigs.[48] A CIA agent himself, Bennett
met with his own Agency case officer Martin Lukoskie
on July 10, 1972, less than four weeks after the burglary.

---

46 Bernstein and Woodward, 197-8.

47 Oglesby, *Yankee-Cowboy War*, 297. It is also worth pointing out that
burglar Frank Sturgis had been both a friend and a 'contact' for
Washington syndicated columnist Jack Anderson since the Bay of Pigs.
Anderson was also a friend and protégé of JCS mole Charles Radford.
Anderson was also the journalist who published a leak concerning the
White House's tilt away from India and towards Pakistan during the East
Pakistan War in 1971, infuriating both Nixon and Kissinger. Colodny and
Gettlin, 18-20 and 14-16.

48 Hougan, fn. 11 265; 273.

Later that month, Lukoskie submitted a hand-written memorandum of his most recent meeting with Bennett directly to CIA director Helms; 'Mr. Bennett related that he has now established "back door entry" to the Edward Bennett Williams law firm which is representing the Democratic Party in its suit for damages resulting from the Watergate incident.'[49] And in March 1973, Lukoskie's supervisor, Eric Eisenstadt, submitted his own memorandum on Bennett to Helms.

> Mr. Bennett said…that he has been deeding stories to Bob Woodward of the Washington Post with the understanding that there is no attribution to Bennett. Woodward is suitably grateful for the fine stories and by-lines which he gets and protects Bennett (and the Mullen Company)… [Bennett also] said that, if necessary, he could have his father, Senator Bennett of Utah, intercede with Senator [Sam] Ervin [head of the Senate committee investigating Watergate]. His conclusion then was that he could handle the Ervin Committee if the Agency can handle Howard Hunt.[50]

Just as Phase I of NIXON/WATERGATE came down to parapolitical nomadicism of two covert agents (Hunt and McCord), it would appear that Phase II was the handiwork of other equally clandestine doubles.

BOB WOODWARD: THE MOORER-RADFORD AFFAIR

"In this matter, nothing is beyond the realm of possibility."—Richard M. Nixon

---

49 Ibid, 331. The official Senate Watergate Report stated that Bennett 'served as the point of contact between Hunt and Liddy during the two weeks following the Watergate break-in.' Haldeman, 141.
50 Hougan, 333-4.

It is today fairly well established that Bob Woodward, the iconic 'heroic' reporter most closely identified with 'the story of Watergate,' was an agent of Naval Intelligence (NIS) throughout his journalistic career. After graduating from Yale in 1965, Woodward enlisted in the Navy and was assigned to serve as communications officer aboard the *USS Wright*, the designated National Emergency Command Post Afloat (NECPA), the President's command vessel in the event of 'national emergency'.[51] In 1969, under the tutelage of Admiral Robert O. Welander, Woodward was assigned to the Pentagon, where he served as the communications duty officer for then Chief of Naval Operations (CNO), Admiral Moorer. In Hougan's own words

> It was a fascinating assignment for someone so young. In his new position, Woodward presided over all communications traffic going to and from the CNO's office. This included top–secret communiques from the White House, the CIA, the National Security Agency (NSA), the State Department, the Defense Intelligence Agency (DIA) and the NSC...He held, in other words, a position of strategic trust within the intelligence community; while others of much higher rank and longer service labored within the constraints of the 'need to know' stricture, Woodward was in an oversight position vis-à-vis a broad spectrum of interagency intelligence operations.[52]

Possibly of even greater significance was the 'political' relationship between Woodward's commanding officer, Admiral Moorer, and the Nixon White House; what made Moorer an exceptionally powerful CNO 'was his

---

51 Ibid, 293-4.
52 Ibid, 294-5.

ability to get along well with two of the administration's most powerful figures, [Attorney-General] John Mitchell and Henry Kissinger. Because he was trusted by them, very little was kept from him, and the man through whom much of that information passed was Lieutenant Woodward.'[53]

The complicated, and still shadowy, history of NIXON/WATERGATE as a deep event illuminates clearly the covert dimensions of the crusader journalist-hero Bob Woodward. In December 1971, the White House was made aware of a covert military intelligence ring operating within the NSC. The locus of the operation was with the JCS liaison office to the NSC, headed, at that time, by Admiral Robert O. Welander. Under Welander's direction, Navy Yeoman Charles Edward Radford had penetrated the inner workings of the NSC as a mole, and had begun passing on sensitive NSC documents to the JSC; most of these documents appear to have related to the groundwork negotiations for Détente II. Radford's materials were handed over to Welander in person, who then physically conveyed them to Admiral Moorer, who had been appointed Chief of the JCS by Nixon the previous July.[54] According to NIXON/WATERGATE researchers Len Colodny and Robert Gettlin,

> Radford knew that his actions gave his superiors 'an excellent overview of what was going on in the White House…Knowledge is power and the more they knew about all this peripheral data [regarding the White House's operations] the more they were able to circumvent and to maneuver and to accomplish their own ends.' And what, we asked him, did he think those ends were? He told

---

53 Hougan, 295.
54 Colondy and Gettlin, 1-28, generally.

us, 'Well, bringing Nixon down. Really, getting rid of Kissinger—Kissinger was a real monkey wrench in things.'[55]

Commenting to both investigators about Radford's behavior, Rear Admiral Gene R. LaRocque remarked that 'You have to understand...that with the military it's "us versus them." The Navy in particular. Civilians are all to be feared and distrusted and guarded against...So that reading their traffic...was all considered legitimate.'[56] What LaRocque did not helpfully ruminate upon was the fact that Welander was Woodward's commanding officer on the young lieutenant's second posting, the *USS Fox*.[57] Furthermore, from 1969-70, Woodward served as the JCS briefing officer to General Alexander Haig, Kissinger's chief aide on the NSC, [58] and someone who was closely connected to Radford—in December, 1970, Radford was appointed military aide-de-camp to Haig during the General's trip to Saigon and Phnom Penh. And it was Haig, as JCS liaison to Kissinger at the NSC, who helped establish the military back-channel that permitted the National Security Adviser to by-pass both the Departments of State and Defense.[59] From all of this, I can only conclude the following: if Woodward continued an informal connection with the JCS during the time of the Watergate scandal (as both Hunt and McCord apparently did with the CIA), then it increases the possibility that the *Washington Post*'s coverage of the story, even if only unintentionally, formed part of a managed false-flag spectacle. The exact same, in fact, seems to have

55 Ibid, 28.
56 Ibid, 13.
57 Ibid, 76.
58 Ibid, 83.
59 Ibid, 24-5.

been the case with the FBI.

DEEP THROAT/W. MARK FELT

'I suspect that in [Mark Felt's] *mind I was his agent.'*—Bob Woodward

'I want every fucking cocktail party in Georgetown talking about this [Watergate].'—Ben Bradlee

Until former FBI Associate Director W. Mark Felt's 'outing' as Deep Throat in 2005,[60] Woodward had always strenuously denied that his cryptic source 'Deep Throat' (spectacularly portrayed by Hal Holbrook in the equally spectacular film of NIXON/WATERGATE, Alan Pakula's *All The President's Men*, a blockbuster adaptation of the spectacular 'tell-all' book of the same title, co-authored by Woodward and Carl Bernstein) had been a member of the intelligence community. This, of course, was disingenuous; 'The FBI has always been responsible for domestic counter-intelligence operations, and a member of the intelligence community ever since that term became part of Washington parlance.'[61] Although Woodward repeatedly presented Felt's motives as ones of unabashed patriotism and civic virtue, Hougan claims to have discerned a revealing pattern of fake altruism to Deep Throat's well-timed leaks.[62]

---

60 Felt served as Associate Director of the Bureau from May 1972 to June 1973.

61 Holland, 181.

62 The almost visceral effects of Felt's strategic campaign of the clandestine is well conveyed by Haldeman: 'It took bombshell after bombshell...to destroy a powerful President. What is fascinating in

It may be...that [Deep] Throat remains anonymous [as of 1984] because if he was identified our perception of him and of the *Post's* Watergate reportage would change. That is, it may be that Throat's position within the Nixon administration was such that he would stand revealed as a Machiavellian figure moved more by his own ambitions than by any concern for fair play in national politics. In which case, Woodward and the *Post* would seem to be mere tools in a power struggle. So there is reason to be skeptical. While Woodward and Bernstein prefer to believe in Deep Throat's altruism, we should not trust their judgment on the matter: the *Post's* reporters, after all, have an important stake in the selflessness of their source.[63]

Much more recently, Max Holland has also challenged the authenticity of Felt's nobler form of patriotism by arguing for the careerist motivation of his leaking: angered at being passed over for promotion to the Directorship of the FBI in favor of Justice Department official (and Nixon lackey) L. Patrick Gray III, Felt attempted to force the White House to reverse itself by illuminating Gray's incompetence through a series of selective leaks to the press, primarily *The Post* and Time-Life.[64]

The portrait of Felt that emerges when we follow

---

reconstructing the true story of Watergate is both the *timing* of those bombshells and the surprise twists which made their shock even more effective. Nixon was never prepared. Time and again after he thought he had stabilized his ship of state, and knew every danger lurking in the waters, another torpedo would explode amidships and Nixon and his crew, including me, would frantically be shoring up bulkheads against a sea of outrage.' Haldeman, 232.

63 Hougan, 281.

64 In *All the President's Men*, Woodward provides several examples, perhaps unknowingly, of Felt's multiple strategic leaking; see Bernstein and Woodward, 197-8.

this thread does not resemble any of Bob Woodward's depictions [of Deep Throat]. Felt held the
news media in contempt and was neither a high-
minded whistle-blower, nor was he genuinely
concerned about defending his institution's integrity. He was not even hopelessly embittered—just
calculating. A single-minded determination drove
him, even as his chances [to be named Director],
slim to begin with, evaporated...A key part of the
argument here is that Mark Felt had no thought of
bringing Nixon down...Nixon's downfall was an
entirely unanticipated result of Felt's true and
only aim.[65]

Of course, a potentially fatal flaw with Holland's robust
advocacy of the careerist theory of Deep Throat is that
Holland himself may be a CIA asset embedded in the
media, as has been argued by Mark Lane.[66] If this is cor-

---

65 Holland, 10-11.

66 Lane, 105-32 and 133-6. Although listed in the Bibliography, there is no
reference made to *Secret Agenda* in the copious endnotes of *Leak*.
According to the author of the now standard history of the Watergate
scandal, mainstream historian Stanley L. Kutler, 'Hougan has established
the most thorough reconstruction of the crime.' Kutler, 202. Kutler
himself is something of an agnostic concerning domestic counter-
intelligence: 'Questions regarding the CIA appear in various segments of
the Watergate story. The Agency's role, however, seems destined to
remain shadowy.' Ibid, 203. Kutler does concede, however, that Nixon's
'entanglement with Watergate surely allowed the Agency to escape
confrontation with a President apparently bent on tightening his own
command and control of it.' Ibid. For his part, Holland re-cycles the long
since worn out 'official' explanation for the break-in: 'The purpose of the
June 17 re-entry was to fix the bug on the telephone of [DNC Chairman]
Larry O'Brien's secretary; it had been initially installed on May 28.'
Holland, fn. 8, 227. For a contrarian opinion, see Haldeman, 121 and
127; 'every professional politician in Washington (including Nixon and
myself) knew that no political knowledge of any value could ever be
found in party headquarters. The candidate's headquarters contained all
the vital information. The Democratic National Committee, like its
Republican counterpart, is little more than a ceremonial shell before the
convention takes place...To isolate the break-in as a simple political
intelligence action is to require sweeping under the rug an absolute

rect, what effect does this have on the veracity of Holland's not implausible critique of Deep Throat-as-selfless-patriot?

The best answer may be that Felt's covert stratagems constitute a possible continuation of the parapolitical fall-out prophesized by Hoover following the announcement of the Huston Plan. As Holland himself recognizes, 'The Huston Plan threatened to encroach on the FBI's turf and prerogatives from Hoover's vantage point. And in point of fact, the White House was [apparently] completely unaware of the extent of the FBI's vigorous counter-intelligence program (COINTELPROs) designed to disrupt, confuse, and ultimately vitiate domestic groups deemed subversive.'[67] It is also worth keeping in mind the memorandum of the Watergate saboteur James McCord, submitted on May 7, 1973 to Federal prosecutors and the Senate Watergate Investigating Committee:

> When...I saw [what was] happening to the FBI under Pat Gray—political control by the White House—it appeared then that the two Government agencies which should be able to prepare their reports, and to conduct their business with complete integrity and honesty in the national interest, were no longer going to be able to do so. That the nation was in serious trouble has since been confirmed by what happened in the case of Gray's leadership of the FBI.[68]

COINTELPRO was organized into six divisions: the

---

mountain of conflicting evidence'.

67 Holland, 206 fn. 5.

68 Haldeman, 144. Cf. Haldeman on McCord's memo: 'What he wrote in arcane bureaucratic language is that the CIA feared Nixon would preempt the CIA as it [sic] had the FBI.' Ibid.

U.S. Communist Party (1956-71); the Socialist Worker's Party (1961-71); the Puerto Rican national independence movement (1960-71); the KKK and affiliated 'white hate' groups (1964-71); the Black Panthers and allied 'black militant' groups (1967-71); and the generic 'New Left' (1968-71).[69] Felt was a senior coordinator of these programs, and it is not difficult to see, as does Holland, that Felt's theatrical assumption of the covert role as Deep Throat was a direct continuation of his earlier counter-intelligence efforts.

> He stayed at the Bureau [after Gray's appointment] and worked for almost a year on what might be called his own psychological warfare plan... [COINTELPRO] was designed to disrupt and confuse his adversaries and manipulate those in power. Pat Gray and [Associate Director William Sullivan] were the intended victims. The White House, and to a lesser extent, Congress, were the targets of his manipulations, and the press was his instrument of choice. The bulk of Felt's effort would consist of trying to prove to the White House, through anonymous links to the media, that Gray was dangerously incompetent and incapable of running the Bureau. Felt was supremely confident that because of his extensive counter-intelligence experience, he could keep his hand invisible.[70]

Also worth noting was that leaking information 'to "certifiably reliable" reporters and columnists was a central component in all the FBI's COINTELPRO [programs] and also used as part of its orchestrated effort to discredit Martin Luther King, Jr.'[71] Apparently, Felt's second fa-

---

69 Holland, 206 fn. 5.
70 Ibid, 9.
71 Ibid, 209 fn.6.

vorite 'reliable' reporter, after Bob Woodward, was organized crime reporter Sandy Smith of *Time* magazine;
'one criticism of Smith that would eventually be leveled
was that he was *too* close to the FBI—he would later be
identified as one of the reporters who regularly received
COINTELPRO leaks.'[72] And Time Inc. was owned by
Clare Luce Booth, the widow of founder Henry Luce,
both of whom were CIA assets; during the Cuba Project,
both *Time* and *Life* magazines provided extensive coverage of the 'private' commando raids 'staged' by the extremist paramilitaries Alpha/66 and Commandos L.[73]
The more that I explore the COINTELPRO dimensions
of Felt's career, the more convinced I become that Deep
Throat was a singularly spectacular persona within a
much wider network of parapolitical affiliations centered
around the Huston Plan;[74] rather than simple careerism,
Felt was acting to subvert Nixon-appointee Gray as one
part of a much larger deep event.

> What really mattered [to the FBI] was that Gray
> was loyal to Nixon personally and might even put
> the president's interests and desires above the
> Bureau's…Given that Gray's only Washington
> experience was in… [the Department of Justice],
> his appointment suggested that Nixon was going
> to at least try to assert greater control over the

---

72 Ibid, 212 fn. 22.

73 Fonzi, 53-4. Through his private endorsement of these 'renegade'
groups, Luce, 'the great editorial innovator, invented a new form of
journalism for which he is yet to be credited…paramilitary journalism.'
Hinckle and Turner, 187. In an interesting anecdote about Clare, Fonzi
relates that Luce 'hadn't thought about her boat crew [of 'sponsored'
anti-Castro terrorists] until the day that President Kennedy was killed.'
Ibid, 54.

74 Holland provides ample grounds for more advanced parapolitical
speculation about Deep Throat than he himself offers in his main
narrative, although most of this is assigned to the Endnotes of *Leak*.

Bureau via his political appointees in the Justice Department.[75]

But, in an even 'deeper' sense, there may have been an overriding impulse to prevent disclosure of the full extent of the COINTELPRO programs; most disturbing is the case of Arthur Bremer, the unsuccessful 'lone gunman' of the assassination attempt against Governor George Wallace of Alabama, who, although clearly acting alone, appears to betray some signs of counter-intelligence manipulation. According to Holland

> Nixon wanted to depict Bremer as a pro-McGovern radical, even though he was generally a-political and basically a nihilist [sic]. The president discussed with Charles Colson the possibility of planting left-wing tracts in Bremer's apartment, and Colson was in frequent contact with Mark Felt the night of the attempted assassination [May 15, 1972]. The Associated Press, interestingly, distributed a story that evening (citing a source close to the investigation) that alleged scraps of paper in Bremer's apartment 'showed he aligned himself with "left-wing causes."'[76]

An obvious question to ask at this stage is given the intensely pluralistic nature of the Dual State, could both the CIA and the FBI have been running independent but parallel cover-up operations (Phase II) during NIXON/WATERGATE? The FBI feared that Nixon's penetration of the Bureau would lead to the White House's discovery of deep COINTELPRO operations rendering senior Bureau members subject to political

---

75 Holland, 21 and 23. The same had long been suspected about JFK in his appointment of his brother RFK as Attorney-General.

76 Ibid, 210 fn.9. I discuss the issue of Bremer in more detail, below, this chapter and Chapter Five.

blackmail, allowing Nixon to exert by other, and even more insidious means, that unprecedented degree of political control sought through the Huston Plan. And the CIA feared the ultimate unravelling of Phase II of JFK/DALLAS; reputedly, Richard Helms 'was particularly exercised by five stories written by *New York Times* reporter Tad Szulc in late June 1972... [whose] consistent theme was that the parties culpable for the break-in were the same people responsible for the Agency's Bay of Pigs operation in 1961, that is CIA officers and anti-Castro Cubans.'[77] A striking confirmation of Oglesby's hypothesis of Dealey Plaza and the Watergate as somehow serving as parapolitical doubles.

PARAPOLITICAL SYMMETRIES: JFK/DALLAS AND NIXON/WATERGATE

'The main enemy is within.'—Guy Debord

If I ask the question posed by Oglesby's work—'what are the parapolitical symmetries between the Kennedy and Nixon administrations?'—then my answer must be that they managed to alienate both the Yankee and the Cowboy factions simultaneously. As a result, both administrations fell victim to a 'silent' *coup d'etat*, Kennedy's by a spectacular assassination, Nixon's by an equally spectacular constitutional crisis self-consciously stage-managed as a media-event.[78] Roger Morris' highly

---

77 Ibid, 217 fn.3.

78 If my musings are even remotely accurate, then the logic of spectacular power would explain why Nixon was not assassinated—it would have been one public execution too many, following JFK, RFK, Martin Luther King, Malcolm X and the myriad victims of COINTELPRO, such as Fred Hampton. By the same token, however, it does cast in a new light the still very shadowy affair of Arthur Bremer—a psychotic loner and

suggestive comments regarding JFK/DALLAS are equally applicable to NIXON/WATERGATE.

> The means and methods [of the respective coups] are appropriate to the setting. No conspirators steal away to some secret command post. No tanks crouch among the tree-shaded streets behind the Capitol. We are witnessing the classically American genus of the coup d'etat, achieved by folly as well as cunning, by commercial calculus and public relations, by both the manipulation of institutions and their craven abdication, by cold intention and no little inadvertence, and—perhaps most essential—at no sacrifice of the popular mythology. (A distinguishing mark of the American coup is that it should remain concealed from its victims and history even *after* its successful execution.)[79]

For Kennedy, his unsuccessful attempt to synthesize both through the JFK-LBJ/Massachusetts-Texas coalition led to interminable instability within the executive branch; for Nixon, Kennedy's weird twin, his fervid double-crossing of both factions culminated in the 'deep' triple-cross of the clandestine para-government of the Nixon-Kissinger White House. On this second point,

---

apparent would-be presidential assassin—who was reputedly stalking Nixon in 1972 before being 'deflected' towards Governor George Wallace of Alabama. Most striking is that Colson personally ordered none other than E. Howard Hunt to burglarize Bremer's apartment after the Wallace shooting; according to the two *Washington Post* reporters, an anonymous attorney informed them that "'Hunt said Colson wanted him to fly to Milwaukee immediately and break into Arthur Bremer's apartment and bring back anything that might help in connecting Bremer to left-wing political causes.'" See Bernstein and Woodward generally, 326-30. Among Hunt's other clandestine accomplishments during the Nixon years was the forging of diplomatic cables that falsely implicated JFK in the sanctioning of the murder of President Ngo Diem of South Vietnam. Ibid, 306.

79 Roger Morris cited in Colodny and Gettlin, xiii.

Haldeman is quite enlightening on the profoundly alien-ating effect of both the 'Super-Cabinet' and the Huston Plan upon the essential 'power blocs' of Washington

> Re-organization is the secret story of Watergate. That re-organization in the winter of 1972—very little known to the American public—eventually spurned into action against Nixon the great power blocs of Washington [mass media, the bureau-cracy, the Congress, and the intelligence services]. All of them saw danger as the hated Nixon moved more and more to control the Exec-utive Branch from the White House, as he was constitutionally mandated to do. What they feared was real.[80]

An imperially covert Presidency demanded a clandestine resistance; the White House 'was the focal point of an extraordinary degree of clandestine surveillance during the Nixon years', including the possible 'bugging' of Nixon himself by the Plumbers.[81]

> One might be inclined to dismiss such reports with a shrug because, after all, they cannot be confirmed. But the leitmotif of bugging is so pre-valent in the Watergate affair that it would be naïve to reject such reports out of hand. Indeed, as Nixon's memoirs make clear, he himself suspec-ted that he was the victim of electronic eavesdrop-ping. Kissinger, too, fretted about ensuring the secrecy of White House communications. In fact, the President's National Security Adviser was so concerned about the privacy of his communica-tions, and the leaks bursting around him, that he rejected the usual communications channels avail-able to his office. Rather than relying upon White

---

80 Haldeman, 168-9.
81 Hougan, 60.

House, State Department or CIA channels, Kissinger approached Admiral Thomas Moorer, then Chief of Naval Operations, and requested a medium that neither the CIA nor any other intelligence service could penetrate. Moorer accommodated the request by giving Kissinger access to the supersensitive SR-1 channel used by the Navy's top-secret spy unit, Task Force 157.[82]

And, of course, it was none other than Lieutenant Bob Woodward who was monitoring Kissinger's multifarious 'back-channel' communications.

The communiques that Woodward handled [while seconded to the CNO] included those that were transmitted on the top-secret SR-1 channel assigned to Task Force 157…What is uncertain, however, is whether the channel was being used by Kissinger during the time that Woodward processed its contents: the summer of 1969 until June of 1970. While Kissinger is known to have used the channel to make arrangements for his mid-1971 visit to Peking, it is unclear whether this was the first occasion on which he began to use the channel or, indeed, just when those arrangements were made. Still, the Nixon administration's first year, coincident with Woodward's tour of duty at the Pentagon, was a critical one in terms of national security, and there were many secrets to which Woodward became privy. Besides Nixon's vision of a rapprochement with the People's Republic of China, efforts were under way to initiate secret negotiations with North Vietnam, and clandestine meetings were being held with the Soviets to prepare the way for SALT talks and, it was hoped, détente. Henry Kissinger's plate was full. So was Moorer's. And so, on a much lower

---

82 Ibid, 61. Task Force 157 was responsible for the global monitoring of Soviet nuclear vessels.

level, was Woodward's.[83]

What is so frequently overlooked is that both Presidents, whatever their external differences, were at one in attempting to extract, or dis-embed, the Executive from the parapolitical networks of the Yankee-Cowboy symmetry.[84] In practical terms, this was manifested through the near-total breakdown in the relationship between the White House and the pluralistic and fragmenting networks of intelligence agencies.[85] Although one can only guess what conversations took place within the clandestine spaces of the Kennedy administration, one would be able to conclude from the direct evidence of the paper trail, that a de facto collapse in relations between the Presidency and the intelligence services, both civilian and military, had taken place immediately following the failure of ZAPATA. This is established with exceptional clarity in the two National Security Memorandums that were both issued on June 28, 1961 designating paramilitary warfare as a central pillar of national defense policy

---

83 Hougan, 295.

84 Although it may be pushing the similarities with Nixon's Plumbers too far, it would appear that JFK had cultivated his own private, and parallel, unit of informal operatives: the 'Irish Mafia', whose members included Kenny O'Donnell, Dave Powers, William Walton, Edwin Guthman, John Seigenthaler and Richard Goodwin,

85 Interestingly, the only other U.S. President known to have seriously alienated the CIA—Jimmy Carter—also appears to have been politically undermined by the Agency. Following the 1977 dismissal of more than 800 covert operatives (or 'cowboys' in Agency-speak) by Carter's select pick as CIA Director Admiral Stansfield Turner, rank and file intelligence officers defected to the Reagan-Bush election campaign, and covertly undermined Carter's re-election efforts through a series of 'dirty tricks'; CIA personnel 'not only stole Carter's briefing book before his television debate with Reagan, [but] they also set up Carter's brother Billy to look like a cheer-leader for Libya, planted moles in the National Security Council, and even used the White House situation room to spy on Carter's every move and waking thought.' Hinckle and Turner, xxxii and xxxiv.

while simultaneously transferring operational responsibility exclusively to the Pentagon.

National Security Action Memorandum No. 56

> It is important that we anticipate now our possible future requirements in the field of unconventional warfare and paramilitary operations.[86]

National Security Action Memorandum No. 57

> [The] Department of Defense will normally receive responsibility for overt paramilitary operations. Where such an operation is to be wholly covert or disownable, it may be assigned to CIA, provided that it is within the normal capabilities of the agency. Any large paramilitary operation wholly or partly covert which requires significant numbers of military trained personnel, amounts of military equipment which exceed normal CIA-controlled stocks and/or military experience of a kind and level peculiar to the Armed Services is properly the primary responsibility of the Department of Defense with the CIA in a supporting role.[87]

Aggravating the intelligence establishment even further was the issuance of The Inspector General's Survey of the Cuban Operation in October 1961, authored by Lyman Kirkpatrick. In response to the Survey, Deputy Director of the CIA, General Charles Cabell circulated a secret memo within the Agency on 15 December 1961,

---

86 Stone and Sklar, 535.
87 Ibid, 544.

214 | THE SPECTACLE OF THE FALSE-FLAG

declaring that 'The report misses objectivity by a wide margin. In unfriendly hands [JFK or RFK?], it can become a weapon unjustifiably to attack [sic] the entire mission, organization, and functioning of the agency.'[88] Cabell's response was neither a-typical nor exaggerated; according to Colonel Jack Hawkins, '"the CIA high command of that time seemed to reject the report out of hand, dismissed it as worthless and a threat to the CIA's very existence.'"[89] The Agency's worst fears were subsequently realized through the intensification of JFK's commitment to covert operations, flexible response, and counter-insurgency as pseudo-compromise, an effort to resolve the Yankee-Cowboy split in a manner that truly satisfied no one and yielded the intolerable outcome of the structural and operational subordination of civilian intelligence to military.

> JFK had...moved to transfer CIA 'operations' to the American military in Vietnam. He was focusing covert military operations on Army Special Forces rather than CIA para-military. His 1963 Cuban initiatives were being built around interdepartmental (Army and State) efforts, placing the CIA operations staff (such as JM/WAVE) in a supporting rather than [a] controlling role. All of these moves were a direct blow to CIA operational autonomy and would not have gone unnoticed by individuals in roles such as David Morales at JM/WAVE...[90]

And as Nixon himself seemed to be aware, Cuba was the parapolitical key to JFK's fate-as-spectacle, the very one that he tried so desperately to avoid for himself.

---

88 Kornbluh, 242.
89 Ibid, 20.
90 Hancock, 365.

'THE WHOLE BAY OF PIGS THING...'

"Well, I've never understood, myself, what Cubans were doing there."—H.R. Haldeman

"Nixon and Helms have so much on each other, neither of them can breathe."—Senator Howard Baker

Although written from 'the inside' as one of the major participants of the events it purports to describe, Haldeman's memoirs of NIXON/WATERGATE are nevertheless highly compelling, precisely because he so constantly highlights the parapolitical background of the Watergate 'scandal'. Almost alone in the literature, Nixon's former chief of staff consistently stresses the importance of the 'deep politics' of Nixon's administrative assault upon both the Federal bureaucracy and the intelligence establishment.

> The Huston Plan, even though it failed, brought home to the intelligence agencies a new threat. They feared that White House 'interference' could result in [the] disembowelment of their power. I believe that from that point on the CIA, for example, began monitoring the White House very, very closely through 'plants,' and perhaps other intelligence agencies, too. Were there CIA 'plants' in the White House?...I leave the question to rest as a part of a great mystery the significance of which may one day overshadow even Watergate: the manipulation of this nation by members of an intelligence agency.[91]

---

91 Haldeman, 109-10. There has long been speculation as to the role of Alexander Haig, Kissinger's military liaison with the NSC, in Watergate

The utterly tangled nature of Nixon's relationship with the secret services reached its apogee in Nixon's brazen attempt to politically blackmail CIA Director Helms into assisting the White House's Watergate cover-up operations by threatening to (counter-) leak damaging material concerning the Agency's actions against Cuba. In some extraordinarily opaque manner, the Bay of Pigs was to serve as Nixon's 'hook', which, when placed in historical context, provided the perfect nexus point between the false-flags theatres of Dealey Plaza and the Watergate Hotel.

In order to convey the full clandestine significance of this complicated sequence of events, I need to reproduce the history of the covertly taped White House conversations in some detail.

June 23, 1972. 10:00 am: meeting in the Oval Office between Nixon and Haldeman to discuss the Watergate burglary. This meeting constitutes the 'smoking gun' of NIXON/WATERGATE, where Nixon conspires to obstruct justice by attempting to compel the CIA to shut

---

and his possible connections with either the CIA or the DIA. Also highly suspect is Air Force Colonel Alexander Butterfield, who oversaw the installation and maintenance of the secret taping systems of the Nixon White House. On July 13 1973, Butterfield voluntarily informed the Senate Watergate committee as to the existence of the 'Nixon tapes'; his exact words to the investigators were: "'This is all something I know the President did not want revealed, but you asked me, and I feel it is something you ought to know about in your investigations. I was told no one was to know about the information I have told you.'" Ibid, 327-8. Previously, Butterfield had served for several years as the Defense Department's liaison with the CIA in Australia. Ibid, 323. Butterfield seems to have been especially close to Haig. During the Johnson administration, after several months of working together, Butterfield took over two tasks from Haig: overseeing the re-settlement of captured Bay of Pigs veterans that had been ransomed from Cuba and serving as Robert McNamara's liaison with the White House; Butterfield 'had what he described as a "strange role" that involved "a lot of undercover stuff."' Ibid, 322-3.

down the FBI investigation of the break-in. During this session, Nixon makes two highly elliptical comments linking Hunt to anti-Castro CIA activities.

> Of course, this Hunt, that will uncover a lot of things. You open that scab, there's a hell of a lot of things, and we just feel that it would be very detrimental to have this thing go any further. This involves these Cubans, Hunt, and a lot of hanky-panky that we have nothing to do with ourselves. [Oglesby, 47]...When you get in—when you get in (unintelligible) people, say, 'Look, the problem is that this will open the whole, the whole Bay of Pigs thing, and the President just feels that, ah, without going into the details—don't, don't lie to them [the CIA] to the extent to say there is no involvement [by the White House in the burglary], but just say this is a comedy of errors, without getting into it, the President believes that it is going to open the whole Bay of Pigs thing up again. And ah, because these people are plugging for (unintelligible) and that they should call the FBI in and (unintelligible) don't go any further into this case period! ...'[92]

It should be obvious by now that when Nixon cryptically references 'the whole Bay of Pigs', he is not merely uttering a crude (albeit disguised) threat against Helms— he is unconsciously providing a gloss upon the defining parapolitical dynamic of the Kennedy administration.

> 11:40 am—Haldeman makes arrangement for a meeting between himself and both the Director (Richard Helms) and Deputy Director (General Vernon Walters) of the CIA in the offices of Presidential advisor Erlichmann.[93]

---

92 Oglesby, *Yankee-Cowboy War*, 47-8.
93 Powers, 301.

1:00 pm—second meeting between Nixon and Haldeman. Nixon once again re-visits the Bay of Pigs.

OK, just postpone (unintelligible)...Just say (unintelligible) very bad to have this fellow Hunt, ah, he knows too damned much, if he was involved— you happen to know what? If it gets out that this is all involved, the Cuba thing would be a fiasco. It would make the CIA look bad, it's going to make Hunt look bad, and it is likely going to blow the whole Bay of Pigs thing, which we think would be very unfortunate—both for the CIA, and for the country, at this time, and for American foreign policy. Just tell him [L. Patrick Gray, the Director of the FBI] to lay off.[94]

1:30—meeting of Haldeman, Erlichman, Helms, and Walters.

Haldeman then said 'it was the President's wish that Walters call on Acting FBI Director Patrick Gray and suggest to him that since the five suspects [McCord, Martinez, Barker, Frank Sturgis, and Virgilio Gonzalez] had been arrested that this should be sufficient and that it was not advantageous to have the enquiry pushed'...Helms said he had already discussed the investigation with Gray the day before, and had assured him the CIA was not involved and that none of the suspects were working for the Agency.

At this point Haldeman ventured the gambit [of Nixon]. 'The President asked me to tell you this entire affair may be connected to the Bay of Pigs, and if it opens up, the Bay of Pigs may be

---

94 Hougan, 48.

blown...'

Helms' reaction was immediate. He gripped the arms of his chair, leaned forward, and shouted: 'The Bay of Pigs had nothing to do with this! I have no concern about the Bay of Pigs!'[95]

Haldeman was taken aback by the vehemence of Helms' reaction. 'I'm just following my instructions, Dick,' he said. 'This is what the President told me to relay to you.'[96] [Powers, 302.]

2:20 pm—third meeting between Haldeman and Nixon.

Haldeman: 'Gray called Helms and said I think we've run right into the middle of a covert CIA operation.'

Nixon: 'Gray said that?'

Haldeman: 'Yeah. And (unintelligible) said nothing we've done at this point and ah (unintelligible) says well it sure looks to me like it is (unintelligible) and ah, that was the end of that conversation (unintelligible) the problem is it tracks back to the Bay of Pigs and it tracks back to some

---

95 Presumably this is Helm's coded reference to the CIA suspension of its own investigation of Dealey Plaza following the release of the FBI report on December 9, 1963? Kurtz, 20-1. Also of possible significance was that very soon after assuming the Presidency in 1969, Nixon demanded 'all the facts and documents the CIA had on the Bay of Pigs, a complete report on the whole project.' After being repeatedly stonewalled by the CIA, Nixon held 'a long secret conversation' with Helms in the Oval Office, after which he ordered his aides Ehrlichman and Haldeman 'to cease and desist' from trying to obtain the CIA files. Haldeman, 25-6.

96 Powers, 302.

other, the leads run out to people who had no involvement in this, except by contracts and connection, but it gets into areas that are liable to be
realized.'[97]

Haldeman makes clear in his memoirs that by the end of
the Watergate scandal he had come to believe that 'the
Bay of Pigs' was Nixonesque code for JFK/DALLAS;
'It seems that in all those Nixon references to the Bay of
Pigs, he was actually referring to the Kennedy assassination.'[98] Offering an opinion shared by many assassination investigators (Lane, Russo), Haldeman speculates
that Oswald was actually a Cuban agent who killed JFK
under orders from Castro as retaliation for the assassination component of OPERATION MONGOOSE.

> [W]hen Nixon said, 'It's likely to blow the whole
> Bay of Pigs' he might have been reminding
> Helms, not so gently, of the cover-up of the CIA
> assassination attempts on the hero of the Bay of
> Pigs, Fidel Castro—a CIA operation that may
> have triggered the Kennedy tragedy and which
> Helms desperately wanted to hide.[99]

In Haldeman's view, Phase II of JFK/DALLAS was really an effort by the CIA to disguise both Oswald's own
clandestine affiliations with central intelligence as well
as the Agency's wider involvement in regional assassination conspiracies.

After Kennedy was killed, the CIA launched a

---

97 Oglesby, *Yankee-Cowboy War*, 48

98 Haldeman, 39. Of course, a somewhat more pedestrian explanation
could be that Nixon was referencing the Cuba Project more generally,
and the multifarious CIA and Mafia linkages and assassination plots in
particular.

99 Ibid, 40.

fantastic cover-up. Many of the facts about
Oswald unavoidably pointed to a Cuban
connection…In a chilling parallel to their cover-
up at Watergate, the CIA literally erased any
connection between Kennedy's assassination and
the CIA. No mention of the Castro assassination
attempt was made to the Warren Commission by
CIA representatives. In fact, Counter-Intelligence
Chief James Angleton of the CIA called [Deputy
Director] Bill Sullivan of the FBI and rehearsed
the questions they would give to the Warren
Commission investigators, such as these samples:

Q. Was Oswald an agent of the CIA?

A. No.

Q. Does the CIA have any evidence showing that
a conspiracy existed to assassinate Kennedy?

A. No.[100]

The evidence presented by Haldeman is perfectly consistent with that false-flag; proof of the collusion between the CIA and FBI highlights the underlying
parapolitical continuity of both JFK/DALLAS and
NIXON/WATERGATE, two singular deep events embedded within the far greater parapolitical landscape of
clandestine governance.

---

100 Ibid, 39-40.

[Movie Poster: Robert Redford and Dustin Hoffman star as Watergate scandal journalists Bob Woodward & Carl Bernstein in Alan J. Pakula's 1976 film "All the President's Men"]

5 | The Spectacle of Conspiracy

'Everything is supposed to be something.
But it never is. That's the nature of
existence.'—Don DeLillo

Modernity can perhaps be usefully understood as the perfect inversion of the Roman Empire—in the place of the spectacle of brutality, we collectively witness/endure the brutality of the spectacle. For parapolitical scholars such as Scott, the traumatizing infliction of the cognitive dissonance that is the grotesque body of the deep event becomes virtually identical with the social consciousness of the Society of the Spectacle[1]: 'the spectacle's domination has succeeded in raising a whole generation molded to its laws.'[2] This inconvenient truth of (post) modern History accounts for not only the scarring traces of the lurking presence of the clandestine but also the emergence of the discourse of 'conspiracy theory' as the dominant epistemo-political apparatus of the era of spectacular power; for Debord, the psychic result of the integrated spectacle is that 'we live and die at the confluence of innumerable mysteries.'[3] Any radical criminology that takes seriously the notion of criminal

---

1 See Wilson, 'Crimes Against Reality'.

2 Debord, *Comments*, 7.

3 Ibid, 55.

sovereignty must therefore also need to come to terms with what I might call the 'political economy of cognitive dissonance',[4] which rests upon two central modes of spectacular production. The first is 'the conceit of the illusion of transparency': the (seemingly) unlimited freeflow of (apparently) uncensored information—currently the main trading commodity of the consumer (-ist) media industry/service provider—is itself the camouflage of the networks of parapolitical governance. Herein, the importance for the clandestine of the virtually unlimited corporate penetration of all domains of the garbage dump of 'social media 'simply cannot be overestimated. The second is the exceptionally risk-adverse nature of contemporary forms of governance, both public and private, that Debord denotes as the *'fragile perfection'* of the Society of the Spectacle.

> Once it attains the stage of the integrated spectacle, self-proclaimed democratic society seems to be generally accepted as the realization of *a fragile perfection*. So that it must no longer be exposed to attacks, being fragile; and indeed is no longer open to attack, being perfect as no other society before it. It is a fragile society because it has great difficulty managing its dangerous technological expansion. But it is a perfect society for governing...Wherever the spectacle has its dominion the only organized forces are those which want the spectacle. Thus no one can be the enemy of what exists, nor transgress the *omerta* which applies to everything.[5]

---

4 Cognitive dissonance may be defined as 'a psychological phenomenon occurring when new ideas or information conflict with previously formed ideologies, accepted beliefs, and corresponding behaviours.' Manwell, 854.

5 Debord, *Comments*, 21.

A conspiracy of a silence of a very unique kind, one which is served not by censorship but by an unregulated (free market?) proliferation of speech that renders critical theory impotent 'not because it is in hiding but *because it is hidden* by the ponderous stage-management of diversionary thought.'[6] The integrated spectacle is the ideal medium for a strikingly Debordean notion of *disinformation* which is tantamount to 'ordinary' speech acts within the spectacular domain; 'disinformation now spreads *in a world where there is no room for verification.*'[7] In reality, Debord's disinformation is no different from *gossip*, the free dissemination of unverified informal knowledge. In a Cultural Studies[8] work infused with quasi-Debordean insights, *Knowledge Goes Pop: From Conspiracy Theory to Gossip* (2006), Clare Birchall outlines the historical coupling of gossip as semi-legitimate social praxis with the saturation of popular consciousness with mass media (digital or otherwise).

> For rather than gossip interrupting the knowledge economy—and that economy's associated neo-liberal open market and erosion of the value of knowledge beyond a notion of 'utility'—gossip could also be thought to facilitate and be facilitated by the rise of information networks and the knowledge economy...We seem more and more comfortable...with the idea that knowledge cannot be traced back to an ultimate source (as is often the case with gossip). We seem more and more willing to allow information to accrue simply through circulation. If we read or hear something enough in enough contexts, it will as-

6 Ibid, 53-4.

7 Ibid, 48.

8 A difficult to define discipline, but one which might usefully be thought of as the University-based vanguard of the totalizing commodification of popular culture—Situationism ossified as academic 'discourse'.

> sume the status of knowledge in spite of an ab-
> sence of authority or method of verification. A
> great deal of knowledge today seems to have
> taken on something of the status of gossip. It is
> neither true nor false, knowledge or non-know-
> ledge, but somewhere [sic] in between.[9]

It is obvious that what is commonly known as conspiracy theory is, in many critical respects, both structurally
and functionally identical with gossip—the exteriority
that guarantees the boundaries of 'legitimate' or 'orthodox' forms of political reason and speech.[10] Within both
of the classic (and negative) works on the discourse of
conspiracy—that of Karl Popper[11] and Richard Hofstadter[12]—conspiracy theory is deployed as a form of al-

---

9 Birchall, 126. For cyber-technology and the high speed circulation of
'false' derivatives commodities as the cause of the GFC see Wilson,
'Criminogenic Cyber-Capitalism' generally. Compare Birchall with Jodi
Dean on digital information: a 'world where more information is
available, and hence, a world where we face daily the fact that our truths,
diagnoses, and understandings are incomplete—click on one more link,
check out one more newscast, get just one more expert opinion...[We]
should expect large-scale feelings of anxiety, suspicion and conspiracy
theorizing.' Cited in Husting and Orr, 142. At issue here, of course, is not
the nature of the true but the *social value* of Truth; knowledge as
commodity equals (self-) validation.

10 'The category *conspiracy theory* polices the borders of legitimate versus
risible statements, and intellectually competent actors versus paranoiacs.'
Husting and Orr, 141.

11 The purpose of conspiracy theory is 'exactly the opposite of the true aim
of the social sciences...It comes from abandoning God and then asking:
"Who is in his [sic] place?" His place is then filled by various powerful
men and groups—sinister pressure groups, who are to be blamed for
having planned the great depression and all the evils from which we
suffer.' Popper, 14. For an effective rebuttal of Popper's summary
dismissal, see Pigden generally.

12 'Although American life has rarely been touched by the most acute
varieties of class conflict, it has served again and again as an arena for
uncommonly angry minds...I call it the paranoid style simply because no
other word adequately evokes the qualities of heated exaggeration,
suspiciousness, and conspiratorial fantasy that I have in mind.'

terity that ensures the validity of the accepted thing through the perpetual verification of difference(s) with the refused thing.[13] What is less obvious, however, is the degree to which disinformation has evolved into a form of 'cultural material' of an entertainment industry that constitutes its own form of spectacular governance. Although hardly a Situationist, the work of neo-Marxist literary theorist Frederic Jameson is of great usefulness on this point. Whether in literary or cinematic form the 'conspiracy text', for Jameson, is a key sign of the cultural hegemony of the geo-political unconscious, that which 'now attempts to re-fashion national allegory into a conceptual instrument for grasping our new being in the world.'[14] Every text constitutes a political fantasy of some kind, recapitulating the social totality of the 'political unconscious', that which sets the parameters of the collective imaginary.[15] This has never been more so the case than in our contemporary post-modern era, [16] with the unbounded hyper-commodification of all cultural forms acting as the aesthetic complement to globalization and the institutionalization of a world-wide corpo-

---

Hosfstadter, 3.

13 See Birchall Chapter Two and Three generally. See also Husting and Orr on the rhetorical deployment of the term 'conspiracy theorist' as a category of deviant personhood'; 'Much discourse about conspiracy has become almost inseparable from Hofstadter's creation of the paranoid mind. His "conspiracy theorist" has become a condensed symbol saturated with constellations of taken-for-granted meanings.' Husting and Orr 133 and 140.

14 Jameson, 3.

15 'For Jameson, every text is at its most fundamental level a political fantasy which in contradictory fashion articulates both the actual and potential social relations which constitute individuals within a specific political economy.' MacCabe, xi.

16 'Post-modernism is not fundamentally a question of subject-matter or themes but of the full entry of art into the world of commodity production.' Ibid, xii.

rate network.[17] The master political fantasy of our globalized contemporaneity is paranoia on the international plane and conspiracy theory at the national level: the expansion of political space into infinity (globalization) permits the emergence of the parapolitical 'nameless' (the unseen, that which is beyond perception). As Jameson shows, the necessary cultural precondition to the discourse of conspiracy theory is communication, experienced (or endured) in social terms as *connectivity*. Is there any faction or sub-state entity of any kind in the world that exists in a state of incommunicability with any other? Anyone in the world, including the private citizen, can 'conspire' with Joseph Kony and The Lord's Resistance Army—all that one needs is access to the Internet. Not surprisingly, the conspiratorial text 'whatever other messages it emits or implies, may also be taken to constitute an unconscious, collective effort at trying to figure out where we are and what landscapes and forces confront us in a late twentieth century whose abominations are heightened by their concealment and their bureaucratic impersonality.'[18] As a cultural artefact of postmodernism, then, Jameson's conspiracy theory bears two signature characteristics. Firstly, it displays a remarkable affiliation with Birchall's association of conspiracy-theory-as-gossip with Cultural Studies. Secondly, and more importantly, it represents an attempt 'to think a system so vast that it cannot be encompassed by the natural and historically developed categories of perception [local; nationalist] with which human beings normally orient themselves'—in other words, the *sublime*.[19]

---

17 Jameson, 4.

18 Ibid, 3.

19 Ibid, 2.

'TWICE AS BIG AS YOU CAN IMAGINE...': 9/11[20]

'We're beyond politics now.'—Richard
Nixon (Anthony Hopkins) in *NIXON*

Debord's reading of the conspiracy transgresses onto dangerous ground for it is precisely within this space of the order of magnitude of both the spectacle and the parapolitical—or, in simpler terms, the 'size' of the conspiracy—that the grotesque is revealed as the dark twin of its (falsely) assumed opposite: the sublime. The architect of the onto-epistemological foundations of what is laughingly known as 'The Enlightenment', Immanuel Kant, 'doubles' as Modernity's premier aesthetician. This should come as no surprise, as Kant's entire metaphysical system ultimately serves an end both aesthetic and epistemological: to organize the World in such a way as to make it the grounds for objective understanding and absolute knowledge; in other words, to thoroughly serve 'the purposive'—in Heideggerian terms, the reduction of both Self and Object to 'correctness'.

For Kant, the perception of the world ('the transcendental deduction') requires a synthesis of what appears before us within both time and space. The synthetic project of 'pure Reason' requires three operational concepts, or 'unities of synthesis': apprehension, reproduction, and recognition. Within the Kantian scheme, all knowledge and understanding is ultimately anthropocentric, in that all things must be reduced to 'units of measure' that are compatible with Human understanding

---

20 The sub-heading is taken from Frank Miller's seminal graphic novel *The Dark Knight Returns* (1985), the first volume of which features the airborne attempt by psychotic gangster Harvey 'Two-Face' Dent to blow up Gotham City's Twin Towers—just one of many striking anticipations within the popular culture of the 1980s and 1990s of September 11 2001.

(*cogito*); 'A tree [the height of] which we estimate with reference to the height of a man, at all events gives us a standard for a mountain...'[21] The categories of pure Reason guaranteeing both the unity of phenomena as well as the ontological unity of the perceiving subject constitutes the 'transcendental unity of apperception'[22] ; 'In other words, it is not so much that I perceive objects; it is rather my perception that presupposes the [unitary] object-form as one of its conditions.'[23] For Kant, 'the real (synthetic) formula of the *cogito* is: I think myself, and in thinking myself, I think the object in general to which I relate a represented diversity.'[24] Therefore, the operations of the *a priori* categories of synthetic understanding need to be supplemented by the work of an additional faculty, Judgment, which is responsible for subordinating all of the inherent 'sensible diversity' of spatio-temporal objects to the operational requirements of the synthetic categories of transcendental Reason; 'The only use which the understanding can make of these [concepts] is to judge by means of them.'[25] From this follow two consequences, one phenomenological the other aesthetic. In terms of the former, the human body itself is the final source not only of the units of measurement but of the operational constraints of the synthetic categories of Pure Reason.

> This primary (subjective, sensory, immediate, living) measure proceeds from the [human] body. And it takes the body as its primary object...*It is the body which erects itself as a measure.* It

---

21 Kant, 118.

22 Smith, xvii.

23 Ibid, xvi.

24 Deleuze, *Kant's Critical Philosophy*, cited in Smith, xvi.

25 Kant, cited in Smith, xvi.

> provides the measuring and measured unit of
> measure: of the smallest and largest possible, of
> the minimum and the maximum, and likewise of
> the passage from the one to the other.[26]

In terms of the latter, the 'lived evaluation' of space-time imparts a necessarily aesthetic dimension to judgment, as the operation of perception is inseparable from the appreciation and evaluation of form, which is the domain of the 'aesthetic' properly defined; 'All estimation of the magnitude of objects of nature is in the last resort aesthetic (i.e., subjectively and not objectively determined).'[27] And it is the intrinsically aesthetic nature of judgment that gives rise to one of Kant's seminal concepts: the sublime. Although an aesthetic concept, the sublime is not identical with the beautiful; it is, in fact, antithetical to it. Whereas the beautiful dwells within the realm of intuition—that is, the natural accordance of the spatio-temporal object with the synthetic categories of *cogito*[28]—the sublime is better understood as a form of sensory trauma, the catastrophic, or chaotic, sundering of the immediacy of perception from the transcendental unity of apperception.

> The Sublime, on the other hand, is to be found in
> a formless object, so far as in it or by occasion of
> it *boundlessness* is represented, and yet its totality
> is also present to thought…that which excites in
> us, without any reasoning about it, but in the ap-
> prehension of it, the feeling of the sublime, may
> appear as regards its form to violate purpose in re-
> spect of the Judgment, to be unsuited to our

26 Derrida, 140.

27 Kant, cited in Smith, xviii.

28 'Natural beauty…brings with it a purposiveness in its form by which the object seems to be, as it were, pre-adapted to our Judgment, and thus constitutes in itself an object of satisfaction.' Kant, 102-3.

> presentative faculty, and, as it were, to do viol-
> ence to the Imagination; and yet it is judged to be
> only the more sublime.[29]

Two aspects of Kant's notion of the sublime and their relevance to the grotesque are particularly important. Firstly, as we would expect, the Kantian sublime is remarkably, almost viscerally, phenomenological in nature: 'Nature is therefore sublime in those of its phenomena whose intuition brings with it the Idea of its infinity.'[30] Essential to the concept of the sublime is not merely the heightening of the *cogito*'s self-awareness of the grounding of perception upon the Body, but the abject 'insult' inflicted upon the anthropocentric unit of measurement: 'We call that *sublime* which is *absolutely great...what is great beyond all comparison...the sublime is that in comparison with which everything else is small.*'[31] Secondly, the subjective experience of the sublime is not the objective perception of the immediately unassimilable sensible diversity of the sublime object but rather the traumatic inducement of a crisis of confidence in the witness' existential faith in the efficacy of judgment.

> [T]rue sublimity must be sought only in the mind
> of the [subject] judging, not in the natural Object,
> the judgment upon which occasions this state...
> Consequentially it is the state of mind produced
> by a certain representation with which the reflect-
> ive Judgment is occupied, and not the Object, that
> is to be called sublime...*the sublime is that, the
> mere ability to think, which shows a faculty of the*

---

29 Ibid, 102-3.
30 Kant, 116.
31 Ibid, 106 and 109.

mind surpassing every standard of Sense.[32]

Where Kantian aesthetics and parapolitical analysis part ways is at the aesthetic dis-juncture that renders the sublime and the grotesque irreconcilable: Kant ultimately preserves the *cogito* by investing the unities of synthesis with the potency to ultimately reduce all phenomena to the requirements of Reason, while parapolitics, following the logic of the grotesque, ultimately seeks to shatter faith in the rationality of the political. But what phemonenologically unifies the two poles is the irreducible element of visceral trauma. Scott's reflections upon 9/11 clearly demonstrate this: the chaotic irruption of a clandestine reality through that catastrophic event resulted in the

> [C]reation of a partly illusory mental space, in which unpleasant facts, such as that all western empires have been established through major atrocities, are conveniently suppressed. (I suspect in fact that most readers will be tempted to reject and forget [parapolitical events]... as something which simply 'doesn't compute' with their observations of America.) I say this as one who believes passionately in civilization, and fears that by excessive denial our own civilization may indeed be becoming threatened.[33]

The great practical joke that Debord plays on the 'progressive' politics of the Enlightenment (about whose long-term prospects he came to increasingly despair during the last years of his life) lies with the incontrovertible proof he provided that the future of Democracy

---

32 Ibid, 117 and 110.

33 Scott, *Deep Politics and the CIA Global Drug Connection*, 2-3. I will discuss the parapolitical trauma of 9/11 in more detail below, this chapter.

belongs to the Right.[34] Since at least the time of Karl Marx it has been the supreme conceit of the Left that it is the true vanguard of History precisely because only it was able to correctly decipher the objective laws of History; it was always able to act more quickly than the Right because it was able to predict more accurately—or, to see the Future *sooner*. Understood in terms of imagery and perception, it becomes clear that the political equation between Left and Right is reducible to more foundational issues of perception, speed, velocity, and acceleration: who sees first strikes first and, just as in War, 'wins'.[35] Speed itself, therefore, facilitates change of a wholly 'virtual' form of reality that effectively supersedes the notions of legality and political accountability. The crucial point—a supremely Debordean one—is that it is not the Right but the Left that has become *reactive*; 'the establishment of spectacular domination is such a profound social transformation that it has radic-

---

34 Just as it was, ironically, the ultimate fate of Situationism to become just one more commodity for 'chic' or 'hip' consumerism, as pseudo-Situationist slogans of (narcissistic) rebellion—'"take your dreams for reality"'—became a central feature of corporate advertising in the mid-1980s. 'In a telling inversion the Situationists...became the role model of the hedonistic, conspicuous consumer of contemporary city life, perfectly in tune with a culture that feeds on contradiction and contrast, that advertises through anti-adverts and that promotes art through anti-art... What now could be the point of an avant-garde when, within the capitalist economy, transgression and shock were recognized as necessary stimulants towards increased consumption?' Ford, 157-8. Wark dates the beginning of the appropriation of radical philosophy by consumerism with the appearance of the 'paperback' industry—the mass production and consumption of universally circulated texts—in the 1950s. Wark, 77. Absolutely nothing, not even 'poetry in the street', can ultimately evade capture by Capitalism, which is both fast-moving and wholly predatory; after all, it was Walt Disney himself who said "If you dream it, you can do it."

35 As McKenzie Wark expresses it, 'Hegel's owl of Minerva no longer flies at dusk, because the shotgun of Dick Cheney fired at first light.' Wark, 153.

ally altered the art of government. This simplification, which has quickly borne such fruit in practice, has yet to be fully comprehended in theory.'[36] The wider parapolitical implications of speed as the 'rate' of political perception are made clearly manifest by the comments of an anonymous White House aide to the journalist Ron Suskind. Discussing the U.S. invasion of Iraq in 2003, the aide said that 'guys like him' were 'in what we call the reality-based community', which he defined as people who 'believe that solutions emerge from your judicious study of discernible reality.'

> We're an empire now, and when we act, we create our own reality. And while you're studying that reality—judiciously, as you will—we'll act again, inventing other new realities, which you can study too, and that's how things will sort out. We're history's actors…and you, all of you, will be left to just study what we do.[37]

Which complements Debord perfectly.

---

36 Debord, *Comments*, 87. Compare this with Debord's much earlier clarion call to the orthodox Left made in 1957: 'In a given society, what is termed culture is the reflection, but also the foreshadowing, of possibilities for life's planning. Our era is at heart characterized by the great distance at which revolutionary political action lags behind the development of the modern potentialities of production, which demands a superior organization of the world…Capitalism is devising new forms of struggle… [that has] been able to preserve familiar social relations in the great majority of highly industrialized countries, thus depriving a socialist society of its essential material foundation.' No doubt Debord had Jackie Gleason and 'The Honeymooners' in mind when he wrote that 'One of the reasons for the American working class's incapacity to become politicized should likely be sought amidst this abundance of televised baseness.' Debord, 'Report on the Construction of Situations', 29 and 46.

37 Ron Suskind, 'Without a Doubt', *New York Times*, 17 October, 2004, cited in Klein. This brings to mind the words of Celine: 'For the time being only the facts count and even this for not much longer.' Cited in Virilio, *Desert Screen*, 49.

> Not only are the subjected led to believe that to all
> intents and purposes they are still living in a
> world which in fact has been eliminated, but the
> rulers themselves sometimes suffer from the ab-
> surd belief that in some respects they do too. They
> come to believe in a part of what they have sup-
> pressed, as if it remained a reality and had still to
> be included in their calculations. Their backward-
> ness will not last long. Those who have achieved
> so much so easily must necessarily go further. It
> should not be thought that those who have been
> too slow to appreciate the pliability of the new
> rules of their game and its form of barbaric
> grandeur, will last forever like some archaism in
> proximity to real power. It is certainly not the
> spectacle's destiny to end up as enlightened des-
> potism.[38]

The Debordean notion of political victory as the fruit of
the shaping of perception is central to the work of contemporary critical theorist Paul Virilio, much of whose
oeuvre may be not misleadingly understood as an open-
ended gloss on *The Society of the Spectacle*; 'To
progress would be to accelerate...After the *century of
the Enlightenment*, there would be the century of the
speed of light and soon, our own century—the century of
the *light of speed*.'[39] Virilio closely follows Debord in
equating spectacular power with the death of a genuinely
progressive discourse; he approvingly quotes Saint Au-
gustine who, when commenting upon the public seduction of theatrical spectacles, caustically remarked that as
'One sees oneself in those who seem transported by such
objects, one soon becomes *a secret actor in the
tragedy*.'[40] And for Virilio there can be no greater

---

38 Debord, *Comments*, 87-8.
39 Virilio, *Ground Zero*, 15. Emphases in the original.
40 Ibid, 40.

tragedy today than the emergence of the 'ideal type' of a new breed of the criminal sovereign, what we might term the 'parapolitician': the 'media tycoon', enshrined in cinematic culture as Citizen Kane and embodied within real-time as Silvio Berlusconi, the once (and perhaps yet again) Prime Minister of Italy.[41]

Berlusconi's 'capture' of the Italian State was an act of inherently spectacular power.[42] It is not the least of the ironies of Berlusconi's criminal sovereignty that he hid 'in plain sight'. As in a *mafiosi*'s selective reading of Poe's 'The Purloined Letter', Berlusconi 'escaped' into the public domain precisely in order to avoid the detection (=prosecution) of his (private) criminal/covert identity.[43] Yet, this self-same act of parapolitical 'camouflage' effected the optical re-configuration of the Italian government into a simulated 'virtual state'. So uncannily perfect is the fusion of simulation with spectacle in Berlusconi's Italy that if this parapolitician did not exist, Virilio would have found it necessary to invent him.[44]

---

41 Ginsborg, 138.

42 See generally Wilson, 'Crimes Against Reality'.

43 In the words of Fedele Confalonieri, president of Berlusconi's television company Mediaset, 'If Berlusconi hadn't entered politics, we would have ended up sleeping under a bridge, on trial for Mafia crimes.' Stille, 138.

44 The more one studies Berlusconi the more he assumes the guise of a living parody of the power criminal. Not the least of his spectacular propensities is his frequent use of fake quotations. 'If you want to convince someone [Berlusconi] told his sales force, make up a quotation and attribute it to some renowned authority. "So use this method: 'As Bill Paley of CBS says. As Plato said. As Abraham Lincoln said'...Who's ever going to go and look it up? ...People are incredibly gullible, they love quotations."' Stille, 16. The same technique is a central feature of Al Pacino's hyper-kinetic portrayal of the arch-gangster boss 'Big Boy' Caprice in Warren Beatty's 1990 film *Dick Tracy*. Unnervingly, Caprice makes frequent bogus references to both Plato and Lincoln.

[T]he election of Silvio Berlusconi as head of the Italian government in 2001 has opened up a *trans-political* era of a new kind. After his failed try-out of 1994, 'Il Cavaliero' has in fact just carried out a *coup détat*, and Italy has just toppled over into a two-party system of the third kind in which the alternative is no longer between classical Left and Right, but between politics and media...No longer content with occupying the stage of daily life with its great ('Big Brother'-style) game shows, *telereality* is now invading the sets of the *Res publica*. And for the first time in Europe we are looking on, mesmerized, at the unprecedented victory of the champion of *telecracy* over representative democracy's man, the triumph of audience ratings over universal suffrage.[45]

Of critical importance to the radical criminologist is the notion of the parapolitician as the site of a convergence between clandestine agency and the alteration of political perception through cinematic technique.

To grasp the real importance of the 'analyser' that speed, especially audio-visual speed, now represents, we must turn again to the philosophical definition: 'Speed is not a phenomenon but a *relationship between phenomena.*' In other words it is the very *relativity* or transparency of the reality of appearances, but a 'spatio-temporal transparency' that here supersedes the spatial transparency of the linear geometry of the optical lenses— hence the term *trans-appearance* to designate the transmitted electronic appearances, whatever the space interval separating them from the observer. This subject or *subjugated* observer thus becomes inseparable from the observed object, because of the very immediacy of the interface, of the aptly named 'terminal', that perfects the extension and

---

45 Virilio, *Ground* Zero, 30.

duration of a world reduced to man-machine com-
mutation, where the 'spatial depth' of perspectival
geometry suddenly gives way to the 'temporal
depth' of a *real-time perspective* superseding the
old real-space perspective of the Renaissance.[46]

In an unintentionally revealing interview with journalist
Alexander Stille, Berlusconi re-presented himself as the
incarnation of the post-Debordean telematic analyser:
Berlusconi's official position within the public state is
determined by his unofficial domination of virtually all
forms of televisual communication. This yields a 'cognitive dissonance' of parapolitical dimension—as Stille
himself clearly perceives.

I...found Berlusconi to be psychologically one of
the strangest people I had ever met. I had never
before interviewed anyone who told so many obvious untruths with such enthusiastic conviction[47]
...in grappling with Berlusconi's curious relationship with factual truth, it began to dawn on me
that what I was encountering was a deep anthropological difference. My obsession with factual
accuracy, documentation, objective truth was all
part of my baggage as a print journalist, the quaint
and naive and old-fashioned credo of the age of
Gutenberg and the Enlightenment, while Berlusconi is a man of a different age, of the age of
television and mass media, in which image and
perception are all that really matter. Berlusconi is
decidedly a creature (and creator) of the post-
modern world where it doesn't matter what actually happened, but what people think happened.
'Don't you understand,' he told one of his closest
advisors, 'that if something is not on television it
doesn't exist. Not a product, a politician or an

---

46 Virilio, *Polar Inertia*, 56-7.
47 Stille, 18.

> idea.' And because the things we were discussing
> —his conflicts of interest, the crimes of which he
> and his associates have been accused (and, in
> some cases convicted)—have not been aired in
> Italian television, they, too, did not exist.[48]

Although every politician utilizes television as a political instrument, Berlusconi is the first parapolitician to
evidence a belief in television as a social force, in a
manner unnervingly reminiscent of Futurism.[49] The
'true' irony of Berlusconi's tele-Futurism—a revolutionary form of post-Democratic governance in which politics is effectively reduced to trivia, or 'e-tainment'[50]—is
the speed in which it transits from the epistemological
(simulation) to the ontological (the absence of Being),
an irony that is only furthered when we recall that the
temporal site of the emergence of the Dual State is the
Italian Renaissance. It is not a coincidence that the virtual re-presentation of the State-as-optical-phenomenon
was spawned by the same 'Re-Birth' that gave us modern politics and linear perspective. As Virilio observes,
Renaissance painting (linear perspective; depth) lays the
foundation for the Enlightenment 'anthropic principle,
which regards the existence of any observer as inseparable from the existence of rationally observed phenomena'[51] The elaborate civic rituals of *Il Stato* established
the iterability of the State as both an agent of perception
and as an object of sight: public procession generated
the simulacra of the 'transparent' State, whose Truth/Be-

---

48 Ibid, 20.

49 Ginsborg, 33, 92-3, 185-7 and 189-90.

50 Contemporary identity politics' might best be understood as the North
American variety of this—both Fox News and MSNBC as pseudo-
journalist 'infommercials' targeted at rival groups of consumers.

51 Virilio, *Polar Inertia*, 51. See Cubitt for 'Virilio's claim that Renaissance
geometry was the basis for all subject-object relations and therefore of all
critical thought and ultimately all human values.' Cubitt, 86-92.

ing was commensurate with its entry into the collective gaze of *Il Popolo*.[52] Berlusconi as a post-Futurist 'virtual prince' provides the parodic gloss upon Renaissance civic ritual: his procession through public space is commensurate with his parapolitical manipulation of judicial and parliamentary immunity. Berlusconi's public representation is itself the highly self-conscious—if not cynical[53]—parapolitical simulation of lawful authority. The space that separates the Renaissance ritual *Stato* from Berlusconi's 'virtual state' is the difference between the illusory and the delusional; 'The state's only original existence is as a visual hallucination akin to dreaming.' The political crisis of legitimacy of the disappearance of the Italian public state into the (politicised) aesthetics of the 'virtual state', occasioned by Berlusconi's dual capture of both the government and the media, is the real-time occurrence of the epistemic crisis of Renaissance epistemology described by Virilio.

This *indirect light* [of telecommunications] is ulti-

---

52 Muir 1981 and Trexler 1980. In placid Venice, 'the ducal procession was the constitution' (Muir, 190), while in volatile Florence public processions 'were used after aborted conspiracies and when illegitimate governments were toppled' Trexler, 337. Compare the accounts of Muir and Trexler with Debord's critical comments on the documentary film in his own anti-documentary *Critique of Separation*, produced in 1961: 'Society broadcasts to itself its own image of its own history, a history reduced to a superficial and static pageant of its rulers—the persons who embody the apparent inevitability of whatever happens.' Debord, *Critique of Separation*, 33.

53 Here, I adopt Peter Sloterdjik's definition of cynical reasoning as especially appropriate for Berlusconi's Italy. 'Cynicism is *enlightened false consciousness*. It is that modernized, unhappy consciousness, on which enlightenment has labored both successfully and in vain. It has learned its lessons in enlightenment, but it has not, and probably was not able to, put them into practice. Well-off and miserable at the same time, this consciousness no longer feels affected by any critique of ideology; its falseness is already reflectively buffered...It is the stance of people who realize that the times of naiveté are gone.' Sloterdjik, 5.

mately the result of the fusion of optics and kin-
ematics, a fusion which now embraces the whole
range of ocular, graphic, photographic and cine-
matographic representations, making each of our
images a kind of *shadow of time*—no longer the
customary 'passing time' of historical linearity
but the 'exposed time' which...surfaces. This is
the time of Niepce's photographic development,
the time of the Lumiere Brother's cinematograph-
ic resolution of movement, but now above all *the
time of videographic high definition* of a 'real-
time' representation of appearances which cancels
the very usefulness of passive (geometric) optics
in favour of an active optics capable of causing
the decline of the direct transparency of matter.
What is inordinately privileged by this process is
the indirect (electro-optical) transparency of light
or—to be even more precise—of the light of the
speed of light...Thus, after the nuclear disintegration of the space of matter which led to the political situation that we know today, the disintegration of *the time of light* is now upon us. Most
likely, it will bring an equally major cultural shift
in its wake, so that the depth of time will finally
win out over the depth of spatial perspective inherited from the Renaissance.[54]

One can scarcely hope for a better Debordean metaphor
than 'the disintegration of the time of light'. Within Berlusconi's virtual state, political meaning, or 'truth', had
been suspended by the optical negativity of the telematic. Herein, the 'Dual' State—a metaphorical composition
of space, crime, and light (deep = dark = crime)—disappears through the sensory bombardment of the high-
speed circulation of post-political simulacra.[55] As with
Stille's mournful invocation of the obsolete cognitive

---

54 Virilio, *Polar Inertia*, 61.
55 Jones, *The Dark Heart of Italy*, 127-8.

tools of the Enlightenment, any lingering normative outrage over the parapolitical substance of the Dual State is
unveiled as yet one more archaic metaphysical supersti-
tion.

> The idea that the real forces behind or underneath
> the screen can be revealed is...based on the pre-
> sumption that the media themselves do not have
> power, but instead are tools in the hands of ma-
> nipulating third parties...the quest for hidden
> power not only underestimates the feature of me-
> dia power, it also sticks to the rules of old power,
> which has in fact disappeared within the media.[56]

Here I am reminded of Jean Baudrillard's famous account of the alibi: the substitution of the false image as
validation of the perceived absence of the thing-that-is-
true. For Baudrillard, the two-party system is an 'alibi'
for the one-party state; in Italy, the parapolitical one-
party state is the 'alibi' of both the multi-party system
and the transpolitical spectacle that it both spawns and is
sustained by. Once again, we encounter Tunander's ad-
monition of the failure of liberal political discourse to
encounter parapolitical tele-reality. With the criminal
sovereign Berlusconi as our exemplar, we can now appreciate more readily the criminological relevance of
Virilio's radical and subversive optics.

> To admit that for the human eye the essential is
> invisible and that, since everything is an illusion,
> it follows that scientific theory,[57] like art, is
> merely a way of manipulating our illusions, went
> against the political-philosophical discourses then
> evolving in tandem with the imperative of convin-
> cing the greatest number, with its accompanying

56 Geert Lovink cited in Cubitt, 142.
57 Political Science?

> desire for infallibility and a strong tendency to-
> wards ideological charlatanism. Publicly to point
> to how mental images are formed, including the
> way their psycho-physiological features carry
> their own fragility and limitations, was to violate
> a state secret of the same order as a military
> secret, since it masked a mode of mass production
> that was practically infallible.[58]

If the correlation between spectacular power and speed-politics is correct, then the entire phenomenon of para-politics, quite literally, can be viewed in terms of optical considerations of 'high resolution' or 'high definition' as factors governing the invisibility of the power crime 'event'; a constant, and rapid, alteration between foreground and background, between the visible and the invisible.[59] Conversely, the state, as the final arbiter of all definitional thresholds of criminality, may be re-conceptualized in terms of its existence as an 'optical effect'; juro-political truth is mediated through surveillance and transparency. Virilio has made this point clearly through a striking example taken from the modes of political control developed during the French Enlightenment.

> It is no longer the body of the army that passes
> back and forth in tight ranks beneath the regard of
> the intendant, now it is the inspector general that
> files past in review of the provinces, aligned as in
> a parade. Yet the repetition of these reviews that
> triggers *the unfolding of the regional film is only
> an artifice, only a cinematic special effect* which
> benefits the itinerant observer. Perceiving the se-
> quence of geographic locations in this isolated
> fashion, the general loses sight of the local realit-
> ies and immediately demands the reform of the

---

58 Virilio, *The Vision Machine*, 23.

59 Virilio, *Negative Horizons*, 26-38.

common law in order to advance the administrative standard.[60]

The state is 'real' precisely to the degree that it is capable not only of perception but, also, to the same degree
and in the same manner, that it is capable of being perceived. The state, in order to be 'real', must necessarily
exhibit some degree of virtuality;[61] not the 'de-realized'
projection of an illusory reality, but 'a change of identity,
a displacement of the centre of ontological gravity of the
object considered'.[62] The paradox, then, of the 'surveillance society' is that its optical hegemony, the expansion
of surveillance always stands in inverse relationship to
the visibility of the State. The State creates its own virtual existence through time by means of the continuous re-
circulation of the externalized signs of its visibility
through space; the processions of the intendant's entour-
age through the geo-spatial territory of the state *both
sees and is seen*. This ritualistic act of mutual constitution, however, serves as the grounds of a dangerous
metaphysical 'trap' for the state: in effect, the reality of
the state is reduced to its virtual *appearance*. Here, of
course, 'real' means 'lawful'. The prejudice of modern
Liberalism is that the mutual conditionality of the reality
and the legality of the state is guaranteed by the state's
co-determinate existence with the visible, or 'public',
realm, the onto-epistemological encumbrance inherited
from the linear perspective of the Renaissance.[63] In fact,

---

60 Ibid, 68.

61 Kroker, 44-50.

62 Levy, 26.

63 The Enlightenment's 'prejudice' in favour of the optical may be the
ideological basis of Liberalism's refusal of 'conspiratorial' views of the
State. The universal criticism of 'conspiracy theory' is 'lack of evidence';
that is, the absence of visible, and, therefore, detectible historical traces.
See discussion above, this chapter.

every State is a parapolitical entity that auto-defines its own parameters through its control over the discourse of legality and the praxis of visibility.[64] It is important to recall here that International Law lacks a formal theory of the State. Instead, it substitutes hermeneutics—the close reading of the sign-systems of the State—for a juridical ontology. The resultant metaphysical lacuna allows for the occupation of the empty discursive space of the rule-of-law State by the parapolitical, and intensely heterogeneous Dual State. Virilio, like Debord, is highly cognizant of this parapolitical truth: 'The State apparatus is in fact simply an apparatus of displacement [*déplacement*], its stability appears to be assured by a series of temporary gyroscopic processes of delocalization and relocalization'.[65] The demarcation of the political body of the state rests largely upon its successful deployment of its arsenal of optical devices. Panoptical technique and its variables, most crucially its velocity, serve as the parameters within which the state regulates the politics of appearance; 'What we see arises from what is not apparent.'[66] Such control of a high-velocity virtual reality would operationally double as the control of the invisibility, or 'disappearance' of the parapolitical reality. And Virilio himself could not improve upon the final paragraph of *Comments on the Society of the Spectacle*.

> We must conclude that a changeover is imminent and ineluctable in the co-opted cast who serve the interests of domination, and above all manage the protection of that domination. In such an affair, innovation will surely not be displayed on the spectacle's stage. It appears instead like lightning,

---

64 See generally Wilson, 'Deconstructing the Shadows'.
65 Virilio, *Negative Horizons*, 56.
66 Ibid, 136.

which we know only when it strikes. This
changeover, which will conclude decisively the
work of these spectacular times, will occur dis-
creetly, and conspiratorially, even though it concerns those within the inner circles of power. It
will select those who will share this central exi-
gency: that they clearly see what obstacles they
have overcome, and of what they are capable.[67]

As the reader may be aware, the year 2001 marks two
seminal events in the operation of spectacular power: the
election of the politician of spectacle Berlusconi and a
major architectural disaster in New York City.

On September 11 2001, the Manhattan skyline became the front of the new war. The anonymity of
those who initiated the attack merely signals, for
everyone, the *rise of a global covert state*—of the
unknown quantity of a private criminality—that
'beyond-Good-and-Evil' which has for centuries
been the dream of the high priests of an icono-
clastic progress.[68]

For Virilio—as for Debord if he were alive today—the
two catastrophes signify a remarkable cultural convergence.

As the attack on the World Trade Centre was being broadcast live, many TV viewers believed
they were watching one of those disaster movies
which proliferate endlessly on the TV screens. It
was by switching channels and finding the same
pictures on all the stations that they finally understood that 'it was true'.[69]

---

67 Debord, *Comments*, 88.

68 Virilio, *Ground Zero*, 82.

69 Ibid, 38 fn. 5. A personal anecdote might be in order here. In February
2010 I was in New York City for the first time since 9/11. Naturally, I

The spectacle of the Twin Towers serves as the primal imagery of The War on Terror, experienced on the national plane as an irrevocable shift in the constitutional balance of power to the Executive, commensurate with a parallel acceleration of executive/military decision-making.[70] 'Let us make no mistake about it, the modernity of "Big Brother" and its clones is the direct successor to the multi-media presentation of the Gulf and Kosovo conflicts...an image strategy which preceded the perfectly orchestrated strategy of the terror attacks of September 2001' says Virilio.[71]

> Here as elsewhere, what is troubling about the covert state of trans-national terrorism—that unknown quantity—is its growing subordination to a techno-scientific progress which is, itself, un-authored and dependent on the development of its own audiovisual media and platforms. The scientific imagination ultimately suffers the same fate as 'e-tainment'; it comes to resemble that of those TV viewers who thought the attacks on the World Trade Centre on September 11 was merely another disaster movie, or that of Islamist suicide attackers no doubt dying happy at becoming actors in a global super-production in which *reality would tip over* once and for all *into electronic nothingness*.[72]

Scott's distinctive parapolitical poetics and his emphasis upon the irrationality of the Dual State are strikingly psycho-analytical in nature, creating (perhaps deliber-

---

asked as many New Yorkers as possible concerning their experiences on September 11. Literally all of them who witnessed the Twin Towers attack in person likened the event to 'watching a movie'.

70 See Wilson, 'Speed/Pure War/Power Crime', generally.

71 Virilio, *Ground Zero*, 42.

72 Ibid, 68. Emphases in the original.

ately) a series of meaningful associations: repression, denial, the unconscious, guilt, transference. Missing though, but synonymous with all of the above, is the notion of *dream*. Revealingly, 'dream', in German, is *traum*, which evokes 'trauma'; trauma, in turn, is etymologically derived from the Greek word for 'wound', a rupturing-by-force that serves as sign of combat and violence. If the essence of neurosis is conflict, then every act of repression is a self-inflicted wound; every dream that symbolically announces the presence of the repressed is a signifier of trauma.

THE SITUATION OF THE MASS MEDIA

'The world is going to ruin... [and] *man's feeling of superiority triumphs in the expectation of a spectacle to which only contemporaries are admitted.'*—Karl Kraus

'All experts serve the State and the media and only in that way do they achieve their status.'[73] Although Debord does not actually reduce the Spectacle to mass media, the instruments and channels of mass communication have emerged as the uncontested arena for the staging of both the spectacle and any possible situation; 'Rather than talk of the spectacle, people often prefer to use the term "media". And by this they mean to describe a mere instrument, a kind of public service which with impartial "professionalism" would facilitate the new wealth of mass communication through the mass media...'[74] The cultural truth of mass media within the Society of the Spectacle is fundamentally identical

---

73 Debord, *Comments*, 16.
74 Ibid, 6.

with Jameson's notion of the political unconscious as social totality: 'For the final sense of the integrated spectacle is this—that it has integrated itself into reality to the
same extent as it was describing it, and that it was reconstructing it as it was describing it.'[75] To test the validity
of this hypothesis, I will now examine several of the key
depictions of two of my spectacular events—JFK/DAL-
LAS and NIXON/WATERGATE—as 'media events'. I
will ignore the third false-flag, LBJ/TONKIN, precisely
because it has not been the object of either literary or
cinematic re-presentation, a telling historical omission
that no doubt reflects that spectacle's status as a thoroughly proven conspiracy; since it is completely known,
it cannot serve as an example of the parapolitical sublime that acts as the indispensable aesthetic conceit of
the conspiracy text.

THE UNKNOWN QUANTITY (OF A PRIVATE CRIMINALITY): LIBRA

*'That's only fitting because in this city at
this particular time, black is white is black.
In other words, people are playing havoc
with the categories.'*—Don DeLillo, *LIBRA*

The most striking thing about Don DeLillo's *LIBRA*
(1988), by far the most artful post-modernist novel ever
written about conspiracy (with the possible exception of
Thomas Pynchon's *The Crying of Lot 49*), is the uncanny manner in which it inhabits the landscape of the
grotesque as first assayed by Kayser. It is, in fact, the

---

75 Ibid, 9.

perfect literary exemplar of two of the three signs of the grotesque. The first is 'the grotesque as the estranged world'; 'It is our world which has to be transformed. Suddenness and surprise are essential elements of the grotesque.' The second is 'the Grotesque as a Play with the Absurd', signified by the operational hegemony of determinism (natural or otherwise) and the concomitant manipulation of reality by occult forces: 'the unity of perspective in the grotesque consists in an unimpassioned view of life on earth as an empty, meaningless puppet play or a caricatural marionette theatre.' Although ostensibly about the assassination of John F. Kennedy, the novel is in fact a literary free-for-all with the defining tropes of the genre of the crime novel, defined by Tony Hilfer in the following manner.

> 'The central and defining feature of the crime novel is that in it, self and world, guilt and innocence are problematic. The world of the crime novel is constituted by what is problematic in it'...A crime novel maneuvers its reader into various forms of complicity, managing to subvert the reassurances of the detective novel by 'put[ting] the signification process into doubt or even exploit[ing] the gap between socially accepted signification and ultimate reality.'[76]

Consistent with its narrative foregrounding of the liminal and the nomadic, the crime novel adopts a strictly anti-representational approach to language and reason, in which the ontologically privileged is not sameness but difference; as a result, to the degree that 'the crime novel puts the signification process into doubt or even exploits the gap between socially accepted signification and ultimate reality, it subverts the reassurances of the detective

---

76 Tony Hilfer, cited in Sherwin 52 fn. 50. Emphasis in the original.

novel,'[77] which, by contrast, is ultimately predicated upon the intelligibility of both World and Self. The post-modernist implications of crime fiction has perhaps been most thoroughly explored by Baudrillard, in his seminal essay entitled (not surprisingly), *The Perfect Crime* (1996).

> The perfect crime is that of an unconditional real-ization of the world by the actualization of all data, the transformation of all our acts and all events into pure information: in short, the final solution, the resolution of the world ahead of time by the closing of reality and the extermination of the real by its double.[78]

As we should expect, *LIBRA* is the literary drama that enacts Baudrillards's radically anti-Humanist anthropo-logy.

The main narrative conceit of this conspiracy text is that Dealey Plaza was the (in part, unintentional) out-come of a series of overlapping networked linkages be-tween retired and middle-level CIA officers and American paramilitaries who were operating small teams of Cuban snipers. Apart from Lee Harvey Oswald himself, the three main protagonists are disguised liter-ary composites of historical actors: Walter Everett, Jr., who is 'really' Richard Bissell, innovator of the U-2 spy plane program and director of planning for ZAPATA; Laurence Parmenter, a hybrid of Tracy Barnes, Bissell's Assistant Director of Plans for the Cuba Project, and Theodore (aka, 'The Blond Ghost') Shackley, director of JM/WAVE;[79] and T.J. Mackey, a synthesis of CIA case

---

77 Tony Hilfer, cited in ibid, 48.

78 Baudrillard, *The Perfect Crime*, 25.

79 There is, in fact, a partial overlap between Everett/Bissell and

officer Grayston Lynch[80] and paramilitary/mercenary William (aka 'Rip', 'Carlos', 'Alligator', and 'Tinka') Robertson'.[81] It is Everett/Bissell, artfully doubling as a pseudo-parody of mainstream conspiracy theory, who announces the grand strategy of the false flag.

> 'The movement [the Cuba Project] needs to be brought back to life. These operations the Agency is running out of the Keys are strictly pinpricks. We need an electrifying event. JFK is moving toward a settling of differences with Castro. On the one hand he believes the revolution is a disease that could spread through Latin America. On the other hand he's denouncing guerilla raids and trying to get brigade members to join the U.S. Army, where someone can keep an eye on them. If we want a second invasion, a full-bore attempt this time, without restrictions or conditions, we have to do something soon. We have to move the Cuban matter past the edge of all these sweet maneuverings. We need an event that will excite and shock the exile community, the whole country. We know Cuban intelligence has people in Miami. We want to set up an event that will make it appear they have struck at the heart of our government. This is a time for high risks. I'm saying be done with half-measures, be done with evasion

---

Parmenter/Shackley; DeLillo has it that it was Everett who 'was putting people of his own into Zenith Technical Enterprises [based on the University of Miami campus in the early 1960s], the burgeoning Miami firm that provided cover for the CIA's new wave of operations against Cuba.'DeLillo, 24. It would be doing DeLillo's extraordinary novel disservice by treating it as a literal 'reconstruction' of the secret history of JFK/DALLAS, the moral conceit that ultimately destroys Stone's bombastic *JFK*; the novel's real significance, as I will show, lies in its sophisticated application of Debordean discourse.

80 For the direct parallels between Mackey and Lynch, compare DeLillo at 70-3 with Rasenberger, 230-3.

81 Albarelli, 249-52.

and delay.'[82]

'Some things we wait for all our lives without knowing it. Then it happens and we recognize at once who we are and how we are meant to proceed. This is the idea I've always wanted...We want to set up an attempt on the life of the President. We plan every step, design every incident leading up to the event. We put together a team, leave a dim trail. The evidence is ambiguous. But it points to the Cuban Intelligence Directorate. Inherent in the plan is a second set of clues, even more unclear, more intriguing. These point to the Agency's attempts to assassinate Castro. I am designing a plan that includes elements of both the American provocation and the Cuban reply[83]...We script a person or persons out of ordinary pocket litter. Shots ring out, the country is shocked, aroused. The paper trail leads to paid agents who have disappeared in Venezuela, in Mexico. I am convinced this is what we have to do to get Cuba back. The plan has levels and variations I've only begun to explore but it is already, essentially, right. I feel its rightness. I know what scientists mean when they talk about elegant solutions. This plan speaks to something deep inside me. [84] It has a powerful logic. I've felt it unfolding for weeks, like a dream whose meaning slowly becomes apparent. This is the condition we've always wanted to reach. It's the life-insight, the life-secret, and we have to extend it, guard it carefully, right up to the time we have

---

82 DeLillo, 27.

83 This from a professorial office in the basement of Texas Women's University, where Everett had been retired/exiled to following the 'fiasco' of the Bay of Pigs.

84 Reputedly, Bissell's 'idea of fun was reading railroad timetables and rate schedules from around the world, many of which he committed to memory.' Rasenberger, 58.

shooters stationed on a rooftop or railroad bridge.'

There was a silence. Then Parmenter said dryly, 'We couldn't hit Castro. So let's hit Kennedy. I wonder if that's the hidden motive here.'

'But we don't hit Kennedy. We miss him,'' Win said.[85]

In classic noir fashion (which the novel is very much a knowing parody of) a 'fly-in-the-ointment' soon (and unexpectedly) emerges: the more that operational control is conferred to the low-level Mackey, who begins to move towards the Cubans and the cipher-like 'Leon' Oswald—who functions throughout the novel as an inverted double of JFK[86]—the more homicidal the original

---

85 DeLillo, 27-8. The notion of the shooter deliberately missing JFK (or merely wounding him) is, of course, completely consistent with the false flag scenario offered by both DeLillo and myself (he as a plot device, me as a criminological hypothesis). The minimal requirement for a successful false-flag was a public spectacle of parapolitical significance, although JFK's death may have served as the guarantee of the desired outcome (plus pay back). See Hancock, 219-20 and 298. I confess to a personal fondness for a theory propounded by the television series *Quantum Leap*: that Oswald's intended target was Jacqueline Kennedy; fitting this into the false-flag scenario, we can speculate that the President's grief at the loss of the First Lady would provoke a homicidal rage against Castro. This 'theory' has two advantages: firstly, it is consistent with a series of complaints that Oswald made several weeks prior to Dealey Plaza concerning alleged FBI harassment of his Russian émigré wife Marina, raising the possibility of Jacqueline as the pay back (Shenon, 26); secondly, it would confirm Oswald's reputation as a terrible marksman and his Mannlicher-Carcano rifle as a pathetic weapon —he was gunning for Jackie but kept on hitting Jack.

86 'Coincidence. Lee was always reading two or three books, like Kennedy. Did military service in the Pacific, like Kennedy. Poor handwriting, terrible speller, like Kennedy. Wives pregnant at the same time. Brothers named Robert.' Ibid, 336. The mimetic logic that culminates in Oswald's deliberately murderous act is that he is actually eliminating his own Other. The metaphysical joke, of course, is that in the assassin's sleep-waking semi-consciousness it is Oswald who is the original and Kennedy

plot becomes. This is revealed with great clarity through the meditations of 'Frank Vasquez' (a composite of possible second shooters Eladio del Valle Gutierrez and Sandalio Herminio Diaz Garcia) on assassination with a telescopic lens.

> On his fourth day with Castro he shot a government scout, aiming through a telescopic sight. It was uncanny. You press a button and a man drops dead a hundred meters away. It seemed hollow and remote, falsifying everything. It was a trick of the lenses. The man is an accurate picture. Then he is upside down. Then he is right side up. You shoot at a series of images conveyed to you through a metal tube. The force of a death should be enormous but how can you know what kind of man you've killed or who was the braver and the stronger if you have to peer through layers of glass that deliver the image but obscure the meaning of the act? War has a conscience or it's ordinary murder.[87]

A literary touch that Debord would take to heart: neither a completely false form of consciousness nor a mere question of technology, the spectacle is 'far better viewed as a weltanschauung that has been actualized, translated into the material ream—a world view transformed into an objective force...the spectacle epitomizes the prevailing model of social life.'[88] Strikingly, *LIBRA*'s two onto-epistemological premises are essentially Debordean: (i) the spectacle (which is the social totality of contemporary Reality) is inherently indeterminate and therefore, 'infinite', or 'endless'; and (ii) the sum total of

---

the copy, an ironic twist of Baudrillard's perfect crime, which is 'the extermination of the real by its double...'

87 DeLillo, 297-8.

88 Debord, *Society*, 12-13.

perceptual apparatuses within the Society of the Spectacle are exclusively governed by a thoroughly cinematic imaginary that creates the (false?) consciousness of psychically meaningful coincidence, or synchronicity ('the occult forces' of Kayser's 'the Grotesque as a Play with the Absurd'). The infinity of the spectacle is personified by Nicholas Branch, 'retired senior analyst of the Central Intelligence Agency[89] and 'covert' historian of the JFK assassination whose real (but unstated) function is to re-assemble all available data on Dealey Plaza in order to insure its ultimate indecipherability.[90]

> Branch must study everything. He is in too deep to be selective.

> He sits under a lap robe and worries. The truth is he hasn't written all that much. He has extensive and overlapping notes—notes in three-foot drifts, all these years of notes. But of actual finished prose, there is precious little. It is impossible to stop assembling data. The stuff keeps coming. There are theories to evaluate, lives to ponder and mourn. No one at the CIA has asked to see the work in progress. Not a chapter, a page, a word of it.[91]

The governing conceit here is that the inherent un-readability of Dealey Plaza—ordinarily the prime sign of the inherent meaninglessness of a given event—is, even if

---

89 Ibid, 15.

90 'The case will haunt him to the end. Of course they've known it all along. That's why they built this room for him, the room of growing old, the room of history and dreams.' Ibid, 445. Although the primary unifying thread, both narratively and metaphysical, of the novel, the scenes with Branch only occupy a total of seventeen pages: 14-16, 57-60, 298-302, 376-79, 440-45.

91 Ibid, 59.

only by serendipity, the mark of Everett's design to create a hermeneutical 'cloud of unknowing' that is itself the signifier of the deeper design—which ultimately cannot be reconstructed. The irony is only deepened through Branch's wholly asymmetrical (and non-dialogic) relationship with the invisible but seemingly omniscient Curator who continually sends him more data but never requests a final (or 'finite') summation of the truth. Branch's narrative function, in essence, is to serve as an ironical juxtapose to Everett's pseudo-providential manipulations.

> There's something they aren't telling him. The Curator delays, lately, in filling certain requests for information, seems to ignore other requests completely. What are they holding back? How much more is there? Branch wonders if there is some limit inherent in the yielding of information gathered in secret. They can't give it *all* away, even to one of their own, someone pledged to confidentiality. Before his retirement, Branch analyzed intelligence, sought patterns in random scads of data. He believed secrets were childish things. He was not generally impressed by the accomplishments of men in clandestine service, the spy handlers, the covert-action staff. He thought they'd built a vast theology, a formal coded body of knowledge that was basically play material, secret-keeping, one of the keener pleasures and conflicts of childhood. Now he wonders if the Agency is protecting something very much like its identity—protecting its own truth, its theology of secrets.[92]

And, of course, the presence of Theology—or, more subversively, the Theology of Presence—is precisely

---

92 Ibid, 442.

what leads into the novel's second major metaphysical gimmick: the ubiquity of synchronicity and 'high strangeness'.

> Branch has become wary of these cases of cheap coincidence. He's beginning to think someone is trying to sway him towards superstition. He wants a thing to be what it is.[93] Can't a man die without the ensuing ritual of a search for patterns and links?

> The Curator sends a four-hundred page study of the similarities between Kennedy's death and Lincoln's.[94]

The most fundamental metaphysical paradox of the Society of the Spectacle is that it is both radically empirical ('sight is all that there is') and radically idealistic ('all seeing is conveyed through the collective consciousness

---

93 A sentiment which is neatly inverted by the brutal, and irreducible, materialism of the 'pornography' of the autopsy photographs and post-mortem reports that 'flood' Branch's office. 'He doesn't know why they are sending him this particular grisly material after all these years. Shattered bone and horror. That's all it means to him. There is nothing to understand, no insights to be had from these pictures and statistics, from this melancholy bullet with its nose levelled and spread like a penny left on trolley tracks. (How old he is). The bloody goat heads seem to mock him. He begins to think that this is the point. They are rubbing his face in the blood and gunk. They are mocking him. They are saying in effect, "Here, look, these are the true images. This is your history. Here is a blown-out skull for you to ponder. Here is lead penetrating bone." They are saying, "Look, touch, this is the true nature of the event. Not your beautiful ambiguities, your lives of the major players, your compassions and sadnesses. Not your roomful of theories, your museum of contradictory fact. There are no contradictions here. Your history is simple. See, the man on the slab. The open eye staring. The goat head oozing rudimentary matter." They are saying, "This is what it looks like to get shot."' Ibid, 299-300.

94 Ibid, 379.

of mass media') simultaneously.[95] The 'default' position of such an interminable alterity is, of course, the cinematic, which all of the characters of *LIBRA* are hopelessly enslaved to. T.J. Mackey, for example, remembers—and, therefore, 're-lives'—the entirety of the Bay of Pigs in expressly cinematic terms: ' The memory was a series of still images, a film broken down to components. He couldn't quite make it continuous.'[96] Under the aegis of spectacular power, neither Thought nor Meaning are lost —rather, they are both thoroughly subsumed under 'Editing'; the truth/meaning of any event is identical with the 'correct' re-assemblage of the tele-reality within the correct sequence, both optical and libidinal. Everett himself makes the duality of the Society of the Spectacle, both ocular and erotic, clear to his wife.

> 'U-2 planes. The planes that spotted the missiles the Soviets were putting into Cuba. We used to call the photos pornography. The photo interpreters would gather to interpret. "Let's see what kind of pornography we pulled in today." Kennedy looked at the pictures in his bedroom as a matter of fact…I'll tell you what it means, these orbiting sensors that can hear us in our beds. It means the end of loyalty. The more complex the system, the less conviction in people. Conviction will be drained out of us. Devices will drain us, make us vague and pliant.'[97]

In a world that is wholly ocular, paranoia becomes the only form of 'connectivity' available to us—the close reading of visual sequences for the purposes of estab-

---

95 Debord's onto-epistemology closely resembles that of George Berkeley: every sensation is an idea and every idea is a sensation, perfectly conceived.

96 Ibid, 72.

97 Ibid, 77.

lishing the true nature of the relationship between Self and Other. Not only are all of the major characters in *LIBRA* wholly given over to a paranoid 'world-view' (an occupational hazard within national security work) but they employ paranoid reconstructions as a narcissistic/infantile form of emotional gratification. In Jungian terms, an unexpected coincidence (real or imaginary) that induces a profound psychic transformation is known as synchronicity and, synchronicity, as should be obvious, is very much a matter of the psychic editing of an interrupted and inherently chaotic flow of sensory input. This becomes clear in a conversation between David Ferrie (portrayed in the novel as the 'waking', rational Self of the somnambulistic Oswald) and the Mafiosi Carmine Latta (Carlos Marcello) and the generic Tony Astorina.

> Tony said, 'Speaking of Cuba, a couple of weeks ago I dream I'm swimming on the Capri[98] roof with Jack Ruby. The next day on Bourbon Street, who do I fucking see? You talk about coincidence.'

> 'We don't know what to call it, so we say coincidence. It goes deeper,' Ferrie said. 'You're a gambler. You get a feeling about a horse, a poker hand. There's a hidden principle. Every process contains its own outcome. Sometimes we tap in. We see it, we know. I used to run into Jack Ruby now and then. What was he doing in New Orleans?'[99]

The seduction of 'tapping into' the cosmic joke of synchronicity is, of course, the moment of supreme danger

---

98 The Mob owned Capri Hotel in Havana.
99 Ibid, 172.

for the parapolitical scholar, just as it perennially is for Nicholas Branch: at the precise instant that 'conspiracy theory' discourse enters into the mainstream media it is instantaneously appropriated by the operatives of the universalist circulation of 'freedom of information' and subsequently transformed into just one more 'spectacle'. As Debord has theorized and as I have (partially) demonstrated, the revealing of clandestine truth(s) invariably provokes the counter-move of disinformation.

THE ULTRA-IDIOCY OF NAÏVE REALISM: JFK

> 'Remember, fundamentally people are suckers for the truth, and the truth is on your side, 'bubba.'—Colonel X (Donald Sutherland) to Jim Garrison (Kevin Costner), in *JFK*

> 'In a world that has **really** been turned on its head, truth is a moment of falsehood.'—Guy Debord

> 'I'm lost boss. What are we saying here?'—Bill Broussard (Michael Rooker), in *JFK*

Perhaps the greatest parody of Frank Capra's *Mr. Smith Goes to Washington* (1939; Columbia Pictures) humanly conceivable, Oliver Stone's (aka, 'the Wagner of Hollywood'[100]) film *JFK* (1991; Warner Brothers) has been described by the Kennedy dynasty's greatest toady Arthur Schlesinger Jr. as "...a virtuoso exercise in postmodernist film making."[101] The choice of the word 'postmodernist' is illuminating, for that elusive term is the

---

100 Robert Sam Anson in Stone and Sklar, 209.
101 Stone and Sklar, 393.

key to interpreting Stone's monumental and bombastic epic, a cinematic spectacle that is not only a media event in its own right, but the source of a parallel spectacle of public discourse that operated concurrently within the journalistic establishment. Anyone who spends any time investigating Dealey Plaza comes to recognize clearly the ultimate political issue at stake in Dallas.

> How we make sense of the assassination of John F. Kennedy is directly related to how we make sense of American public life...The events of Nov. 22, 1963, have thus become a kind of national Rorschach test of the American political psyche. Those six seconds of gunfire in Dallas' Dealey Plaza serve as an enigmatic inkblot into which we read our political concerns.[102]

The assassination is not simply an unclassified fragment of parapolitical reality but the fulcrum of a crisis of political legitimacy.

> That's no small part of the reason why Stone and the conspiracy theorists are contrasted so fiercely today. Those who do believe Oswald acted alone are not only defending the anti-conspiratorial theory advanced by the Warren Commission. They are also defending the credibility of senior US government officials, the integrity of US law enforcement and intelligence agencies and the capabilities of the national media. (If there was a conspiracy, then the media has thus far failed to uncover it.) The lone-gunman theory of Kennedy's death, in its own way no less implausible than some of the conspiracy theories, depends on confidence in the legitimacy of national political authority.[103]

102 Jefferson Morley in Stone and Sklar, 231.
103 Ibid, 232. Compare this with the insight of arch-conservative pundit

It is worth mentioning here the release by the CIA in January 1967 of a directive to its numerous contacts and assets within the media on how to proceed in framing the parameters of the debate over conspiracy theory. I provide the most relevant portions below.

> CIA document 1035-960 [4 January 1967][104]
> RE: Concerning Criticism of the Warren Report
>
> 1. This trend of opinion [46% of the American public did not think that Oswald acted alone] is a matter of concern to the US government, including our organization. The members of the Warren Commission were naturally chosen for their integrity, experience, and prominence. They represented both major parties, and they and their staff were deliberately drawn from all sections of the country. Just because of the standing of the Commissioners, efforts to impugn their rectitude and wisdom tend to cast doubt on the whole leadership of American society. Moreover, there seems to be an increasing tendency to hint that President Johnson himself, as the one person who might be

---

William F. Buckley: 'The general scepticism on the question who killed JFK is really in the nature of a cognate question: who really ordered Watergate? Who really was guilty of aggression at the Tonkin Gulf? Who really started the Cold War? What were the motives of the Founding Fathers?' Cited by David Klinghoffer in ibid, 286.

104 The 'book dispatch' was written by Western Hemisphere Division Chief Bill Broe at the request of Richard Helms. Morley, 243. See Lane, 114-18. Lane offers this account on the CIA's penetration of the mass media: 'This is the method now employed. An independent publication is chosen to mask the source. A CIA puppet is placed there and given an impressive title. The CIA then provides the propaganda. It appears as an independent concept when published. The CIA, employing its official website, cia.gov, then cites the "independent" writer and the "independent" publication as the source as it spreads its false allegations throughout the world. In the intelligence world some refer to this as sheep-dipping. Their wolf had been dipped into a sheep's bath and came up smelling quite neutral.' Lane, 105.

said to have benefited, was in some way responsible for the assassination. Innuendo of such seri-
ousness affects not only the individual concerned,
but also the whole reputation of the American
government.

2. Action

a. To discuss the publicity problem with [?] and
friendly elite contacts (especially politicians and
editors), pointing out that the Warren Commission
made as thorough an investigation as humanly
possible, that the charges of the critics are without
serious foundation, and that further speculative
discussion only plays into the hands of the opposition. Point out also that parts of the conspiracy
talk appear to be generated by Communist propa-
gandists. Urge them to use their influence to dis-
courage unfounded and irresponsible speculation.

c. A conspirator…would hardly choose a location
for a shooting where so much depended on conditions beyond his control; the route, the speed of
the cars, the moving target, the risk that the assassin would be discovered. A group of wealthy conspirators could have arranged much more secure
conditions.

e. Oswald would not have been any sensible person's choice for a co-conspirator. He was a
'loner,' mixed up, of questionable reliability and
an unknown quantity to any professional intelligence service.[105]

The release of *JFK* in December of 1991 ignited an outburst of journalistic opprobrium of such intensity that it

---

105 Ibid, 115-17.

can only be likened to a sort of 'moral panic', the sort of counter-culture gossip-mongering that normally accompanies shock realizations of Satanic ritual abuse or repressed memory syndrome. I reproduce some of the most outstanding examples of the vituperation of the official commentariat below; note the 'sliding' conflation of otherwise incompatible agendas—moral(istic), political, and artistic.

> Whether or not it is a gift, artistic talent conveys a responsibility. Those who can sway emotions ought to know what they are talking about, lest emotions be swayed towards foolishness.[106]

> But [*JFK*] is not parody,[107] and it is not funny. It could spoil a generation of American politics just when sanity is returning.[108]

> And it is the business of those who do care about the future generations, to worry, if they wish, about how Stone's legacy is a dose of heightened distrust and paranoia.[109]

> The children of the video age get their information more from images than from words. They tend to believe uncritically what they see... They'll swallow *JFK* whole. Society cannot police art for inaccuracies; film makers are free to take whatever liberties they wish. But society can denounce bogus history—and study honest his-

---

106 John Margolis, in Stone and Sklar, 189.

107 This is incorrect; *JFK* can be very easily read as a carnivalesque inversion of a Frank Capra film.

108 Daniel Patrick Moynihan, ibid, 331. The film was released in December 1991, so presumably the return of political sanity refers to the presidential election of Bill Clinton.

109 *Chicago Sun-Times*, in ibid, 332.

tory. That means reading, critically. Otherwise, Hollywood becomes the culture's historian by default.[110]

The rancor over *JFK* arises from around the realization that historical lies are nearly impossible to correct once movies and television have given them credibility.[111]

Although many in the media have lambasted the movie as a travesty of history...many moviegoers probably will not read their critiques, and the movie version is likely to become their reality. Numerous studies show that when people have no independent information on a subject...a mention in the media is more likely to be powerful, more likely to be remembered and more likely to be influential.[112]

In an age when most young Americans have no sense of history or geography and don't like to read much, there is the real potential that Oliver Stone's spine-tingling mythopoetic [sic] of John Kennedy's tragic death will replace the Warren Commission as the next popular perception.[113]

One of the most insightful responses to this avalanche of panicked bile was that offered by Bob Katz, channeling the spirit of Berlusconi a full ten years before the actual event.

Who but an ivory-tower pedant still believes in the primacy of 'facts'? The so-called facts are as

---

110 Brent Staples, in ibid, 312.
111 Brent Staples cited by Edward S. Herman, in ibid, 450.
112 Katharine Seelye, 373.
113 Robert Hennelly, in ibid, 415.

> susceptible to the sleek techniques of promotion and spin control as the new Infiniti or candidate Dan Quayle. Our Age of Innocence with respect to the truth is over; history will be whatever the majority of people—and our proxy, the viewing public—chooses to believe. Lacking all faith in our ability to discover truth, we raise our hands in abject surrender to await polling results.[114]

The 'truth' of our post-modern condition ('the children of the video age') is not that no one is able to differentiate between truth and falsehood; it is, rather, that everyone has been traumatized by the omnipresence of simulation and simulacra. Therefore, by default, 'truth' becomes reduced to a commodity, the value of reality validated not by an objectivist epistemology but by the economic imperative of the un-decidability of a subjectivist freedom of consumer choice. The crisis of the post-modern condition is not one of perception, but of value; not the nature of Reality but the (exchange-) value of Truth. It is quite true, as Debord indicates, that 'Spectacular domination's first priority was to eradicate historical knowledge in general; beginning with just about all rational information and commentary on the most recent past.'[115] But it is also and equally true that 'the reign of the perpetual present'[116] becomes our historically 'correct' domain of reference through the valorization of life-as-freedom-of-choice. The authentic grounds of the moral panic within the anti-Stone media campaign is not that *JFK* 'distorts' the truth of Dealey Plaza in any significant (long-lasting) way, but that it

114 Bob Katz, in ibid, 280.

115 Debord, *Comments*, 13-14.

116 'As much as any single feature, Debord sees the core of the spectacle as the annihilation of historical knowledge—in particular the destruction of the recent past. In its place is the reign of a perpetual present.' Crary, 463.

demonstrates how easily a possible deep event can be transformed into, and commodified as, 'entertainment'. The capacity of the film for disinformation, even if wholly unintentional, is directly proportionate to the extent of its embedding within the circulatory capillaries of the mass media.

> The prospect that an issue deep and dear will be adjudicated by the carnival barkers of Tinseltown is indeed troubling...The unsolved murder of the century has entered the realm of myth...History as defined by box-office returns may strike many as a deplorable development, but we have been heading in that direction a long, long time.[117]

And, of course, as Jameson well understood, the seductive appeal of 'being in the know' (or counting oneself as 'hip' to use James Ellroy's terminology, a neo-noir crime writer who is acutely aware of the drawing power of voyeuristic occultism) is identical with the 'promise of a deeper inside view [that] is the hermeneutic content of the conspiracy thriller in general...'[118] DeLillo makes exactly the same point through the mouth of the perennially hapless Nicholas Branch.

> If we are on the outside, we assume a conspiracy is the perfect working of a scheme. Silent nameless men with unadorned hearts. A conspiracy is everything that ordinary life is not. It's the inside game, cold, sure, undistracted, forever closed off to us. We are the flawed ones, the innocents, trying to make some rough sense of the daily jostle. Conspirators have a logic and a daring beyond our reach. All conspiracies are the same taut story of

---

117 Bob Katz, in Stone and Sklar, 281.
118 Jameson, 15.

men who find coherence in some criminal act.[119]

As Jameson further demonstrates, the entirety of the historical weight assigned to Dealey Plaza (including this book that you are reading) rests upon the labyrinthine overlapping between JFK and the Press, especially television journalism.

> [W]hat ensured the well-nigh permanent association of assassination in general with this particular historical one was the experience of the media, which for the first time and uniquely in its history bound together an enormous collectivity over several days and vouchsafed a glimpse into a Utopian public sphere of the future which remained unrealized...henceforth assassination and the question of the media are representationally related and mutually implicit (in ways in which they were not in popular or collective representations of Sarajevo, for example, or of Lincoln's death).[120]

The real aesthetic paradox of *JFK*, that ultimately undermines the film's claim to serious cinematic art, rests with its stylistic incoherence that is a direct result of a skewed attempt to unify two inherently incompatible literary and filmic genres: the crime story and the detective story. The basic pattern of the detective film, in stark contrast to the crime film which radically relativizes both Truth and the World, is the *search*.

> These tales have... 'goal-oriented plots', patterns of action to which investigation is key. Mysteries and detective films often mete out clues in small, progressive portions, so that the viewer's process

---

119 DeLillo, 440.
120 Jameson, 47-8.

of discovery parallels the investigator's. Sometimes...they conceal the object of the search, such
as the villain's identity, as long as possible...At
other times the goal of the search is clear from the
start, and the investigator's job is to find the thing
that is missing.[121]

The epistemological frame of the detective film is a
strictly representational theory of language, yielding a
hero-protagonist who reassures 'us of an ultimate rationality, "a benevolent and knowable universe," "a world
that can be interpreted by human reason, embodied in
the superior intellect of the detective"...The detective's
skill is precisely the ability to code "seemingly unrelated
data into a coherent system of signs, a text identifying
the malefactor."'[122] Therefore, the function of the detective hero 'is to guarantee the readers' absolution from
guilt. This is basic to the genres' wish fulfillment...What
matters is the detective's revelation, not the murderers'
punishment, for in this myth of rationality truth takes
priority over justice.'[123] If the detective film has a philosophical prejudice, it is *naïve realism*, 'the tendency to
believe that oneself always sees and responds to the
world objectively, and thus when others do not agree, it
is because their cognitions or behaviors are not based on
reality.'[124]

JFK's fatal flaw, and Stone's lethal conceit, is that the
film aspires to be a post-modernist detective story; its almost operatic deployment of the pseudo-documentary
technique subliminally asserts itself as objectively factual, and, therefore, as historically accurate. Yet, its entire

---

121 Rafter, 190.
122 Tony Hilfer, cited in Sherwin, 48.
123 Tony Hilfer, cited in ibid, 52 fn. 49.
124 Manwell, 863.

content, both substantive and stylistic, clearly marks it as a crime film; the *text* of *JFK* is the detective story, while the *sub-text* is the noir tale of criminality. In many ways, *JFK* resembles the seminal 'true crime' but post-modernist documentary by Errol Morris, *The Thin Blue Line* (1988) which concerns the false conviction of an apparently innocent man for the killing of a Texas highway patrolman; both films suffer from the same stylistic incoherence through the self-undermining fusion of post-modernist film making with a strictly modernist epistemology and morality. Richard C. Sherwin has provided some exceptionally insightful criticism of Morris' work.

> But on an allegorical level, the film depicts a battle that rages back and forth, moment by moment, across a thin blue line of representational order. It is a battle against chaos, fate, and deception, forces that could easily destroy human agency and makes individual responsibility impossible. Metaphorically, the film asks a fundamental and daring question: Who (or what) polices meaning? It is a daring question that Morris does not quite see through. For in the end, the [post-modern] counterplot does not take hold.[125]

'In Morris' film the truth is knowable'[126] ; yet the cinematic 'tension' within the film that Sherwin rightly identifies is precisely the incommensurability between the detective and the crime genres. *The Thin Blue Line*'s

> [P]arodic, post-modern, self-conscious images are eventually overwhelmed by the linear detective plot. The viewer resists the invitation to find problems in the film's linear plot. We refuse to entertain the possibility that the purported 'docu-

125 Sherwin, 64.
126 David Denby, cited in ibid, 53 fn. 53.

mentary' nature of the film is itself merely another dramatic re-enactment. We reject the parody
and prefer to play it straight.[127]

Why does the text, in the end, overwhelm the sub-text?
Here the moral and epistemic relativism (or the 'im-
morality') of post-modernism is thwarted by the political
morality (and moralism) of the legal drama: the discovery of Truth and the triumphant elevation of Innocence.
The sub-text/counter-plot 'fails in the same way that
skeptical post-modernism is likely to fail in law and
lawyering generally.'

> In a legal context, the reality that it portrays is
> aesthetically and psychologically untenable. In
> matters of life and death, whether it be the execu-
> tion of the accused or the possibility of his killing
> again, we instinctively reject the message of skep-
> tical post-modernism. Human traits like prejudice,
> deceit, greed, abuse of power, and the reality of a
> deliberate frame-up are things we can understand.
> But mystification, time's circularity, fate, and co-
> incidence defeat the practical demands of human
> judgment.[128]

Which is, of course, absolutely no problem for DeLillo,
whose conspiracy text faithfully abides by the narrative
requirements of the crime genre, albeit in extreme form.
But it proves artistically fatal for Morris, as it does for
Stone, who is also excavating the truth concerning a
murder in Texas.

> Chaos is disorienting and unpleasant, especially
> in matters of life and death. Decisions of such
> consequence are no time for epistemological

127 Ibid, 70.
128 Ibid.

> conundrums or aesthetic musings. Thus, once
> nestled in the sobering frame of a criminal trial,
> storytelling fictions such as Morris' self-con-
> sciously cartoonish images and their playful inter-
> ference with the linear documentary have a boom-
> erang effect. These caricatures of reality only
> send us running back to the 'truer' reality, the
> reality that the linear plot alone is able to provide.
> Faced with untenable disorder on the one hand,
> and a meaningful drama on the other, there is no
> choice.[129]

Sherwin's final judgment of *The Thin Blue Line*—that its 'aesthetic and psychological failures offer a cautionary lesson about the art of persuasive legal story-telling: the law has little use for the kind of skeptical, radically sub-versive post-modernism that has been featured of late in some legal and much non-legal scholarship'[130]—can equally be levelled against *JFK*, although within a slightly different aesthetic context. Although Morris de-tails a conspiracy, it would be doing violence to Jame-son's terminology to classify *The Thin Blue Line* as a conspiracy text. Stone's film, however, is gloriously so and, as a narrative of a wounded survivor's account of a traumatic encounter with a deep event, must comply with the aesthetic directives concerning the re-presenta-tion of the grotesque. But the internal incoherence ex-hibited by *The Thin Blue Line* is doubled in the case of *JFK*: the incompatibility of Truth with Relativism is compounded by the irreconcilability of two views of the grotesque violently forced into a single but dis-unified narrative: 'the grotesque as the estranged world' ('It is our world which has to be transformed. Suddenness and surprise are essential elements of the grotesque') and the

---

129 Ibid, 71.
130 Ibid.

grotesque 'as an Attempt to Invoke and Subdue the Demonic Aspects of the World' ('In spite of all the helplessness and horror inspired by the dark forces which
lurk in and behind our world and have the power to estrange it, the truly artistic portrayal effects a secret liberation. The darkness has been sighted, the ominous
powers discovered, the incomprehensible forces challenged').

The first issue that must be dealt with, then, is the
problem of Stone's undigested post-modernist (self-) re-
flexivity. In part, *JFK*'s aesthetic incoherence is not just
due to Stone but to the nature of the original spectacle itself—the televised nature of the event(s) and the penetration of Dallas by the audio-visual, not least Abraham
Zapruder's spectacular 8mm home movie[131] and the trau-

---

131 Cultural material of clearly dubious value; when viewed for the very
first time without preconception one realizes immediately that this
'proof' provides no certainty as to the number, rate, or direction of shots
fired. Even worse, the notorious 'head splatter' frames allow for no clear
determination of the bullet's trajectory; when I saw the film for the first
time (while watching *JFK*), my initial impression was that Kennedy had
been shot from the front but from the *left*, not from the grassy knoll
which was to his right. I believe that the greatest forensic value of the
film is that it strongly hints at a discernible time gap between President
Kennedy's throat shot and Governor Connally's back shot. The film
indicates that Kennedy was shot through the throat no sooner than at
frame 210 and Connally shot through the shoulder/back at no later than
frame 240, a time gap of close to two seconds; the 'single-bullet theory'
offered by the Warren Commission, which establishes Oswald as the lone
gunman, requires that the bullet that exited Kennedy's throat entered
Connally's shoulder. In any event, the absolute earliest that Connally
could have been shot at was at frame 207; most likely he was shot at
some point between frames 207 to 225. Given that the muzzle velocity of
the sniper's bullet was 2200 feet per second, and that it would have
entered Kennedy's body at 2000 feet per second and exited Kennedy's
body at 1900 feet per second, both Kennedy and Connally would have
had to have been shot simultaneously—a time gap of anything above the
infinitesimal is troubling. If we place Kennedy's neck wound at frame
210 and Connally's shoulder wound at 225, this is a difference of 15
frames—well short of simultaneous. In the alternative, if we abandon the

matic on-air assassination of Oswald by Jack Ruby, was ideal stimulus to the post-modern imagination. Making things worse was the narrative unreliability of the official version, the Warren Commission Report, an unstable admixture of disclosure and cover up; as Todd Gitlin has argued, the 'more corrupt the public language, the more people want the luxury of suspending disbelief. For all our post-modern sensibilities, our everyday cynicism, we want to believe there remains a truth that hasn't been re-touched. Curiously, no one believes in truth like a person surrounded by liars.'[132]

> Those who are enraged at Oliver Stone's film
> *JFK* for its heavily fictionalized blending of various assassination theories are missing the point.
> As Stone has apparently grasped in his blockhead populist way, the JFK killing has been fiction for a long time. It is the creation myth we use to understand the discords of contemporary America: the tale of the fall from grace, for which we keep vainly seeking redemption. If it hadn't happened, we would have had to invent it... But it was on that autumn day in Dallas that post-modernism came here to roost. Dallas seemed like a magic trick, or the culmination of some elaborate practical joke; it traumatized us because we couldn't figure out how it worked. We still feel that if we go through it one more time we'll see the concealed wires leading to the book depository window, spot the clown on the grassy knoll, decode

---

single bullet, this means that Oswald would have had to re-cycle, aim and fire his weapon and then actually hit both Connally and Kennedy with separate shots in under a maximum time of two seconds, a physical impossibility. Shenon, 254 and 262-71. Although he publicly endorsed the findings of the Warren Commission, until the end of his life Connally maintained that he was hit by a separate shot; he also insisted that only three shots were fired and that they all came from the rear. Ibid, 270-5.

132 Todd Gitlin, in Stone and Sklar, 454.

the umbrella man's secret message. But it's still
the same stale pie in our face, all over again.[133]

But the turbulent waters of Dallas are only roiled further
by Stone's own auteur-like conceit, a manifestation of
his narcissistic self-identification as Jim Garrison's real
life double. Over the years Stone's own self-commentary
on *JFK* has proven voluminous, running every known
rhetorical position imaginable, from the pejorative to the
self-exculpatory. Here is Stone on the post-modernist nature of History.

> What is history? Some people say it's a bunch of
> gossip made up by soldiers who passed it around
> a campfire. They say such and such happened.
> They create. They make it bigger, they make it
> better. I knew guys in combat who made up shit.
> I'm sure the cowboys did the same. The nature of
> human beings is that they exaggerate. So, what is
> history? Who the fuck knows?[134]

Next is Stone on History as Trauma.

> The murder of President Kennedy was a seminal
> event for me and for millions of Americans. It
> changed the course of history. It was a crushing
> blow to our country and to millions of people
> around the world. It put an abrupt end to a period
> of innocence and great idealism.[135]

Finally, there is Stone on History as Myth.

> Unlike children's fairy tales, myths have always
> expressed the true inner meaning of human
> events. Myths are dynamic. They reinterpret his-

133 Andrew O'Heir, in ibid, 270-1.
134 Oliver Stone cited by Robert Sam Anson, in ibid, 208.
135 Oliver Stone, in ibid, 199.

> tory in order to create lasting, universal truths. For example, artists for centuries have tackled exactly the same historical and religious stories and produced a Christ with a thousand faces. From Griffith to Kubrick, moviemakers have operated on the principle that the dramatic force of story transcends the 'facts'. With *JFK*, we are attempting to film the true inner meaning of the Dallas labyrinth —the mythical and spiritual dimension of Kennedy's murder—to help us understand why the shots in Dealey Plaza still continue to reverberate in our nightmares.[136]

The personal trauma undergone by Stone while in Vietnam is self-servingly repeated by Jim Garrison in a scene that was deleted from the theatrical release.

> Jim: Just think…just think. What happened to our country…to the world…because of that murder… Vietnam, racial conflict, breakdown of law, drugs, thought control, assassinations, secret government, fear of the frontier…[137]

By this time it should be obvious to even the most casual viewer that *JFK* actually works as a cinematically splendid act of *gossip*—both in high and low places. Stone, like Morris, chaotically mixes fragmentary truths into the narrative structure of the epic, resulting in the hyperinflation of (crypto-documentary) reality, now re-presented as an un-true Truth ('we are attempting to film the true inner meaning of the Dallas labyrinth') that fortuitously is identical with Myth ('the mythical and spiritual dimension of Kennedy's murder'). This reaches its epitome (epiphany?) in Jim Garrison's seemingly interminable summation to the jury of the Clay Shaw trial—

---

136 Oliver Stone, in ibid, 356.
137 Stone and Sklar, 183.

not only is this one of the longest monologues in the history of film, it is also marred by the pummeling, or 'bullet-like', nature of Kevin Costner's delivery.

> **Jim:** The President was murdered by a conspiracy planned in advance at the highest levels of the United States government and carried out by fanatical and disciplined Cold Warriors in the Pentagon and CIA's covert operation apparatus—among them Clay Shaw before you. It was a public execution, and it was covered up by like-minded individuals in the Dallas Police Department, the Secret Service, the FBI, and the White House—all the way up to and including J. Edgar Hoover and Lyndon Johnson, whom I consider to be accomplices after the fact.[138]

According to Stone, 'Contradictions are the nature of reality.'[139] In his discussions of *JFK* over the years, he has made occasional reference to Akira Kurosawa's masterpiece *Rashomon* (1950), that supremely artful presentation of four inherently incompatible but equally persuasive accounts of a single event, a murder. What Stone seems to have forgotten is that a film narrative such as Kurosawa's *requires* the unmediated juxtaposition of the conflicting narratives and antagonistic voices of the diverse witnesses—precisely what *JFK* fails to provide. Instead, *JFK* is *aletheia* (the detective story), the uncovering of a concealed truth which, like the infamous 'magic bullet', remains inexplicably pristine. Stone's self-proclaimed (and mass marketed) filmic capture and faithful reproduction of the 'inner meaning' of Dallas is, through his bombastic cinematic vehicle, irreversibly transformed into spectacle. And, quite suitable

---

138 Ibid, 177-8.
139 Stone in ibid, 200.

for Stone's own purposes, the moral panic of the journalistic establishment (whether they were following CIA directives or not), because they were circulated as part of the 'media event', passively collude with that self-same spectacle, tantamount to a form of disinformation.

But perhaps the greatest artistic 'give away' of *JFK* is the one narrative technique that has drawn the most ire not only of media pundits but conspiracy researchers—the hyper-inflation of the size, scope and complexity of the conspiratorial machinery. On the one hand, the density of the evil plot (or the vast breadth of the grotesque landscape) is simply a by-product of naïve realism—the cover up has been so extensive the now unconcealed truth must be of commensurate magnitude.[140] More perniciously, the bogus erudition displayed by the director is nothing more than a calculated sensory bombardment designed to blot out any realization in the mind of the audience that Stone is nothing more than the huckster purveyor of conspiracy gossip. Debord appreciated very well the underhanded intent of information overload: 'There is a contradiction between the mass of information collected on a growing number of individuals, and the time and intelligence available to analyze it, not to mention its actual interest.'[141] At times Stone even appears to be partially conscious of his own onanistic gamesmanship; this may explain his decision to (merci-

---

140 Curiously Stone's technique of cinematic hyper-inflation ironically parallels Jim Garrison's judicial one. 'Some of his staff became alarmed about his behavior. He would call meetings, then disappear into the men's room for a while, emerge with a new theory and send aids to try to prove it.' Kenneth Auchincloss, Ginny Carroll, and Maggie Malone, in ibid, 293. For a compelling critique of Garrison, see James O'Byrne, in ibid, 234-40.

141 Debord, *Comments*, 81. Perhaps Stone's key error is that he conflates Phase I of JFK/DALLAS with Phase II; if we assume that the killers were also the liars, then conspiratorial overload necessarily results.

fully) cut the scene of Jim Garrison being interviewed on the 'Jerry Johnson Show', a thinly fictionalized re-staging of Garrison's notorious interview with Johnny Carson on 'The Tonight Show', January 31, 1968.

> **Johnson**: First we had your charge that the Cuban exiles killed the President, then the Mob, then you said the oil billionaires did it, then you said the Minutemen and the Ku Klux Klan collaborated to do it, now with your latest theory seems to be that the CIA and the FBI and the Pentagon and the White House all combined in some elaborate conspiracy to kill John Kennedy. Let me ask you, is there anyone besides Lee Harvey Oswald who you think did not conspire to kill the President?[142]

What we may hold to be 'disinformation by accident' is also clearly present in another deleted scene, where Lyndon Johnson is personally issuing commands to the Dallas Police Department.

> [Director's Notes] *At the Dallas police station, Dallas Police Captain Will Fritz takes a call from a high official in Washington. In the background we notice Lee Oswald continuing to be questioned by federal agents. We hear Johnson's distinctive Texas drawl but we never see him.*

> **Jim** *(voice over)*: No legal counsel is provided. No record made of the long questioning.

> **High Official voice**: Howdy there, Cap'n. Thanks for taking care of us down there in Dallas. Lady-bird and I will always be grateful.

> **Fritz**: Thank you, Mr. President. We're doing our

---

142 Stone and Sklar, 142.

best.

> **High Official voice:** Cap'n, I know you're work-
> ing like a hound-dog down there to get this mess
> wrapped up, but I gotta tell you there's too much
> confusion coming out of Dallas now. The TVs
> and the papers are full of rumor 'bout conspir-
> acies.[143] Two gunmen, two rifles, the Russkies
> done it, the Cubans done it, that kinda loose talk,
> its scarin' the shit outta people, bubba'. This thing
> could lead us into a war that could cost 40 million
> lives. We got to show 'em we got this thing under
> control. No question, no doubt, for the good of
> our country…you hear me?

> **Fritz:** Yes, sir.

> **High Official voice:** Cap'n, you got your man,
> the investigation's over, that's what people want
> to hear.

> [Author's Notes: *Call to Capn. Fritz. Dallas Po-*
> *lice Chief Jesse Curry told the Warren Commis-*
> *sion: '…nobody would tell me exactly who it was*
> *that was insisting "just say I got a call from*
> *Washington and they wanted this evidence up*
> *there," insinuated it was someone in high author-*
> *ity that was requesting this.'* [WC 4H, p. 195]

---

143 Significantly, the first of the Oswald-as-Communist-agent conspiracy
theories that began appearing in the *Washington Post* on the morning of
November 23 were all floated by the DRE, operating under Phillip's
oversight. Morley, 207 and 212. This was not the DRE's first attempt to
manipulate public opinion as part of an effort to incite a U.S. invasion. In
late October 1962, the *Washington Star* printed a headline story 'Exiles
Tell of Missiles Hidden in Cuban Caves/Refugees Give Location of 7
Camouflaged Sites for Rockets', indicating that the Russians had left
some nuclear missiles behind in Cuba; the 'Exiles' were members of the
DRE and the writer of the article was Jerry O'Leary Jr, a CIA asset and a
very close friend of David Phillips. Morley, 142-3.

[Marr, Crossfire, p.357. Penn Jones, Jr., Forgive
My Grief III, p. 101.] *KXAS reporter Bob Sirkin
claims to have discussed this episode with Cap-
tain Fritz himself. Shortly before Fritz's death,
Sirkin asked him to go public with the story but
Fritz declined.]*[144]

And it is disinformation that underlies the central story
arc of the film: the transposition of conspiratorial intent
from Cuba to Vietnam, which narratively requires the
existence of a sublimely vast but wholly invisible clandestine apparatus. An avowed Kennedy-phile, we can
easily understand Stone's motive in inverting the ambiguous and contested historical record concerning
NSAM-273: the death of JFK as the failure of the Sons
of Light in their contest against the demonic aspect of
the world symbolized by Vietnam flows seductively into
the myth-poetic grandeur that provides *JFK* with its
stunning dramatic power. It is also a remarkably hagio-
graphic way of ennobling Kennedy's gory murder ('a
ghastly pink cloud of bone, blood, and brains...'[145])—
being killed for having attempted to pre-empt the Vietnam War is glorious; being executed for failing to assassinate Castro merely makes one the 'patsy' of
gangsters.[146] This transposition takes place in three distinct stages. The first is the announcement of the false-
flag.

---

144 Ibid, 175.

145 Morley, 204.

146 See Russo, generally. Another personal anecdote if I may: my first
thought after exiting the theatre in Hollywood that was showing *JFK* in
December 1991 was that Stone should have done a straight adaptation of
DeLillo's *LIBRA*. In fact, it appears that Stone successfully campaigned
to stop the production of such a film, telling the assigned director Phil
Joanou that "'my film's more cinematic than yours.'" Robert Sam Anson
in ibid, 219-20.

FLASHBACK to David Ferrie's apartment

> Ferrie [Joe Pesci]: It won't be long, mark my
> words. That fucker'll get what's comin' to him.
> And it can be blamed on Castro. Then, the whole
> country'll want to invade Cuba. All we got to do
> is to get Kennedy out in the open.[147]

The second is when the false flag is inverted; this takes
place in a scene between FBI agent 'Frank' (Wayne Tip-
pit) and Garrison investigator Bill Broussard (Michael
Rooker).

> Frank: Look, we know Oswald didn't pull that
> trigger. Castro did. But if that comes out, there's
> gonna be a war, boy—millions of people are
> gonna die. That's a hell of a lot more important
> than Jim Garrison. [*Suddenly*] Godammit, look at
> me when I talk to you. You're too goddam self-
> opinionated, now *shut up*. If you got a brain in
> your thick skull of yours, listen to me. Listen real
> hard.[148]

The third, the uncovering of Vietnam-as-Truth occurs in
two separate scenes with 'Colonel X' (Donald Suther-
land), who is supposed to be Colonel Fletcher Prouty. In
the original screenplay, this scene, the narrative crux of
the film, was divided into two parts, the first half at the
exact mid-point, the second half serving as the conclusion—and which also delivered the 'big payoff', by revealing the identity of the mastermind of Dealey Plaza,
'General Y': Edward G. Lansdale, the nominal head of
OPERATION MONGOOSE (which was actually being
run by Robert Kennedy).

---

147 Stone and Sklar, 70.
148 Ibid, 105.

COLONEL X, PART ONE

> X: That's the real question isn't it—'Why?'—the
> 'how' is just the 'scenery' for the suckers...Os-
> wald, Ruby, Cuba, Mafia, it keeps people guess-
> ing like a parlor game,[149] but it prevents them
> from asking the most important question—Why?
> Why was Kennedy killed? Who benefitted? Who
> has the power to cover it up?[150]

COLONEL X, PART TWO

> X: I think it started in the wind. Money—arms,
> big oil, Pentagon people, contractors, bankers,
> politicians like LBJ were committed to a war in
> Southeast Asia. As early as '61[151] they knew
> Kennedy was going to change things...He was
> not going to war in Southeast Asia.[152]

NOTE: in the original screenplay, the following scene
was the end of the film; in the theatrical release, it was
moved towards the middle of Garrison's summation to
the jury.

> [Director's Notes] *FLASHBACK TO the White
> House, 1963. Johnson sits across the shadowed
> room with* [US ambassador to Vietnam Henry
> Cabot Lodge] *and others. His Texas drawl rises
> and falls. He signs something unseen* [NSAM-

---

149 Note the deliberate downplaying of the Cuba Project the closer we
   move to the final revelation.

150 Ibid, 110.

151 Presumably an oblique reference to NSAMs 56 and 57 and Kennedy's
   unwavering commitment to counter-insurgency warfare in neo-colonial
   struggles. See above, Chapter Two.

152 Ibid, 180.

273]

Johnson [Tom Howard and John William Galt]:
Gentlemen, I want you to know I'm not going to
let Vietnam go the way Cuba did. I'm personally
committed. I'm not going to take one soldier out
of there 'til they know we mean business in
Asia... *(he pauses)* You just get me elected, and
I'll give you your damned war.

X (voice over): ...and that was the day Vietnam
started.

*CUT TO Documentary footage of—US Marines
arriving in full force on the beaches of Danang,
March 8, 1965...as another era begins and our
movie ends.*[153]

These two scenes, when combined with the deleted
Johnson scene, yield Stone's most brazen conceit: all of
the speculation concerning Cuba and the false-flag is itself a higher form of disinformation, skillfully manipulated by the conspirators of *both* Phase I and Phase II to
disguise Vietnam as the true purpose of JFK/DALLAS
that much more effectively—so effectively, in fact, as to
be virtually untraceable within the historical record. But
the worst is yet to come.

Just before the Final Credits, this dedication:

*DEDICATED TO THE YOUNG,
IN WHOSE SPIRIT THE SEARCH FOR TRUTH
MARCHES ON.*

As Jim Garrison says elsewhere in the film, '...about as
subtle as a cockroach crawling across a white rug.'[154]

---

153 Ibid, 183 and 184.
154 Ibid, 73.

'WHAT'S THE DOPE ON THE WATERGATE?':
ALL THE PRESIDENT'S MEN

'Garage freak? Jesus, what kind of a crazy
fucking story is this?'—Ben Bradlee (Jason
Robards), *All the President's Men*

Artistically superior to *JFK* in almost every way, Alan J.
Pakula's film adaptation of the Bernstein and Woodward
(aka, 'Woodstein') book *All The President's* Men (1976;
Warner Brothers[155]) succeeds where Stone's epic fails
precisely because it deliberately maintains narrative con-
sistency with the onto-epistemological requirements of
the detective story. Although Robert Redford, the producer and lead actor of the film, instantly recognized the
story's quality as a detective thriller, it is Jameson, in his
incisive discussion of the movie, who makes the essential aesthetic observation: the 'detective story presupposes an absolute distinction between the story of the crime
and the story of its resolution: here the distance between
the two has been reduced to an absolute minimum by the
positing of a "crime" as informational and media-cen-
tered as its own solution.'[156] In clear compliance with
Jameson's requirements for the conspiracy text, *All the
President's Men* ostensibly treats with the same forms of
the grotesque as does *JFK*: 'the grotesque as the estranged world' and the grotesque as 'an Attempt to Invoke and Subdue the Demonic Aspects of the World'.
But the film's slide into the realm of spectacle (and dis-

---

155 All of my references to the film version are taken directly from the
Two-Disc Special Edition released in 1976, including several
documentaries about the making of the film and a scene-by-scene voice-
over version with commentary by producer and lead actor Robert
Redford.

156 Jameson, 68.

information) is equal to that of Stone's Wagnerian cinematic bombast, even though it takes place on a more refined level and operates in a far more subtle way: namely, through the transition from book to film, or, in this case, from film to book. As historical fact, it was Redford himself who convinced Woodward and Bernstein to write the book from their own perspective ('two young journalists fighting to uncover the truth') as opposed to their original idea which was to deal with the effects of the unfolding of the Watergate scandal on the White House). Not only was the book version of *All the President's Men* self-consciously framed in terms of cinematic genre(s) prior to its initial production, it was deliberately written with anticipation of the future screenplay (by William Goldman) in mind—in effect, a movie tie-in before the fact.[157] In other words, the alleged 'truth' of the official version of the journalistic investigation, which I have already shown to be almost certainly falsified in many vital respects,[158] is doubly compromised by the self-referential (and narcissistic) need to recast the real-life story in terms of film narrative. Take for example the beat-cop like delivery of the voice-over for the theatrical promo.

> *The story of the two young reporters who broke the Watergate conspiracy...They tripped over clues. And piece by piece they solved the greatest detective story in American history.*

Compare this with Redford's explanation for one of the defining and powerful visual conceits of the film, periodic long shots and aerial views that draw our attention to smaller foreground characters who are always visual-

---

157 The resultant book, *All the President's Men*, even provides a Hollywood style 'Cast of Characters'. Bernstein and Woodward, 9-11.

158 See above, Chapter Four.

ly juxtaposed against a monumentalist architecture/ urban landscape[159]: 'To contrast the hard work they [Woodstein] were doing, way, way, way down at the bottom of things, against the State, the city, even the administration...'. Now compare this with Woodstein's self-portrait of Woodward in the opening scene of the book version.

> Woodward had worked for the *Post* for only nine months, and was always looking for a good Saturday assignment, but this didn't sound like one. A burglary at the local Democratic headquarters was too much like most of what he had been doing—investigative pieces on unsanitary restaurants and small-time police corruption. Woodward had hoped he had broken out of that; he had just finished a series of stories on the attempted assassination of Alabama Governor George Wallace. Now, it seemed, he was back in the same old slot.[160]

Without batting an eye, and apparently impervious to irony, Ben Bradlee holds forth on Woodstein's investigative journalism: 'It's the longest shot I've ever seen in journalism.' Which is my point exactly: it was such a long shot that it could not actually be one. A double layer of disinformation now comes into view: not only do Woodstein dissemble in order to conceal their own clandestine activities—*All the President's Men* was a counter-conspiracy (uncover the cover-up) of an antecedent conspiracy (the cover-up) which was itself a conspiratorial act undertaken in reaction to an even earlier conspir-

---

159 Monumentalism may be usefully defined as the architectonic expression of the will-to-totality.

160 Ibid, 13. Given the involvement of both Coulson and Hunt with Bremer and the possible status of the Wallace shooting as a deep event, this might be a more significant admission than has been previously realized.

acy (the sabotaged burglary, which although classified as a failure was really a success)—but their concealment conforms to the dramatic and narrative requirements of Tinseltown, which, precisely because they are cinematic, acquire a greater veracity through strict compliance with the movie-goers' expectations of the expose film as 'truth.' Jameson has elaborated on this unrecognized 'double movement' brilliantly.

> But the originality of *All the President's Men* is to have staged its chain of events virtually from the outset as the struggle between two conspiracies, two collectivities, two supra-personal organizations; the plumbers versus the newspaper: the White House versus the *Washington Post*; the voices on the telephone versus the in principle equally disembodied voice of 'Deep Throat'; the amoral arrogance of the Nixon officials versus the equally brutal and ruthless determination and ambition of the young reporters.[161]

This is clearly demonstrated by the striking visuality of the newsroom of *The Washington Post*, the only set in the film that is fully lit; Jameson deduces (probably correctly) that Pakula thinks that 'the *Post*'s openness and harsh fluorescent lighting is the sign of Truth itself and everything uncomfortable about it: actually, its light is fully as unnatural as the darkness, and is also in some sense a replay and an unfolding of the primal offices at the Watergate with which we began.'[162]

---

161 Jameson, 67.

162 Ibid, 75. To the best of my knowledge, no critic of the film, including Jameson, has drawn any attention to what is for me one of the most striking features of many of the scenes in the film: the prominence given to framed portraits or paintings, most notably the centrally placed presidential photograph of John F. Kennedy in Democratic Party Headquarters. These may be visual puns—a double entendre on 'truth' as the framing of a story and the conflicting stories of the warring

The political unconscious of post-modernism, epitomized by the conspiracy text requires the re-working of the triptych of the classical detective thriller (the detective/hero, the criminal/villain and the victim) as *collectivities*.[163] Collectivization of dramatic personae is necessary because all agency in a globalized world-system is corporate. Within this banal materialist observation lies concealed a subversive aesthetic truth that was very much operative in NIXON/WATERGATE—the unfolding of the spectacle of Watergate is identical with the suspension of the possibility of any possible future repetition. The spectacle of Watergate proves the efficacy of the rule of law through the judicial removal of the enemy within, yet the clandestine agency at work was to effect an extra-judicial *coup d'etat*: the highest proof that 'the system works' was the covert appropriation of the system by private agency. On the level of personal agency, the gumshoe-like dogged individualism and beat-cop heroism of the solitary investigators constitutes not a new dawn of investigative journalism but its precise moment of expiration; what stands out to us ,'the children of the video age', in watching this film is the historical *obsolescence* of what Redford freely admits are the 'dramatic weapons' of Woodstein: telephone, type-writer, tele-type, and notebook, all of which become 'stronger' over the course of the film as the investigators approach their goal, but remain objects 'which the hermeneutic of detection at once transforms into traces and signs.'[164] For Jameson, following Walter Benjamin, the dramatic deployment of 'archaic technology' constitutes a primary means of 'signaling the lost and, by now, irrelevant past.'

collectivities as the 'framing' of the other.

163 Ibid, 33-4.

164 Ibid, 76.

> At any rate, it seems clear that, in *All the President's Men*, the representability of this narrative material is somehow deeply related to what is already archaic about it, to what is already secretly no longer actual, what is outmoded and already old-fashioned, whether or not the participants or indeed the first viewers are aware of it. It is as though somehow the film bore on itself in a kind of calibration the rate of the trajectory of its own contents into the distant past, the heroic legendary moment of a vanished medium, the newspaper, a news sensation that was always somehow in its generic nature a fairy tale.[165]

As we should expect, the 'grand moment' of both the book and film version, the union of the dramatic and the clandestine, and the spectacle's victorious collapsing of knowledge into gossip is the handling (framing?) of Deep Throat. According to the promo,

> *It was a plot device worthy of a Cold War spy thriller: a shadowy figure, the keeper of the secrets of a national crime, reveals snippets of information to the man struggling to crack the case. Had Hollywood invented it, no one would have believed it.*

Of course, to a very real degree Hollywood did invent it, even more so if we understand Woodstein to have been writing the first treatment of a screenplay in the form of a journalistic novel. The first reference to Deep Throat in the book version is oblique, almost concealed: 'Woodward called an old friend and sometime source who worked for the federal government and did not like to be called at his office. His friend said hurriedly that the break-in case was going to "heat up," but he wouldn't

---

165 Ibid, 77.

explain and hung up.'[166] Deep Throat is not formally announced in the text until almost fifty pages later.

> Woodward had a source in the Executive Branch who had access to information at CRP [Committee to Re-Elect the President] as well as at the White House. His identity was unknown to anyone else. He could be contacted only on very important occasions. Woodward had promised he would never identify him or his position to anyone. Further, he had agreed never to quote the man, even as an anonymous source. Their discussions would be only to confirm information that he had obtained elsewhere and to add some perspective.[167]

As was more or less faithfully reproduced in the film version, the source, now explicitly identified as Deep Throat, later expresses an interest in an alternative mode of communication; 'At first Woodward and Deep Throat had talked by telephone, but as the tensions of Watergate increased, Deep Throat's nervousness grew. He didn't want to talk on the telephone, but had said they could meet somewhere on occasion.'[168] Woodward's investigative success with Deep Throat prompts a rueful response from Bernstein: 'Back at the office, Woodward went to the rear of the newsroom to call Deep Throat. Bernstein

---

166 Bernstein and Woodward, 23.

167 Ibid. Which leads directly to two of the most egregious examples of disinformation in the book version: in the footnote at 112 we read that 'No dissatisfied FBI agent or CRP employee had ever come to Bernstein or Woodward offering information.'; at 177, an unnamed FBI Agent informs Bernstein that '"We went to everybody involved in the money [the slush fund]...we know that 90 percent of your information comes from the Bureau files. You either see them or someone reads them to you over the phone."'

168 Ibid, 71.

wished he had source like that.'[169] As if by magic, he gets one: the mysterious woman (Delphic Oracle?) known only as 'Z'. Bernstein makes first contact with 'Z'; absolutely no context or background is provided.[170]

> The woman was in a position to have considerable knowledge of the secret activities of the White House and CRP...She refused to be interrogated, and laid down the ground rules: she would point the reporters in the right direction to help them fill in some of the right names in the right places—certain hints, key avenues to pursue. She would answer questions only in the most general way, if at all. Much of what she called her 'message' might seem vague, partly because even she didn't understand things completely, and because the information would be difficult to sort out.[171]

This scene appears almost verbatim in Redford's film, except for the fact that the message is not attributed to 'Z' but to Deep Throat; the depiction of Bernstein's first encounter with 'Z' is transposed in toto to Woodward's first nocturnal (and underwordly) interview with Deep Throat (Hal Holbrook), who, however, is equally oracular to the mysterious woman.

> "Your perseverance has been admirable," she said. "Apply it to what I say."

---

169 Ibid, 76.

170 'The reporters returned to more conventional sources. A few nights later, Bernstein signed a *Post* car out of the office garage and drove to an apartment several miles away. It was about eight o'clock when he knocked on the door. The woman he was looking for answered, but when he told her his name, she did not open the door. She slipped a piece of paper underneath it with her unlisted telephone number written on it. "Call me later this evening," she said, adding "Your articles have been excellent."' Ibid, 211-12.

171 Ibid, 212.

> Bernstein, who had no idea what to expect,
> thought she sounded like some kind of mystic.[172]

A case of camouflage by transposition?

Or as Robert Redford put it, 'Tremendous signs all over the place.'

---

172 Ibid. Even worse for the conspiracy junky, just like the iconic 'Play it again, Sam', the equally iconic 'Follow the money 'is never actually said by anyone, in either the film or the book; the source of the cliche is provided in a statement delivered by yet another nameless lawyer who is an associate of E. Howard Hunt's lawyer, William O. Bitttman: "'The money is the key to this thing."' Ibid, 34.

[Washington: August 9th 1974 | Gerald Ford and Henry
Kissinger. Photo via the US Library of Congress]

6 | Conclusion

*Since the Watergate affair, the media think
they can get away with anything.'*
—Norman Mailer

A nd it is this final thought which may best explain
the dogmatic refusal of the Western literati to collectively withhold recognition of the rationality of the
discourse of parapolitics: if true, then the self-proclaimed 'insiders' ('CBS News reporters can now reveal
that...') are, in fact, just one more sub-set of hapless
stooges, not at all unlike *LIBRA*'s Nicholas Branch.

> When advertising in all its forms aspires to
> provide the entire terrain of social reality, one can
> understand why the judiciary, in its turn, distances
> itself from the political sphere, and from a demo-
> cracy presumed to be the guardian of the old mor-
> al order—to seek out....a new popular legitimacy
> based on its tacit alliance with the mass media.[1]

The reality is that the entire social edifice of the social
authority of journalism as an 'elite profession' is wholly
dependent upon the extreme willingness of its members
to be actively co-opted by the clandestine. 'It must not
be forgotten that every media professional is bound by

1 Virilio, 29.

wages and other rewards and recompenses to a master, and sometimes to several; and that every one of them knows he is dispensable,'[2] as Debord enlightens us; therefore, all 'experts serve the state and the media and only in that way do they achieve their status.'[3] A spectacle, then, within a spectacle: the (somewhat naïve) attempts by the parapolitical scholar (or the radical criminologist) to have the clandestine foundations of the Society of the Spectacle formally declared as 'the truth' merely gives rise to yet another endless loop of self-referential circulation.

> Secrecy dominates this world, and first and foremost as the secret of domination. According to the spectacle, secrecy would only be a necessary exception to the rule of the freely available, abundant information, just as the domination in the integrated spectacle's 'free world' would be restricted to a mere executive body in the service of democracy. But no one really believes the spectacle. How then do spectators accept the existence of secrecy which alone rules out any chance of their running a world whose principal realities they know nothing, in the unlikely event that they were to be asked how to set about it? The fact is that almost no one sees secrecy in its inaccessible purity and its functional universality. Everyone accepts that there are inevitably little areas of secrecy reserved for specialists; as regards things in general, many believe that they are *in on the secret*...Someone [i.e., the professional journalist] who is happy to be given confidential information is hardly likely to criticize it, nor to notice that in all that is confided to him, the principal part of reality is invariably hidden. Thanks to the bene-

2 Ibid, 16.
3 Ibid.

volent protection of his deceivers, he sees a few
more of the cards, false though they may be; he
never learns the rules of the game. Thus he immediately identifies with the manipulators and scorns
an ignorance which in fact he shares...Their only
role is to make domination more respectable, never to make it comprehensible. They are the priv-
ilege of *front-row spectators*, who are stupid
enough to believe they can know something, not
by making use of what is hidden from them, but
by believing what is revealed! [4]

I would like to go beyond even Debord on this final
point—not only do the public 'experts' (falsely) believe
themselves to be in on the secret, in an even more vitally
parapolitical manner, they are collectively unable to conceptualize the almost certain possibility that they are actually *outside* of the hermetically sealed inner circle.

For, if such were shown to be the truth, wherein
would lie their 'expertise'?

§

---

4 Debord, *Comments*, 60-1.

Bibliography

Albarelli, H.P., *A Secret Order: Investigating the High Strangeness and Synchronicity in the JFK Assassination Volume One* (Waterville OR: Trine Day, 2013).

Anderson, Benedict, *Imagined Communities* (London: Verso, 1991).

Andrade, Dale and Conroy, Kenneth, 'The Secret Side of the Tonkin Gulf Incident', *Naval History*, 13(4), 1999 at 27.

Armstrong, John, 'Harvey and Lee: The Case for Two Oswalds, Part I', in DiEugenio and Pease (eds.), 91-112.

Armstrong, John, 'Harvey and Lee: The Case for Two Oswalds, Part II', in DiEugenio and Pease, 113-35.

Bakhtin, Mikhail, *Rabelais and His World*. Translated by Helene Iswolsky (Indiana University Press: Bloomington, 1984).

Bamford, James, *Body of Secrets: How America's NSA and Britain's GCHQ Eavesdrop on the World* (London: Century, 2001).

Bartelson, Jens, *A Genealogy of Sovereignty* (Cambridge. Cambridge University Press, 1995).

Baudrillard, Jean, *The Perfect Crime*. Tran. Chris Turner

(London: Verso, 1996).

Baudrillard, Jean, *Simulations* (New York: Semiotext(e), 1983.

Bell, Jeffry A., *Philosophy at the Edge of Chaos: Gilles Deleuze and the Philosophy of Difference* (Toronto: University of Toronto Press, 2006).

Bernstein, Carl and Woodward, Bob, *All the President's Men* (New York: Simon and Schuster, 1974).

Birchall, Clare, *Knowledge Goes Pop: From Conspiracy to Gossip* (Oxford: Berg, 2006).

Blight, James G. and Kornbluh, Peter (eds.), *Politics of Illusion: The Bay of Pigs Invasion Re-examined* (Boulder CO: Lynne Reiner Publishers: Boulder, 1998).

Bohning, Don, *The Castro Obsession: U.S. Covert Operations Against Cuba, 1959-1965* (Washington, D.C.: Potomac Books, Inc., 2005).

Burnham, Greg, 'Introduction to National Security Action Memorandum Number 273', *JFK Lancer*.

Chtcheglov, Ivan, 'Formulary for a New Urbanism', in *Situationist International Anthology*. Edited and Translated by Ken Knabb. Revised and Expanded Edition (Berkeley: Bureau of Public Secrets, 2006), 1-8.

Chomsky, Noam, *Rethinking Camelot: JFK, the Vietnam War, and US political Culture* (Boston: South End Press, 1993).

Coady, David (ed.), *Conspiracy Theories: The Philosophical Debate* (Aldershot: Ashgate, 2006).

Coatsworth, John H., 'Introduction', in Schlesinger and Kinzer, ix-xx.

Colodny, Len and Gettlin, Robert, *Silent Coup: the Removal of a President* (New York: St. Martin's Press, 1991).

Crary, Jonathan, 'Spectacle, Attention, Counter-Memory', in McDonough (ed.), 455-66.

Cribb, Robert, 'Introduction: Parapolitics, Shadow Governance and Criminal Sovereignty', in Wilson (ed.), *Government of the Shadows*, 1-9.

Cubitt, Sean, *Simulation and Social Theory* (London: Sage Publications, 2001).

Davis, Tracy C., 'Operation Northwoods: The Pentagon's Script for Overthrowing Castro', *The Drama Review*, 50/1 (Spring, 2006), 134-48.

Debord, Guy, *Comments on the Society of the Spectacle* (London: Verso, 1998).

Debord, Guy, *Critique of Separation*, in Ken Knabb (ed. and trans.), *Guy Debord: Complete Cinematic Works Scripts, Stills Documents* (Oakland: AK Press, 2003).

Debord, Guy, 'Report on the Construction of Situations and on the Terms of Organization and Action of the International Situationist Tendency (1957)', in McDonough (ed.), 29-50.

Debord, Guy, *The Society of the Spectacle* (New York: Zone Books, 1995).

Deleuze, Gilles, *Kant's Critical Philosophy*. Trans. Hugh Tomlinson and Barbara Habberjam (New York: Continuum, 2008).

Deleuze, Gilles and Guattari, Felix, *A Thousand Plateaus: Capitalism and Schizophrenia*. Trans. Brian Massumi. London: The Athlone Press. 1988.

DeLillo, Don, *LIBRA* (London: Penguin Books, 1991).

Denno, Deborah W., 'Selected Model Code Provisions'(New York: Fordham University School of Law, Fall 2009).

Derrida, Jacques, *The Truth in Painting*. Trans. Geoff Bennington and Ian McLeod (The University of Chicago Press: Chicago, 1987).

Dietche, Scott M., *The Silent Don: The Criminal Underworld of Santo Trafficante Jr.* (Fort Lee NJ: Barricade Books, 2009).

DiEugenio, James, *Destiny Betrayed: JFK, Cuba, and the Garrison Case* (New York: Sheridan Square Press, 1992).

DiEugenio, James and Pease, Lisa (eds.), *The Assassinations: Probe Magazine on JFK, MLK, RFK and Malcom X* (Los Angeles: Feral House, 2003).

Douglass, James W., *JFK and the Unspeakable: Why he died and Why It Matters* (New York: Orbis Books, 2009).

Escalante, Fabian, *The Cuba Project: CIA Covert Operations 1959-62* (Melbourne: Ocean Press, 2004).

Escalante, Fabian, *JFK: The Cuba Files. The Untold Story of the Plot to Kill Kennedy* (Melbourne: Ocean Press, 2006).

Fursenko, Aleksandr and Naftali, Timothy, *'One Hell of a Gamble': Khrushchev, Castro, Kennedy and the Cuban Missile Crisis, 1958-1964* (London: Pimlico, 1999).

Fonzi, Gaeton, *The Last Investigation* (Ipswich MA: The Mary Ferrell Foundation Press, 2008).

Ford, Simon, *The Situationist International: A User's Guide* (London: Black Dog Publishing, 2005).

Freeman, Lawrence, *Kennedy's Wars: Berlin, Cuba, Laos, and Vietnam* (Oxford: Oxford University Press, 2000).

Fulsom, Don, *Nixon's Darkest Secrets: The Inside Story of America's Most Troubled President* (New York: Thomas Dunne Books, 2012).

Galbraith, James K., 'Exit Strategy: In 1963, JFK Ordered a

Complete Withdrawal From Vietnam', *Boston Review*, October/November 2003, http://bostonreview.net/BR28.5/galbraith.html.

Ganser, Daniele, 'Beyond Democratic Checks and Balances: The "Propaganda Due" Masonic Lodge and the CIA in Italy's First Republic', in Wilson (ed.), *Government of the Shadows*, 256-75.

Garrison, Jim, *On the Trail of Assassins: My Investigation and Prosecution of the Murder of President Kennedy* (London: Penguin Books, 1992).

Gentry, Curt, *J. Edgar Hoover: The Man and the Secrets* (New York: Plume, 1992).

Geuss, Raymond, *History and Illusion in Politics* (Cambridge: Cambridge University Press, 2001).

Ginsborg, Paul, *Silvio Berlusconi: Television, Power and Patrimony.* New eedition (London: Verso Press, 2006).

Gleijeses, Piero, 'Ships in the Night: The CIA, the White House and the Bay of Pig', *Journal of Latin American Studies*, 27 (1995), 1-42.

Haldeman, H.R. and DiMona, Joseph, *The Ends of Power* (New York: Times Books, 1978).

Hancock, Larry, *Someone Would Have Talked: Documented! The Assassination of President John F. Kennedy and the Conspiracy to Mislead History* (Southlake TX: JFK Lancer Productions & Publications, 2006).

Hanyock, Robert J., 'Skunks, Bogies, Silent Hounds and the Flying Fish: The Gulf of Tonkin Mystery, 2-4 August 1964', *Cryptologic Quarterly* (no date), 1-55.

Heidegger, Martin, *Identity and Difference*. Trans. Joan Stambaugh (New York: Harper & Row Publishers, 1969).

Heidegger, Martin, *Parmenides*. Trans. Andre Schuwer and Richard Rojcewicz. (Bloomington: Indiana University Press, 1992).

Hershberg, James G., 'Before "The Missiles of October": Did Kennedy Plan a Military Strike Against Cuba?', *Diplomatic History*, 14/2, (1990), 163-98.

Hinckle, Warren and Turner, William, *Deadly Secrets: The CIA-MAFIA War Against Castro and the Assassination of J.F.K.* (New York: Thunder's Mouth Press, 1992).

Hofstadter, Richard, *The Paranoid Style in American Politics and Other Essays* (London: Jonathan Cape, 1966).

Holland, Max, *Leak: Why Mark Felt Became Deep Throat* (Lawrence, KS: University of Kansas Press, 2012).

Hougan, Jim, *Secret Agenda: Watergate, Deep Throat and the CIA* (New York: Random House, 1984).

Husting, Ginna and Orr, Martin, 'Dangerous Machinery: "Conspiracy Theorist" as a Transpersonal Strategy of Exclusion', *Symbolic Interaction*, 30/2 (Spring 2007), 127-50.

Israel, Jonathan I., *Radical Enlightenment: Philosophy and the Making of Modernity 1650-1750* (Oxford: Oxford University Press, 2001).

Jameson, Frederic, *The Geopolitical Aesthetic: Cinema and Space in the World System* (Indianapolis: Indiana University Press, 1992).

Johnson, Wray R., *Vietnam and American Doctrine for Small Wars* (White Lotus Press: Bangkok, 2001).

Jones, Howard, *Death of a Generation: How the Assassinations of Diem and JFK Prolonged the Vietnam War* (Oxford: Oxford University Press, 2003).

Jones, Tobias, *The Dark Heart of Italy* (London: Faber and Faber, 2003).

Kaiser, David, *American Tragedy: Kennedy, Johnson, and the Origins of the Vietnam War* (Cambridge MA: The Belknap Press, 2000).

Kaiser, David, *The Road to Dallas: The Assassination of John F. Kennedy* (Cambridge MA: The Belknap Press, 2008).

Kant, Immanuel, *The Critique of Judgment*. Trans.J. H. Bernard (Amhers, NY: Prometheus Books, 2000).

Kayser, Wolfgang, *The Grotesque in Art and Literature* (Columbia University Press: New York, 1957).

Kinkle, Jeff, 'The Spectacle and the Partisan', in Wilson (ed.), *The Dual State*, 297-314.

Klein, Naomi, *The Shock Doctrine: the Rise of Disaster Capitalism* (London: Penguin Books, 2007).

Kornbluh, Peter (ed), *Bay of Pigs Declassified: The Secret CIA Report on the Invasion of Cuba* (New York: The New Press, 1998).

Kroker, Arthur, *The Possessed Individual: Technology and the French Postmodern* (New York: St. Martin's Press, 1992).

Kurtz, Michael L., *The JFK Assassination Debates: Lone Gunman versus Conspiracy* (Lawrence, KS: University of Kansas Press, 2006).

Kutler, Stanley I., *The Wars of Watergate: The Last Crisis of Richard Nixon* (New York: Alfred A. Knopf, 1990).

Lane, Mark, *Last Word: My Indictment of the CIA in the Murder of JFK* (New York: Skyhorse Publishing, 2011).

Latell, Brian, *Castro's Secrets: Cuban Intelligence, the CIA and the Assassination of John F. Kennedy* (New York: Palgrave Macmillan, 2012).

Levy, Pierre, *Becoming Virtual: Reality in the Digital Age*. Trans. Robert Bononno (New York: Plenum Trade, 1998).

Logevall, Fredrik, *Choosing War: The Lost Chance for Peace and the Escalation of War in Vietnam* (Berkeley: University of California Press, 1999).

MacCabe, Colin, 'Preface', in Jameson, ix-xvi.

Manwell, Laurie E., 'In Denial of Democracy: Social Psychological Implications for Public Discourse on State Crimes Against Democracy Post-9/11', *American Behavioral Scientist*, 53 (2010), 848-84.

Marks, John, *The Search for the 'Manchurian Candidate': The CIA and Mind Control* (New York: McGraw-Hill Book Company, 1980).

Martin, Sean Elliot, *H.P. Lovecraft and the Modernist Grotesque* (Published by Author, 2008).

McDonough, Tom (ed.), *Guy Debord and the Situationist International: Texts and Documents* (Cambridge Mass: The MIT Press, 2002).

Moise, Edwin E., *Tonkin Gulf and the Escalation of the Vietnam War* (Chapel Hill: The University of North Carolina Press, 1996).

Morley, Jeffeson, *Our Man in Mexico: Winston Scott and the Hidden History of the CIA* (Lawrence KS: University of Kansas Press, 2008).

Muir, Edward, *Civic Ritual in Renaissance Florence* (Princeton: Princeton University Press, 1981).

Nairn, Tom, *The Enchanted Glass: Britain and Its Monarchy* (London: Picador, 1988).

Nairn, Tom, *Pariah: Misfortunes of the British Kingdom* (London: Verso, 2002).

Newman, John, *Oswald and the CIA* (New York: Carroll & Graf Publishers, Inc., 1995).

Newman, John, 'Oswald, the CIA and Mexico City: Fingerprints of Conspiracy', in DiEugenio and Pease (eds.), 217-24.

Nisbet, Robert, *The Social Philosophers: Community and Conflict in Western Thought* (London. Heinneman, 1974).

Oglesby, Carl, *Who Killed JFK?* (Berkeley: Odonian Press, 1992).

Oglesby, Carl, *The Yankee and Cowboy War: Conspiracies From Dallas to Watergate* (Kansas City: Sheed Andrews and McMeel, Inc., 1976).

Pease, Lisa, 'James Angleton', in DiEugenio and Pease (eds.), 136-71.

Pease, Lisa, 'James Angleton Part II', in DiEugenio and Pease (eds.), 172-200.

Pigden, Charles, 'Popper Revisited, or What is Wrong with Conspiracy Theories?', in Coady (ed.), 17-44.

Popper, Karl, 'The Conspiracy Theory of Society', in Coady (ed.), 13-16.

Porter, Gareth, *Perils of Dominance: Imbalance of Power and the Road to War in Vietnam* (Berkeley: University of California Press, 2006).

Powers, Thomas, *The Man Who Kept the Secrets: Richard Helms & the CIA* (New York: Alfred A. Knopf, 1979).

Quigley, Carroll, *Tragedy and Hope: A History of the World in Our Time* (San Pedro CA: GSG Associates, 1966).

Rafter, Nicole, *Shots in the Mirror: Crime Films and Society*. Second edition (Oxford: Oxford University Press, 2006).

Rappleye, Charles and Becker, Ed, *All American Mafioso: The Johnny Roselli Story* (New York: Barricade Books Inc., 1991).

Rasenberger, Jim, *The Brilliant Disaster: JFK, Castro and America's Doomed Invasion of Cuba's Bay of Pigs* (New York: Scribner, 2011).

Schlesinger, Stephen and Kinzer, Stephen, *Bitter Fruit: the Story of the American Coup in Guatemala*. Revised and Expanded Edition (Cambridge, Mass: Harvard University Press/David Rockefeller Center for Latin American Studies, 2005).

Schuster, Carl Otis, 'Case Closed: The Gulf of Tonkin Incident', *Vietnam*, 21/1 (June 2008), 29-33.

Scott, Peter Dale, '9/11, JFK, and War: Recurring Patterns in America's Deep Events'. http://www.peterdalescott.net

Scott, Peter Dale, *American War Machine: Deep Politics, the CIA Global Drug Connection, and the Road to Afghanistan* (New York: Rowman & Litlefield Publishers, Inc., 2010).

Scott, Peter Dale, *Deep Politics and the CIA Global Drug Connection: Heroin and the Networks of Domination*. Private Copy (2009).

Scott, Peter Dale, *Deep Politics and the Death of JFK* (Berkeley: University of California Press, 1993).

Scott, Peter Dale, *Deep Politics II Oswald, Mexico, and Cuba: The New Revelations in U.S. Government Files* (Grand Prairie, TX: JFK Lancer Productions and Publications, 1996).

Scott, Peter Dale, 'Systemic Destabilization in Recent

American History: 9/11, the JFK Assassination, and the Oklahoma City Bombing as a Strategy of Tension', *Asia-Pacific Journal: Japan Focus*, September 23, 2012.

Scott, Peter Dale, *The War Conspiracy: JFK, 9/11, and the Politics of War* (New York: Mary Ferrell Foundation Press, 2008).

Sheehan, Neil, et al, *The Pentagon Papers* (New York: Bantam Books, 1971).

Shenon, Philip, *A Cruel and Shocking Act: The Secret History of the Kennedy Assassination* (New York: Henry Holt and Company, 2013).

Sherwin, Richard C., 'Law Frames: Historical Truth and Narrative Necessity in a Criminal Case', *Stanford Law Review*, 47/1 (November, 1994), 39-83.

Simpich, Bill, *State Secret: Wiretapping in Mexico City, Double Agents, and the Framing of Lee Oswald*. http://www.maryferrell.org/wiki/index.php/State_Secret

Sloterdijk, Peter, *Critique of Cynical Reason*. Trans. Michael Eldred (Minneapolis: University of Minnesota Press, 1987).

Smith, Daniel W., 'Translator's Introduction: Deleuze on Bacon: Three Conceptual Trajectories in *The Logic of Sensation*', in Gilles Deleuze, *Francis Bacon: The Logic of Sensation*. Trans. Daniel W. Smith (University of Minnesota Press: Minneapolis, 2003), vii-xxvii.

Stone, Oliver and Sklar, Zachary, *JFK: The Book of the Film*. Research Notes compiled by Jane Rusconi (New York: Applause Books, 1992).

Summers, Anthony, *Not In Your Lifetime: The Defining Book on the Jfk Assassination* (Open Road: New York, 2013).

Talbot, David, *Brothers: The Hidden History of the Kennedy*

Years (London: Pocket Books, 2007).

Theoharis, Athan G. and Cox, John Stuart, *The Boss: J. Edgar Hoover and the Great American Inquisition* (New York: Bantam Books, 1988).

Thomson, Philip, *The Grotesque* (Methuen & Co Ltd: London, 1972).

Trexler, Robert C., *Public Life in Renaissance Florence* (Ithaca: Cornell University Press, 1980).

Tunander, Ola, 'Democratic State vs. Deep State: Approaching the Dual State of the West', in Wilson (ed), *Government of the Shadows*, 56-72.

Valentine, Carol A., 'OPERATION NORTHWOODS: The Counterfeit,' *Public Action, Inc.,* October. http://www.public-action.com/911/northwoods.html

Virilio, Paul, *Desert Screen: War at the Speed of Light*. Trans. Michael Degener (New York: Continuum, 2005).

Virilio, Paul, *Ground Zero*. Tran. Chris Turner (London: Verso, 2002).

Virilio, Paul, *Negative Horizons: an Essay in Dromoscopy*. Trans. Michael Degener (New York: Continuum, 2005).

Virilio, Paul, *Polar Inertia*. Trans. Patrick Camiller (London: Sage Publications, 2000).

Virillio, Paul, *The Vision Machine*. Trans. Julie Rose (Indianapolis: Indiana University Press, 1994).

Virilio, Paul and Lotringer, Sylvere, *Pure War*. Revised edition. (New York: Semiotext(e), 1997).

Waldron, Lamar and Hartmann, Thom, *Ultimate Sacrifice: John and Robert Kennedy, the Plan for a Coup in Cuba, and the Murder of JFK* (New York: Carroll & Graf Publishers, 2005).

Wark, McKenzie, *The Beach Beneath the Street: The Everyday Life and Glorious Times of the Situationist International* (Verso: London, 2011).

Wilson, Eric, 'The Concept of the Parapolitical, in Wilson (ed.), *The Dual State*, 1-28.

Wilson, Eric, 'Crimes Against Reality: Parapolitics, Simulation, and Power Crime', in Stephen Hall and Simon Winlow (eds.) *New Directions in Criminological Theory* (London: Routledge), 292-316.

Wilson, Eric, 'Criminogenic Cyber-Capitalism: Paul Virilio, Simulation, and the Global Financial Crisis', *Critical Criminology*, 20/3 (2012), 249-74.

Wilson, Eric, 'Deconstructing the Shadows', in Wilson (ed.), *Government of the Shadows*, 13-55.

Wilson, Eric (ed.), *The Dual State: Parapolitics, Carl Schmitt and the National Security Complex* (Farnham, Surrey: Ashgate Publishing Limited, 2012).

Wilson, Eric (ed.), *Government of the Shadows: Parapolitics and Criminal Sovereignty* (London: Pluto Press, 2009).

Wilson, Eric, *The Savage Republic: De Indis of Hugo Grotius, Republicanism, and Dutch Hegemony in the Early Modern World-System (c.1600-1619)* (Leiden. Martinus Nijhoff, 2008).

Wilson, Eric, 'Speed/Pure War/Power Crime: Paul Virilio on the Criminogenic Accident and the Virtual Disappearance of the Suicidal State', *Crime, Law and Social Change*, 51/3-4, 413-434.

About the Author

Eric Wilson is a senior lecturer of Law at Monash University, Melbourne, Australia. In 1991 he completed his Doctorate in the history of early modern Europe under the supervision of Robert Scribner, Clare College, Cambridge. In 2005 he received the degree of Doctor of Juridical Science (S.J.D.) from the University of Melbourne. He is the author of *The Savage Republic: De Indis of Hugo Grotius, Republicanism, and Dutch Hegemony in the Early Modern World System (c.1600-1619)*, published by Martinus Nijhoff in 2008. He is the editor of a series of works on critical criminology, the first volume of which was published by Pluto Press in 2009 as *Government of the Shadows: Parapolitics and Criminal Sovereignty*. The second volume in the series, *The Dual State: Parapolitics, Carl Schmitt and the National Security State Complex*, was published by Ashgate in late 2012. He is currently preparing the third volume, which is a study of the covert origins and dimensions of the French and American wars in Viet Nam. His research interests include Law and Literature, critical jurisprudence, the history and philosophy of international law, and critical criminology.

www.ingramcontent.com/pod-product-compliance
Lightning Source LLC
Chambersburg PA
CBHW071730270326
41928CB00013B/2622